THE GREAT IRISH FAMINE

British History in Perspective
General Editor: Jeremy Black

Please note that a sister series, *Social History in Perspective*, is now available, covering key topics in social and cultural history.

British History in Perspective
Series Standing Order: ISBN 0–333–71356–7 hardcover / ISBN 0–333–69331–0 paperback

You can receive future titles in this series as they are published by placing a standing order. Please contact your bookseller or, in case of difficulty, write to the address below with your name and address, the title of the series and the ISBN quoted above.

Customer Services Department, Macmillan Distribution Ltd
Houndmills, Basingstoke, Hampshire RG21 6XS, England

THE GREAT IRISH FAMINE

IMPACT, IDEOLOGY AND REBELLION

Christine Kinealy

First published 2002 by
PALGRAVE
Houndmills, Basingstoke, Hampshire RG21 6XS and
175 Fifth Avenue, New York, N.Y. 10010
Companies and representatives throughout the world

PALGRAVE is the new global academic imprint of
St. Martin's Press LLC Scholarly and Reference Division and
Palgrave Publishers Ltd (formerly Macmillan Press Ltd).

ISBN 0–333–67772–2 hardback
ISBN 0–333–67773–0 paperback

This book is printed on paper suitable for recycling and made from fully managed and sustained forest sources.

A catalogue record for this book is available from the British Library.

Library of Congress Cataloging-in-Publication Data
Kinealy, Christine.
    The great Irish famine: impact, ideology, and rebellion / Christine Kinealy.
        p. cm.— (British history in perspective)
    Includes bibliographical references (p.) and index.
    ISBN 0–333–67772–2 (cloth) — ISBN 0–333–67773–0 (pbk.)
    1. Ireland–History–Famine, 1845–1852.   2. Famines–Ireland–
    History–19th century.
    I. Title.   II. Series.

    DA950.7 .K57 2001
    941.5081—dc21   2001032748

10 9 8 7 6 5 4 3 2 1
11 10 09 08 07 06 05 04 03 02

Printed in China

For Robert

CONTENTS

TABLES

Acknowledgements

This book was written with the assistance of many people. Firstly, I would like to thank the team of the *British History in Perspective* series, especially the general editor, Jeremy Black. My colleagues in the University of Central Lancashire for their support and encouragement, most particularly Anne Brownlow, Susan Burnett, Rex Pope and Geoff Timmins. A special thanks is due to Professor John Walton for his comments and observations on earlier drafts of the text. David Sexton and Robert Langford have offered valuable perspectives and observations on various stages of the manuscript.

I have spent many hours in a variety of libraries and archives and I would like to thank the staff for their help, especially the staff of the County Library in Wexford, the Public Record Office in London, Colindale Newspaper Depository, the National Archives of Ireland, the Royal Irish Academy, Trinity College Library in Dublin, the Linen Hall Library in Belfast, the Presbyterian Historical Society, the National Library of Ireland, the Bodleian Library in Oxford, the Public Library in New York, the National Archives in Washington, the Public Record Office of Belfast. I am grateful also to the Earl of Clarendon for permission to quote from his ancestor's papers.

Inspiration and insights have come from a number of people who themselves have done much to promote an understanding of the Famine – occasionally in fraught circumstances – they include John Leahy and David Valone of Quinnipiac University, Jack Worrall, James Mullin, George Harrison, Senator Tom Hayden, Deborah Peck, Charles Rice, Bill Rogers, Cormac Ó Gráda, Donal Kerr, Brendan Bradshaw, Pat Mac Gregor, Peter Collins, John Waters, Gerard Mac Atasney, Patrick O'Sullivan, Terry Eagleton, Don Mullan, Joel Mockyr, Owen Rodgers, Finbar O'Doherty, Kevin MacNamara MP and Ambassador Ted Barrington. Tony Blair also – whatever his motivation – has made an important contribution to the memory and commemoration of the Famine.

Thanks also are due to Honora and Ray Ormesher, Angela Farrell, Bernadette Barrington, Ray Gillespie, John Brandwood, Steve and Alison Henshall, Séan Sexton, Eileen Black, Peter Collins, Ivan Cooper, Francine Sagar, Peter Roebuck, and Seth and Deirdre Linder. My greatest debt, however, is to those who continue to share a home with me and tolerate my bizarre passion and life-style.

1

REMEMBERING THE FAMINE

The Irish Government wholeheartedly shoulders its responsibilities in acknowledging the importance of the Famine, which so signally marked us as a people, which vastly expanded our diaspora, and in which modern Ireland itself was born.[1]

(Avril Doyle TD Chairperson of Famine Commemoration
Committee in the Republic of Ireland, 1995)

'The Famine was a defining event in the history of Ireland and of Britain. It has left deep scars. That one million people should have died in what was then part of the richest and most powerful nation in the world is something that still causes pain as we reflect on it today. Those who governed in London at the time failed their people through standing by while a crop failure turned into a massive tragedy. We must not forget such a dreadful event'.[2]

(Tony Blair, PM of the United Kingdom, 1997)

Belfast City Council is to erect a stained glass window in memory of those from the city who died in the Great Famine – despite a DUP (Democratic Unionist Party) attempt to block the move ... Councillor Sammy Wilson said there was no evidence that the Famine played a major role in the history of Belfast and said the motion gave succour to anti-British, Sinn Féin propaganda'.[3]

(*Irish News*, Belfast, 4 February 1997)

Few commemorative events have captured the public, private and political imagination as did the 150th anniversary of Ireland's *An Gorta*

Mhór, the Great Hunger or Famine.[4] Significantly, Blair's address provided an open admission that the Great Famine was as much a part of Britain's history as Ireland's. The same point had frequently been made in Ireland. In 1995, the well-respected broadsheet, the *Irish Times*, had declared that 'the Great Famine was the most culpable episode in the troubled rule of Britain and Ireland'.[5] Yet, despite the general acceptance of the awfulness and significance of the Famine, it was rarely taught in Irish schools or universities and little had been published on it. Instead, the dominant school of thought within Irish history, known generically as revisionism, had argued that the Famine was not a significant event in modern Irish history, but that it merely acted as a catalyst for changes which were occurring anyway.[6] Moreover, the Famine was depicted as inevitable and it was suggested that the British government could have done little more than they did to save lives.[7] This interpretation had dominated academic discourse since the 1930s, with varying degrees of intensity. One of its key purposes was to revise the traditional nationalist or popular interpretation of the Famine, whilst claiming that it had no political purpose of its own. Those who challenged it, however, were accused of having a covert agenda or being politically motivated.[8] Clearly, the revisionist interpretation did not exist in an intellectual or political vacuum and its writings – especially by non-academics – were shaped (and constrained) by events within Ireland at the end of the twentieth century, notably, the 'Troubles'. One consequence of revisionism was 'to undermine the basis of Irish nationalism and leave Ireland without the heroes of historical memory . . . [and to] play down the British responsibility for the catastrophic aspects of the Irish experience'.[9] Moreover, the revisionist domination meant that intellectual debate in Ireland was effectively constrained, and to take a counter-position was tantamount to declaring support for the national struggle.[10]

A Forgotten Famine?

The reluctance of Irish historians to engage with the Great Hunger was particularly curious given that the Famine was a watershed in the development of modern Ireland. Moreover, the scale of population loss was remarkable; over one million people died and an even greater number emigrated during a six-year period, thus cutting the population by over 25 per cent. And even after good harvests returned to Ireland, the population decline continued. Until the 1990s, however, the two standard books on the Famine were by Robin Dudley Edwards and Desmond Williams, *The Great Famine: Studies in Irish History*, which was academically acclaimed but of uneven quality, and the academically panned but best-selling, *The Great Hunger*, by Cecil Woodham-Smith. The Taoiseach, Eamon de Valera, commissioned the former in 1944 to commemorate the hundredth anniversary of the Famine. Despite receiving a large subvention from the government, the publication did not finally appear until 1956 and was just over half the size of that which had been agreed. The chapters were uneven in quality and lacked coherence (some lacked footnotes, one set having been lost in a London taxi-cab by one of the editors). The final product was also a disappointment to de Valera, whilst Dudley Edwards admitted that the authors had not paid sufficient attention to it.[11] The editors' introduction (which had been 'ghost' written by a junior historian) captured the spirit of much revisionist writing by refusing to engage with some of the more unpleasant aspects of the disaster, such as mortality and the responsibility of the government. The introduction also criticized popular and folk interpretations for viewing 'the failure of the British government in a sinister light'.[12] Yet, in spite of its many shortcomings, the book sold well and received favourable reviews from fellow acadmics.[13]

In contrast, Cecil Woodham-Smith's *Great Hunger*, published in 1962 and which provided a more comprehensive and meticulously researched view of the Famine by a non-academic, was derided by many Irish historians; one of the examination questions asked of undergraduate history students in University College in Dublin in 1963 was '*The Great Hunger* is a great novel. Discuss'.[14] The author was also attacked on a personal level. Professor Roy Foster, for example, described Woodham-Smith as a 'zealous convert'.[15] Its abundant sales and frequent reprints in Ireland, Britain and America, however, demonstrated not only the gap between popular and academic perceptions of the Famine, but also how deeply entrenched an orthodoxy of the Famine had become within the Irish academic community.

The dearth of Famine publications was followed during the sesquicentenary commemorations with what appeared to be a glut. Between 1995 and 1997 more books were published on the Famine than in the previous 150 years. More significantly, a new generation of historians, mainly from universities outside Ireland, challenged the revisionist school of history, which had dominated academic history since the 1930s, but more intensely since the 1960s. The Famine, which had been ignored or marginalized by Irish historians, suddenly became intellectually admissible. The willingness to revisit the Famine was explained by Mary Daly of University College, Dublin, whose earlier writings on the Famine had been conservative and marked by an attempt to play down the level of mortality and responsibility of the British authorities.[16] In a public lecture in Belfast in 1995 she admitted to having adopted this form of self-censorship saying, 'Now we are in a cease-fire situation, we can talk about aspects of history which we may previously have felt uncomfortable with.'[17] Such an explanation demonstrated the linking of certain sensitive topics in Irish history with the political situation in Northern Ireland. Clearly, the military campaign by the Irish Republican Army and other paramilitary groups had restricted academic debate even in parts of Ireland not directly involved in it.

The political significance of Famine commemorations was increased by the fact that they coincided with an IRA cease-fire between 1994 and 1996, which marked one of the most significant steps towards a peace process since the renewed round of 'Troubles' in 1969. At the launch of its programme in June 1995, the government minister in charge of the Republic of Ireland's Famine Commemoration Programme declared that 'the Peace Process allows us all the more freely to explore the truth. The relations between the two islands have now reached a maturity which allows us to look at our history objectively and to tell the story as it was . . . After all, the Famine is not just an Irish event, it was just as much a British event, a shared experience.'[18] The progress towards peace was intensified with the coming to power in Britain of the Labour Party in 1997, with a resolution of the Troubles being made a political priority. Irish politics and Irish history were discussed in the public domain in a way that had not seemed possible in the highly charged atmosphere of the 1980s and early 1990s.

On the first anniversary of the IRA cease-fire in 1995, an *Irish Times* journalist explained how the revisionist viewpoint had become the accepted dogma, but that just as the political context had changed, revisionism also would have to adapt. He wrote that the cease-fire had changed the politics of both the North and the Republic of Ireland definitively, allowing the removal of power from a powerful clique of anti-nationalists who had attempted to repress all dissent. Radical voices within Ireland or those who tried to critically understand the situation in the North had been denounced as nationalists. Consequently, whilst the conflict continued it had 'the effect of stifling all debate about certain aspects of Irish society', including debates on the Famine. However, the same interests which had nurtured the development of revisionism had responded with 'increasingly vicious attacks on those who advance alternative viewpoints [which] demonstrates a kind of menopausal fear of their own impending obsolescence'.[19]

The Famine commemorations also coincided with a cultural revival within Ireland and further afield. An improbable showcase for Ireland's success was provided by the *Eurovision Song Contest*, which Ireland won a record four times between 1992 and 1997. In 1994 television audiences throughout Europe were exposed to seven minutes of traditional Irish dancing, which borrowed freely from other styles and cultures and which was led by two Irish-American dancers. *Riverdance* did the apparently impossible; it made Irish dancing both sensual and commercially lucrative.[20] More importantly, it was critical in 'redefining Ireland's media image in the world . . . as it jostled for position and exerted its political influence within Europe'.[21]

Two legacies of the Famine were that the role of women was weakened, whilst the position of the Catholic Church was strengthened considerably. Late nineteenth-century society had been increasingly patriarchal – primogeniture and the Catholic Church undermining women's traditional economic role within society – but women found a new voice in Ireland at the end of the twentieth century. Mary Robinson gave Ireland a high-profile president who was intelligent, stylish and, like *Riverdance*, international rather than insular in approach. The birth of the so-called 'Celtic Tiger', by which Ireland was transformed into the fastest growing economy within Europe, consolidated and amplified the newfound attractions of Ireland to an audience that was not merely comprised of emigrants of Irish descent. The Republic of Ireland, with its new found prosperity, poise and popularity was ready not only to take its place on the world stage, but also confident enough to confront the horrors of a lethal famine that had occurred 150 years earlier; an event which had changed the course of modern Irish history yet which had been ignored, marginalized or sanitized by generations of professional historians.[22]

Yet, even before the anniversary and the official commemorations commenced the desire of the Irish people to know more about the Famine was apparent. The publication of *The Famine Diary* in 1992, which provided a narrative account of a famine victim and his wife who emigrated and died on Grosse Ile, the quarantine station outside Quebec, encapsulated and reinforced a popular understanding of the Famine experience. Within two months of publication it was a best-seller, helped by media interest in a 'good story' and endorsements by Irish charities working in the Third World. A few months later, however, the diary was found to be not a contemporary account, but a compilation of newspaper articles that had first been published in 1895 in Canada. A Catholic priest had then reworked it and added a number of new characters.[23] Nevertheless, the diary clearly filled a void, whilst demonstrating that the revisionist interpretation had failed to displace or even adequately challenge the traditional nationalist interpretation of the Famine. A collection of essays by Irish and Irish-American contributors, edited by Senator Tom Hayden and published in 1997, suggested that there existed a moral and spiritual need to remember because 'A Famine repressed breeds an incipient hunger of its own, a hunger to know, to grieve, to hold accountable, to resolve and to honour.' Moreover, he argued, the inability to face up to the Famine was continuing to cast a shadow over the struggle for peace, justice and reconciliation between Irish and British people.[24]

Within Ireland there was initially some doubt as to whether the Government of the Irish Republic would play an official role in the Famine commemorations. The IRA cease-fire in 1994 undoubtedly played a part in the decision to do so. Nonetheless, how could an event so tragic and which had so long been neglected be appropriately remembered? In May 1994, the government set up an inter-departmental committee chaired by the Minister of State, Tom Kitt. Despite a change of government, the project continued, although Avril Doyle TD, Minister of State at the Department of the Taoiseach, replaced Kitt in January 1995. Following the appointment of Doyle, the scale and scope of the Committee increased. In June, the Irish government announced a publicly funded programme drawn up by the recently constituted National Famine Commemoration Committee. The programme was described as 'wide, varied, with a heavy emphasis on education, on scholarships and famine relief projects in the modern world'.[25] Avril Doyle was provided with a budget of £250 000, a substantial portion of which – £115 000 – was given to four Irish historians to supervise new research by a team of post-graduate researchers.[26] She explained this emphasis on the grounds that 'If we understand our history, we can transcend it'. Nine Poor Law unions were chosen for the 'high quality detailed survey' which was to have a special focus on new technologies and methodologies. The research findings were intended to result in a publication and an international conference in 1997 – a timetable that was more in keeping with the schedule of politicians than with the requirements of historical research. In 1997 a conference was held, although the papers and subsequent publication were by established scholars rather than based on the new research financed by the Famine Committee.[27]

Because the Committee believed that the 'story must be told to the widest possible audience through video, TV and the media generally', sponsorship was provided for an RTE documentary and a bilingual schools essay project. Local involvement was actively encouraged, whilst the Famine message was also to be made available to the Irish diaspora. The remaining money was used to assist a limited number of projects not only within Ireland, but also in Britain, the United States and Australia. As a consequence, an eclectic mixture of events was sponsored including an exhibition of art inspired by the Famine, a commemoration concert to include a commissioned 'Famine Suite' and the erection of a national monument. Avril Doyle also undertook a lecture tour of the United States accompanied by a small number of historians and academics, amounting to a famine roadshow.

One of the most ambitious aspects of the Committee's programme was the acknowledgment that the Irish people were still coming to terms with the Famine, Doyle asserting that 'For our own sakes we need the catharsis of a commemoration which fully recognizes the pain and loss the Famine represented. I am confident that the Government's Programme of Commemoration will make a significant contribution to that process.' The Committee also recognized that the Famine was 'an all-Ireland tragedy' and the first national event was to take place in Enniskillen in County Fermanagh on 28 August to mark the place where the blight was first observed.[28] Despite this inclusive assertion, the official commemorations tended to remain located in the Republic and had little impact within Northern Ireland. Also, whilst a number of the events were ecumenical, for the most part the commemorations confirmed the view that the victims of the Famine were predominantly Catholic and that its impact on the north-east of the country was minimal. Also, the divergent interpretation of the unionist community towards the Famine was neglected. In contrast, the British dimension was frequently addressed, with Doyle declaring that 'the Famine is not just an Irish event, it was just as much a British event, a shared experience. Together we will face up to what happened and move forward. It is in a spirit of understanding and reconciliation that we are now commemorating the Great Famine.'[29] Mid-way through the commemorations, the cease-fire came to an abrupt end with the bombing of Canary Wharf at the beginning of 1996.

One of the remarkable features of the Irish Famine was the massive amount of international aid that was sent to the poor, especially in 1847.

During the anniversary there were many references to the generosity of Irish people towards other famine victims. The then President, Mary Robinson, described Ireland as possessing an 'historically informed compassion' as a consequence of the Famine and suggested, following a visit to famine-stricken Somalia, that its memory would serve to 'strengthen and deepen our identity with those who are still suffering'.[30] A number of religious and charitable organizations hoped that a substantial portion of the funds set aside by the government would be used for international aid, but the government decided not to make overseas aid a priority.[31] Only a limited amount of sponsorship was to be given to contemporary famines, including to drought projects in Ethiopia Eritrea and Lesotho, and a scholarship established in one of the recipient countries of Third World aid.[32]

Initially it had been decided that the government's commemorations were to commence on 10 September 1995 – 150 years after the blight was first reported in Ireland – but official commemorations were under way by the summer and Irish newspapers had been writing about the anniversary throughout 1994. The decision to commence the commemorations in 1995 did not take account of the fact that nobody died in the year following the first potato failure in 1845. The Famine proper only really commenced – but almost instantaneously – following the second and far more devastating failure in 1846. Early in 1995, the Irish historian Cormac Ó Gráda counselled against the rush to remember on the grounds that 'at the present dizzy rate of commemorating, the danger is that there will be little energy left by the time the true anniversary of Black '47 comes around'.[33] The vast number of publications, newspaper articles, documentaries and famine events that occurred in the latter part of 1995 appeared to fill the quasi-void of the previous 150 years. By the end of 1995, Eddie Holt, a journalist with the *Irish Times*, claimed that a number of people were feeling famine fatigue and that further research or discussion was not necessary.[34] But one of the positive outcomes of the Famine commemorations and publications was that, as a result, a more rounded and nuanced understanding of the Famine became available to the wider public.

One particularly valuable development was the new research on the impact of the Famine on areas that tended to be regarded as immune, such as Dublin and Belfast and its hinterland. The new research demonstrated that the Famine was a truly national disaster; its impact cut across religious divides – poverty rather than religious affiliation influencing chances of survival.[35] The roles of landlords and merchants have also been reassessed, although more research needs to be carried out on both groups.[36] In regard to the role of the government, the post-revisionist interpretations tended to be closer to the traditional popular understanding rather than to the revisionist interpretation. The new research also utilized new technology and methodological approaches, and more use was made of previously under-utilized archives, such as the Folklore Archive in University College, Dublin. But this and other archives have not been exhausted. As Liam Swords's fine publication has demonstrated, the scale of the tragedy combined with painstaking bureaucratic documentation, means that there is still much that remains unrevealed.[37] Swords, however, in common with many Irish historians, focused only on sources in the Republic of Ireland. Consequently, the vast amount of archives in Northern Ireland and in Britain has been largely neglected. Clearly, historians are only beginning to engage with the archival riches which had for so long been ignored and, although a number of historians have adopted a multi-disciplinary approach, some areas, such as archaeology, remain relatively unexplored.[38] Unfortunately, after 1997 a number of publishers no longer wanted to publish famine books, reflecting the same famine-fatigue that was apparent amongst the media and politicians.

Apart from the high profile attached to many of the government's activities the famine was also commemorated by a number of local and voluntary groups that did not receive financial backing from the government. Other famine events included the making of a four-part drama, *The Hanging Gale*, which was a joint production between Radio Telefís Éireann and BBC Northern Ireland. The BBC also produced a documentary, *The Great Famine*, which was shown on BBC2. The programme was well researched and thoughtfully presented yet, for some of the audience, the complexity of the Famine remained subsumed beneath traditional stereotypes. An extreme example of this interpretation was provided by the television critic in the *Sunday Times*, A. A. Gill, who wrote that the message which he came away with was that the Irish had 'turned their whole country over to a single, low-maintenance crop of tubers, so that they could get on with burning down houses that were nicer than theirs and making sure that every female over 12 was pregnant all the time'.[39]

Even before 1995, the Famine had been regarded as both a tragic example and as a source of inspiration to a number of Irish relief agencies. Since 1989 a small Irish agency, Action from Ireland (AfrI), had organized a ten mile walk from Louisburg to Doolough in a remote part of County Mayo. The walk was a tribute to a group of local paupers from

Louisburg who, according to local tradition, had perished after having been refused relief by Poor Law Guardians who were lunching at the Delphi Lodge, ten miles away. At the same time, the purpose of the walk was to draw attention to the continuing suffering and death of the poor in the Third World, and the parallels with the Irish experience. AfrI also used the walk as a platform for addressing issues of famine and human rights violations in the 1980s and 1990s. The walk attracted an eclectic mixture of people, including Arun Gandhi, one of Mahatma Gandhi's grandsons, returned missionaries, Donal Lunny, the traditional Irish musician, representatives of the Maya people of Guatemala, a member of the Choctaw Nation of Oklahoma, the journalist John Pilger and the actor Gabriel Byrne.[40]

Like many other Third World relief agencies, AfrI sought to draw analogies between the Irish Famine and modern famines. It also argued that memories of the past had made Irish people more generous in their willingness to provide famine relief, and maintained that 'Ireland has a unique role to play in international affairs...Our concern for the world's poor arises out of that experience.'[41] Yet, despite similarities or variations amongst those who had experienced famine, a unique feature of the Irish example was that it was the most lethal famine in modern history in terms of excess mortality and population loss, the death tolls in twentieth-century famines being relatively lower.[42] Nonetheless, a tragic aspect of the Irish Famine was that accurate records were not kept of those who died, leading to accusations at the time that the Whig government was attempting to keep the information unknown. As one Tory politician pointed out, the British State was able to provide accurate statistics on the numbers of pigs and poultry consumed, yet it did not attempt to keep a record of the deaths of its people.[43]

A Dangerous Memory?

The anniversary of the Great Hunger was not without discord. Before Blair's statement, there were a number of calls for the British government, or occasionally Prince Charles, to apologize, including by the leader of the Opposition in Ireland, Bertie Ahern.[44] In 1994 the controversial Irish singer, Sinéad O'Connor, released a Famine 'rap' song questioning the use of the word 'famine' on the grounds that massive quantities of food left Ireland on a daily basis. She also likened modern

Ireland to an abused child who dealt with the pain of the past by denying it, and she argued that healing could not begin until the memory was recovered. Part of the recovery, O'Connor argued, was recognizing that Northern Ireland was an integral part of the child's body. She also believed that the legacy of colonialism was to separate people from their history, memory and cultural identity.[45] O'Connor, who was no stranger to media hostility, immediately found herself under attack from both conservative and anti-nationalist historians and journalists.[46] Whilst the deep psychological damage as a consequence of the Famine was acknowledged by Irish psychologist Dr Anthony Clare, O'Connor's historical interpretation was challenged by Dublin historian Mary Daly who, adopting a revisionist approach, argued that the song was historically inaccurate as, 'the Irish Famine was a natural disaster brought about by the failure of the potato crop and that other food supplies in the country like beef and grain and vegetables would not have provided adequate sustenance even if they had been made available'.[47] The new research, which has appeared since 1994, has largely rejected the viewpoint that the Famine was a natural disaster. As was recognized during the course of the Irish Famine and has been demonstrated by contemporary famine experts, famines are man-made rather than natural disasters. Professor Amartya Sen, the leading contemporary expert on famines, had criticized the over-emphasis by historians and others on the significance of the decline in food availability, arguing that in reality it played a limited role. Instead, he argued, distribution or 'entitlement' to food was the key factor in understanding any famine situation.[48] O'Connor and Daly remained unrepentant about their diverse interpretations.[49] Daly went on to be one of the historians, all based in Dublin universities, who received funding from the government's Famine Committee.

Sinéad O'Connor's explanation found favour with a leading commentator on Irish life, the *Irish Times* columnist John Waters, who praised the fact that she was 'alive and well and determined not to be quiet'. He believed that the anniversary would provide an opportunity to 'reclaim our history, not as a series of facts and details, but in a way so meaningful as to fill the gaping holes in our collective spirit'. The role of academic research was only a minor part of the remembrance, which he viewed as the responsibility of 'politicians, artists, journalists, editors, psychiatrists, intellectuals and all others who claim to contribute to the betterment of this society'. He also believed that the Irish experience of famine provided them with an opportunity to show 'solidarity with the present victims of colonialism and oppression'.[50]

What made the Famine commemorations particularly remarkable was the interest of politicians not only in Ireland, but further afield. This was partly due to the vast Irish diaspora, many members of which left during the Famine or in its aftermath. There were famine events and lectures throughout Britain and the Great Hunger Commemoration Committee in Liverpool planned to erect a famine monument. The committee received a contribution of £5000 from the Irish government, but the British Conservative government refused to make a donation. However, largely due to the efforts of Kevin McNamara MP, in 1997 the new Labour government agreed to do so.[51] In the United States and Australia also, a series of commemorative events were organized. Some of the tensest controversies took place in the United States. A Famine Genocide committee was established in New York in 1995 and, using the expertise of a well-respected law professor, they contemplated taking a retrospective action against the British government on a charge of genocide.[52] In March 1997, the St Patrick's Day Parade in New York was attended with controversy when the Grand Marshal, John Lahey, declared that in 1997 its key purpose would be to 'draw attention to the British government's culpability in the Irish Famine'.[53] The election of a Labour government in Britain and Blair's quasi-apology in 1997, which mirrored much of what Lahey had contended, defused some of the anger that had attended earlier commemorations in the United States.

An attempt to teach about the Famine in schools in the United States caused the most disagreement. An Irish Famine Curriculum Committee, comprising educationalists and Irish activists, attempted to persuade a number of state legislatures to introduce a mandate to incorporate the Irish Famine into the Human Rights Curriculum in public schools, which included other topics dealing with institutional racism and genocide, such as the Holocaust and slavery.[54] New Jersey was the first state to pass a Famine Curriculum and by 1997 it had been adopted by a number of schools, where it was regarded as a valuable educational tool for teaching both history and human rights.[55] A number of British newspapers believed otherwise. The *Sunday Telegraph*, for example, presented the Famine Curriculum as having been the work of 'hard-line Irish American nationalists' who wanted to prove that the Famine was an act of genocide.[56]

The decision to introduce a similar curriculum into New York State aroused more controversy and demonstrated that the Famine continued to be viewed in political rather than historical terms by some of the media. Congressman Mendenez, an American-Cuban, who introduced the bill argued that 'The Irish Famine teaches an important lesson about intolerance and inhumanity and the indifference of the British government to the potato blight that led to the mass starvation of one million people.'[57] In October 1996, the Famine Curriculum was passed in the New York legislature. The reception to the new legislation was mixed, but the conservative press generally disliked it. A common tactic of those who opposed it was to denigrate the implication that the Famine could be compared with the Holocaust, a parallel that had not been suggested by its supporters.[58] The governing Conservative Party in Britain also regarded the curriculum with embarrassment. The British ambassador in the States, John Kerr, registered an official protest and asked the New York legislature not to go ahead with the curriculum.[59] In his official letter he pointed out that 'Unlike the Holocaust, the famine was not deliberate, not premeditated, not manmade, not genocide.' The *New York Daily News*, which largely agreed with Kerr's statement, nevertheless maintained topics like the Famine should be taught and debated in the schools if human rights were to be understood and protected. It concluded that 'Even after 150 years, the British still obviously fear the facts.'[60] The London *Times* accused Governor George Pataki of New York of trying to win the Irish vote and described his knowledge of history as arising from 'the Fenian propaganda version which ambitious American politicians tend to prefer'.[61]

The Irish government was also uncomfortable with the legislation. Avril Doyle of the Irish government's Famine Committee opposed it on the grounds that she was 'not in favour of legislating the way history is taught in schools'.[62] Despite the initial controversy, the legislation went ahead and a team of educationalists at Hofstra University was selected to draw up a famine curriculum that could be used for a variety of ages and abilities.[63] The curriculum was field tested in a number of schools and by the begining of 2001 had been distributed to 8000 public schools in New York.[64] The New York Famine curriculum, however, continued to prove contentious, although its main detractors were from other Irish groups, the president of the New Jersey Famine Committee publicly denouncing it in the *New York Daily News* on 1 April, 2001, as 'A thousand pages of revisionist history'. Nonetheless, the introduction of the New York curriculum encouraged a number of other states to pass similar legislation, including Connecticut. In 2000 also, a Great Hunger Special Collections Room was established at Quinnipiac University in Connecticut to provide a resource both for college students and the wider public.[65] As a consequence, students in some parts of the United States are probably better informed about recent events in Irish history than students in British schools.

From the outset the commemorations of the Famine by the Irish government were due to end in the summer of 1997, allowing a decent interval of a few months before the remembrance of the 1798 uprising could begin. Even before the Famine commemorations were officially 'over' a programme was being prepared for the bicentenary of the 1798 uprising.[66] Initially, it had been planned that the finale of the Famine anniversary in 1997 would be marked with a National Service of Commemoration, attended by the President, the Taoiseach, members of the government, overseas diplomats and representatives of the major religious denominations.[67] By 1997, however, commercialization and celebration, rather than solemn remembrance, had become the main themes of the concluding event of the Famine Committee. Consequently, the official closure was observed by the so-called 'Great Irish Famine Event', a musical festival which took place in Millstreet in County Cork, which mixed commercialism with commemoration in a way that was deemed to be both vulgar and inappropriate. Joe Murray of the aid agency AfrI described it as 'dancing on the graves of the dead', whilst John Waters of the *Irish Times* observed that 'The Famine dead are offered on the altar of Tourism.'[68] The event was widely advertised in the United States and Irish-Americans were encouraged to return 'home' for the occasion. A number of them, however, were offended by the fact that remembering the Famine dead had been transformed into a tourist attraction – replete with alcohol and music.[69] Yet, the event did provide a forum and an international audience for a number of politicians, notably the British Prime Minister and the American President, to extend their sympathy to Ireland. The statement by Tony Blair was a skilful acknowledgment of the behaviour of the government at the time which ended on a predictably upbeat message about the survivors who left Ireland, 'those Irish men and women who were able to forge another life outside Ireland, and the rich vitality and culture they brought with them. Britain, the US and many Commonwealth countries are richer for their presence.'[70] Blair's message amounted to a tacit apology without the word even being mentioned. His message, however, created a torrent of criticism in Ireland and Britain, from historians and from both the Unionist Party (led by David Trimble) and the Democratic Unionist Party (led by Ian Paisley). The *Daily Telegraph* reprimanded Blair for encouraging 'the self-pitying nature of Irish nationalism' and warned that it would serve to feed 'the grievance culture which allows nationalist

Ireland to place the blame for all the country's ills at the door of the Brits, ultimately justifying terrorism'.[71] Despite two years of intensive commemorations, the healing process which had been hoped for had failed to remove some of the deep-rooted prejudices present in both Ireland and Britain.[72]

The conclusion of the government's commemorations in 1997 reinforced a traditional, but erroneous impression that the Famine had ended in 1847 – remembered in folk tradition as 'Black '47'. Moreover, in so-doing the Irish government was reflecting the actions of the British government 150 years earlier when they – prematurely – announced that the Famine was over in August 1847 – at a time when over three million were receiving free daily rations of food. Yet, even in its truncated form, the commemoration represented the longest and most comprehensive historical commemoration by the Irish government. This response was even more surprising as the100th anniversary in 1945 had attracted little notice and the government's response to the 50th anniversary of the 1916 uprising had been particularly restrained. The willingness of the Irish State to involve itself so closely with the Famine, quickly followed by the 1798 commemorations, was praised for being a sign of its new political maturity, one Irish historian arguing that 'the State that doesn't respect its own history is a bankrupt one'.[73] But the thorny question of when ownership becomes control was rarely addressed.[74]

Between 1995 and 1997, history, politics, culture, commemoration and tourism came together in a way that was frequently moving, but occasionally offensive. Nonetheless, the commercialization evident in parts of the commemoration did not tarnish the whole process.[75] The commemorations also showed that remembering the Famine was not the prerogative of academics, but that it had entered popular culture and consciousness in a way that was rare for a historical event. The involvement of Irish Third World organizations was particularly impressive. Some of the most touching events were small local initiatives, such as the recovery of Famine graveyards which had been neglected, or throwing flowers into a quayside to commemorate the Famine dead or those who were lost through emigration.[76] Many local studies also emerged which reinforced the local nature of the crisis and thus provided fresh local insights into the national disaster.

In contrast to the activities of the Irish government, Famine commemorations in Northern Ireland were on a smaller and more local scale, and they were almost totally located within the Catholic community. Significantly, a number of famine wall murals in Belfast were situated in

Catholic west Belfast and not in Protestant Ballymacarrett, despite evidence of far greater suffering in the latter district.[77] Revisionist historians had also played a part in creating an impression that the Protestant experience of famine had been different. For example, Dr Liam Kennedy of Queen's University in Belfast had written, 'Ulster fared better than the average experience of the island ... the Protestant people of that province suffered less severely from famine.'[78] Despite an outpouring of publications between 1994 and 1997, especially of local studies, some areas remained relatively unexplored. One area that proved to be uncomfortable for researchers was that of the six counties which formed Northern Ireland, but which at the time of the Famine had been part of Ireland. Consequently, there were few studies on the impact of the Famine in Ulster and a number of unionist politicians in Northern Ireland clung to an outmoded interpretation of the Famine as being a southern and Catholic phenomenon, and rooted in nationalist propaganda. As a Northern Irish literary critic, Edna Longley, observed, 'Commemorations are as selective as sympathies. They honour our dead, not your dead.'[79]

The decision by Belfast City Council in 1997 to erect a stained-glass window in memory of those who had died in the city during the Famine was opposed by members of the Democratic Unionist Party. Sammy Wilson, a DUP Councillor, argued that to support the proposal would provide a potential propaganda campaign for Sinn Féin, 'the masters of manufacturing and media manipulation'.[80] Also, despite the fact that the proposers of the commemorative window had asked a well-respected local historian, Jonathan Bardon, to provide the Council with a report on the impact of the Famine on the city, Wilson also averred that 'There is no evidence that the Famine played any part in the history of Belfast.'[81] Councillor Hartley of Sinn Féin, who had initially suggested the erection of the window, responded that the intention had been to remember the victims of the Famine, regardless of their religion, and praised other Unionist members for supporting the motion saying, 'This is a small and helpful breakthrough in our endeavours to have the shared history of the city marked in Belfast City Hall.'[82]

The divisive approach to the Famine had its roots in the Famine itself when taxpayers in the north claimed that their prosperity was because they were more hard working than people in the south and west, and because 'we are a painstaking, industrious, laborious people, who desire to work and pay our just debts, and the blessing of the Almighty is upon our labour'.[83] This argument was used to justify their opposition to paying a new national poor rate in 1849. In fact, Ulster as a whole, and some northern areas in particular, suffered greatly during the Famine. Nor was Ulster the county least affected by the ravages of Famine; the average population loss was 17 per cent in Ulster, not far behind the situation in Connaught and higher than in the province of Leinster. Much research remains to be done but three recent studies have demonstrated that Belfast, Newtownards and Lurgan (which lay at the heart of the linen triangle) suffered acutely during the Famine. The three towns, moreover, were predominantly Protestant.[84] Nonetheless, as divisions between nationalists and unionists hardened in the late nineteenth century, the Famine was increasingly viewed by the latter group as not having penetrated to the north. The new Northern Ireland State, which prided itself on its Protestantism and its prosperity, helped to keep alive the myth of a Famine-free zone. In the 1930s, when the southern government undertook a national survey of folk memories of the Famine, officials in Northern Ireland refused to allow it to be extended into the six counties under their jurisdiction.[85]

The Famine in Context

What follows is not intended to be a general history of the Famine or of famine relief, but seeks to provide an examination of the Famine within a broader context of concurrent economic, social and political developments in Ireland – how they shaped the response to the Famine and how the Famine, in turn, moulded them. Fresh perspectives on relatively little researched aspects of the Famine – memory and commemoration, private charity, trade, proselytism, green and orange politics – form the major concern of this publication. The interaction between Ireland and Britain is also a major theme, the paradox of Ireland being part of the United Kingdom – and the British Empire – yet being treated as a separate entity when in the midst of a humanitarian catastrophe. This publication also differs from many earlier publications in that the sources which have been consulted are drawn from archives in Britain, Northern Ireland and the Republic of Ireland, which provides a more complete picture of the Famine in the island of Ireland, thus challenging the myth that sections of the north-east escaped lightly. Moreover, the political, economic and psychological conflicts and convergences that existed between the component parts of the United Kingdom provide an important key to understanding responses to the Famine, both at the time and subsequently. As the recent commemorations have demonstrated, the imprint of the Famine has been deep and its legacy continues to be contentious.

At the time of the Famine, Ireland was governed from Westminster. As a result of the Act of Union of 1801, Ireland had lost her own parliament in Dublin and instead sent a number of MPs to Westminster. As a consequence of the Act, a United Kingdom of Great Britain and Ireland had been created but, as the Famine demonstrated, the political union was far from being united.[86] The 1798 rebellion, which had been a major trigger for the Union to take place, continued to shape politics in Ireland, most notably amongst the Young Irelanders, but also amongst radicals in Britain as an example of the potential of a popular uprising and the capacity of the British government to respond brutally.[87] For the British authorities, the 1798 uprising was an uncomfortable illustration of the danger posed when Catholics and Protestants combined against their authority.[88]

Following the Act of Union, Irish affairs dominated British politics. One of the reasons was due to the large Irish population. By 1841, Ireland accounted for almost one-third of the population of the United Kingdom: the population of England and Wales was 15 929 000; Scotland, 2 622 000; and Ireland, 8 200 000.[89] The economy of Ireland was also different from that of the rest of the United Kingdom and in the decades following the Act of Union, as industrialization advanced in Britain, the differences became more marked. In Ireland, by the 1840s over two-thirds of the labour force continued to depend on agriculture. The majority of these people held little or no land themselves but depended on a system of conacre, in which they would trade their labour for a small plot of land. Potatoes, which grew prolifically even in poor or rocky soil, provided over 50 per cent of the population with an adequate and healthy diet. Industrial production was mostly concentrated in Cork, Dublin and Belfast, but it was Belfast that most proficiently adapted to the new technology.

Official reports into the condition of Ireland confirmed the perception that Ireland was poor and getting poorer, yet showed no sign of curtailing its population growth.[90] For the government in Westminster, the most recent addition to the Union was displaying a tiresome potential for dependency. A constant subject of political discourse, therefore, was the necessity to modernize Ireland; and if this did not occur, she would prove to be an on-going source of dependence on British resources.[91] Ireland's problems were viewed as multiple, cutting across economic and social divisions, with both peasants and proprietors being regarded as obstacles to modernization; peasants because of their perpetuation of a subsistence economy through their attachment to a potato diet, and landlords because of their inertia and unwillingness to improve their estates. But Irish landlords objected to even the moderate changes that had been suggested in the wake of the Devon Commission into landlord and tenant relations. Consequently, the Famine, with its massive social dislocation, presented an opportunity for the desired changes to take place, by removing both poor tenants and impoverished landlords and replacing them with a new class of commercial farmers. But this aspiration could only succeed if government intervention was minimal. Charles Trevelyan of the Treasury, who became the chief administrator of government policy, explained that official assistance needed to be as small as possible because 'The change from an idle, barbarous isolated potato cultivation, to corn cultivation, which frees industry, and binds together employer and employee in mutually beneficial relations... requires capital and a new class of men.'[92] His political master, personal ally and fellow evangelical, Charles Wood, the Chancellor of the Exchequer, endorsed this aim remarking, 'There is no real prospect of regeneration and substantial amendment for Ireland until substantial proprietors possessed of capital and the will to improve their estates are introduced into the country.'[93] Furthermore, the policy of non-intervention coincided with the dominant philosophical orthodoxy that no man should depend on another. By viewing the Famine as either God or nature's way of rectifying the demographic and economic distortions of Irish society, officials in London and Dublin were exempted from any moral responsibility for the consequent suffering.

The survival of the Act of Union was regarded by British politicians as essential to safeguarding the sanctity of the Empire, and successive governments were determined that neither should be lost.[94] Yet despite not wanting the United Kingdom to be splintered, Ireland palpably was not treated as an equal partner within the Union. Proportionately, Ireland had fewer political representatives in Westminster than either England, Scotland or Wales. Also, unlike other parts of the United Kingdom, Ireland's quasi-colonial status was manifested by the continued existence of an Irish administration in Dublin Castle, demonstrating Ireland's lack of integration with the rest of the United Kingdom. Whilst Irish political power transferred to Westminster after 1800, the continuation of the Irish Executive meant that Ireland was not to be governed on an equal footing with the rest of the United Kingdom.

This uneven treatment was also manifested in the introduction of a Poor Law in 1838. Modelled on the English amended law of 1834, the Irish version was deliberately more draconian with no right to relief existing and relief only being provided within the confines of a workhouse. Nor did the Irish Poor Law include a Law of Removal.[95] The differences between the two Poor Laws made it clear that poverty in Ireland was to be treated more harshly than elsewhere and that the Irish poor were even less deserving than the undeserving English poor. Inevitably this attitude shaped responses during the Famine. The point was made on a number of occasions that if the Famine had occurred in England, the political response would have been more generous, as was the accusation that the poor of Ireland were unjustly and unnecessarily being subsidized by the industrial classes in England.[96] Moreover, as the Irish MP, Anthony Lefroy, pointed out in a parliamentary debate regarding providing a grant to promote Irish railways (which was unsuccessful) 'these perpetual contrasts between the interests of England and Ireland, as if they were conflicting, and made by Englishmen too, ought to be deprecated'.[97] As the Famine progressed, the gulf between Ireland and Britain increased. Reports of increasing levels of crime, and an uprising in 1848, which attempted to end the Union, undoubtedly contributed to a hardening of attitude. This was evident in the smallness of the grant asked for by Russell in 1849, which was only given on the understanding that it was to be the final one. Financial, rather than humanitarian, considerations were foremost. A differential treatment was also demonstrated in the response to the potato blight in the Scottish Highlands where – despite the situation being far less critical – relief was provided more promptly and with fewer restrictions.[98] The deployment of the British Laws of Settlement to remove paupers back to Ireland during the Famine and the introduction of the rate-in-aid tax into Ireland only in 1849 reinforced the fact that the United Kingdom was far from united. The treatment of Ireland during the Famine was even more invidious in light of a declaration by Russell at the onset of the famine when he stated: 'I consider the Union [between Britain and Ireland] was but a parchment and an insubstantial union, if Ireland is not to be treated in the hour of difficulty and distress, as an integral part of the United Kingdom.'[99]

Events in Ireland have to be viewed within a wider British, European and transatlantic context. Food shortages were not unique to Ireland after 1845, although famine was. Significantly, historians believe that the last great subsistence crisis across eastern Europe ended in 1819.[100]

Although the potato blight was European-wide, dependence was lower elsewhere than in Ireland and potatoes were not used as much for consumption, but proportionately were used more to produce animal feed, starch or alcohol.[101] Within Europe the potato blight coincided with a more general agricultural crisis in which the more significant corn crop was poor. The bad grain harvest in 1848 also coincided with a crisis in trade and commerce that sent shock waves throughout the British economy and reverberated throughout Ireland, even in Belfast which was regarded as the flagship of Irish industrial development. Whilst Ireland's agricultural sector was regarded as economically backward, especially when compared with Britain, it performed favourably as compared with non-British exemplars; Irish grain and potato yields were higher than in other European countries such as Scotland, France or Belgium.[102] More significantly, Ireland's export sector was highly commercialized, especially in grain and cattle. The rapid expansion of the corn trade after 1790 was largely as a result of war with France and the Corn Laws, which encouraged cultivation despite the damp climate of the country. On the eve of the Famine, Ireland was exporting sufficient corn to Britain to feed two million people. As a consequence, she was regarded as the 'bread basket' of Britain.[103] Policies introduced during the Famine were intended primarily to protect the important trading relationship between Britain and Ireland rather than provide for the destitute in the latter.

The potato failure of 1845 impacted on a country that was familiar with periodic food shortages. Moreover, the Prime Minister, Sir Robert Peel, was not only unparalleled in terms of his knowledge of Ireland, but as Home Secretary had been personally involved in coping with the widespread subsistence crisis of 1821–2. In 1838, a Poor Law had been introduced which meant Ireland was divided into Poor Law Unions, each with its own workhouse and Board of Guardians to manage relief provision. Moreover, both networks of constabulary barracks and of Catholic clergy were present even in the most remote parts of the country. Although the functions of the two bodies were different, they both provided the country with local functionaries who knew the area and the people, and they acted as a valuable intermediary between the local community and the central relief officials.

In 1846, Sir Robert Peel's administration fell, ostensibly over the introduction of an Irish Coercion bill. In reality his premiership ended because he had angered many of his colleagues by repealing the Corn Laws, using the Famine as a pretext for so doing.[104] Peel, who had commenced

his parliamentary career as an MP for Ireland and had spent seven years
as Chief Secretary in that country (the longest period of any officer), was
forced to resign as Prime Minister on an Irish question. Ironically, this
was not the first time that Peel had been forced from office on an Irish
issue. His brief period as premier in 1835 had also ended on a point
relating to Ireland. Moreover, ultra-Protestants had forgiven him
neither for his role in granting Catholic Emancipation in 1829 nor for
his more recent grant to Maynooth College in 1845.[105] The fall of Peel's
government split the Tory Party into Protectionists (led by Lord George
Bentinck) and Peelites.

At the time the blight made its second, more devastating appearance
in Ireland, the British political system was in disarray. Moreover, the
British economy was slipping into a recession, which made financial
retrenchment a major consideration in any subsequent policy formulation. For Ireland, on the verge of a major famine, the repercussions were
significant. Chapter 2 charts the variety of relief measures introduced in
response to the consecutive crop failures. They were repeatedly modified and changed, but increasingly one of their aims was to throw the
burden of relief onto diminishing Irish resources. The mortality and
emigration statistics are the simplest yet most effective benchmark of the
failure of these policies. No excess mortality occurred during Peel's
governance but the scale of shortages facing his successor, Lord John
Russell, was far greater. It was not merely the frugality of many of
the relief measures introduced, but the fact that a large and Byzantine
bureaucracy that absorbed both time and resources hampered them.
But disagreement with the policies and the Whig government's handling
of the situation was substantial.

The opposition expressed by British members of parliament and the
genuine sympathy shown has tended to be overlooked by famine
researchers. Some of the most coherent, incisive and sustained criticisms
of government policy were by Lord George Bentinck, ably supported by
Benjamin Disraeli. It was Bentinck who brought to the attention of the
House that the government had halved the size of food rations arbitrarily; the nonsense of leaving the responsibility for food imports to private
traders and speculators; the government's exaggeration of the quantity
of food imported into Ireland; and the fact that no attempt was made to
collect and collate mortality rates.[106] He was also responsible for introducing a railway bill into Ireland that he hoped would provide employment in the short term and regeneration in the long term.[107] A number
of radicals also made attacks on Irish policy. Irish MPs, however, who

numbered 105, proved to be divided on many of the key measures and were reluctant to act together as a lobby group. The most disappointing performance in parliament, however, was on the part of the Repeal Party. In 1847, death removed Daniel O'Connell from parliament, but even prior to this, his alliance with the Whig Party made his interventions appear feeble and supine. The more spirited attacks by William Smith O'Brien, leader of the radical Young Ireland group, were undermined by his political isolation within the House.[108] Overall, despite debate, policies were shaped by prevailing attitudes to Ireland, the Irish poor and to Irish landlords which had existed before 1845 and which had been exacerbated by famine. Irish people were not only regarded as inferior partners within the United Kingdom, they were low on the international benchmark of civilizations. In 1847, the Lord Lieutenant of Ireland asserted: 'Esquimaux [sic] and New Zealanders are more thrifty and industrious than these people who deserve to be left to their fate instead of the hardworking people of England being taxed for their support.'[109]

In general, the role of the state in the provision of welfare in the nineteenth-century has been the main interest of historians, whilst the role of private philanthropy has received less attention. Yet the late 1840s were regarded as the age of organized charity, with evangelical influence being particularly strong.[110] Most famine studies have focused on the role of the government, paying little attention to the contribution made by private relief. However, not only was private aid considerable, it was effective in targeting those most in need, as it could be given without the bureaucratic or ideological constraints which accompanied much official relief. Private intervention was also regarded as more acceptable than government assistance; the former relief for the purpose of assisting deserving cases and the latter for undeserving paupers.[111] In reality, the distinction was artificial and, during a famine, meaningless. Chapter 3 examines the role of private philanthropy. Most private aid was given in 1847 and, for the most part, it dried up following the harvest. A remarkable feature of this relief was the diversity of those who were involved – cutting across religious and economic divides, and coming from all parts of the world. The geographic range of involvement was particularly impressive in view of the slowness of communications.

Private relief was occasionally controversial and, in some instances, it served to deepen existing divisions within society. The activities of proselytizers also cast a long, dark shadow over the involvement of private relief organizations, the legacy of which was still evident at the end of the

twentieth century.[112] One of the most enduring controversies concerned
the role of Queen Victoria. In January 1847, she gave £2000 to famine
relief, making her the largest individual donor. Yet, she was remembered
by the epithet 'Famine Queen'. In 1880 the nationalist leader, Charles
Stewart Parnell, claimed that 'in 1847 the Queen of England was the only
sovereign of Europe who gave nothing out of her private purse'.[113] In
1900, the political activist Maud Gonne, upon the occasion of Victoria's
third and final visit to Ireland, wrote in the *United Irishman*: 'However
vile and selfish and pitiless her soul may be, she must sometimes tremble
as death approaches when she thinks of the countless mothers who, shel-
terless under the cloudy Irish sky, watching their starving little ones,
have cursed her before they died.'[114] The British authorities banned the
paper in which the article appeared. In 1995, dissension regarding the
contribution of Victoria re-emerged when it was proposed to include a
statue of the Queen in an exhibition marking the 150th anniversary of
Cork University (formerly, one of the Queen's Universities).[115] The acrimonious way in which the dispute was executed was further evidence
that the Famine was a close rather than a distant memory.

The British government and Irish landlords have traditionally been
the villains of the Famine narrative, whilst Irish farmers, who sold their
grain and cattle for export and received massive financial returns, have
been ignored or exonerated. Chapter 4 re-evaluates the impact of government policy in relation to the question of food imports and food
exports, which has remained one of the most disputed aspects of relief
provision. The claims of John Mitchel, more recently echoed by Sinéad
O'Connor in song, which equated food exports with excess mortality
have tended to be associated with a nationalist interpretation of the Famine and, consequently, discredited. Instead, conservative and revisionist
historians have pointed to the vast amount of imports in the spring of
1846, which exceeded exports. The statistics quoted are generally based
on the pioneering work of Austin Bourke.[116] However, what Bourke
himself admitted, and what subsequent interpretations have chosen to
ignore, is that the official returns upon which he based his estimates
were flawed and provided an underestimation of exports. Also, government returns were only concerned with grain and not the vast amounts
of other foodstuffs which left the country.

This distortion of the evidence has meant that even non-revisionist
historians have contended that if the ports had been closed to exports
there would not have been sufficient food in the country to feed the
people.[117] This claim is unsubstantiated given that no attempt has been

made by historians apart from Austin Bourke to compute the quantity of food exported, and even his conclusions are based on the flawed tabulations of the government. Moreover, the fall in grain exports in the winter of 1846–7 was to be expected given that the corn crop had been so poor in Ireland in the 1846 harvest. The reduction in exports also failed to make grain more readily available to the Irish poor as hoarding and forestalling by merchants was widespread, leaving the viceroy to admit that merchants had 'done their best to keep up prices'.[118] It was also pointed out in parliament by Bentinck, and conceded by both the Chancellor of the Exchequer and the Prime Minister, that the amount of food coming into Ireland in the first six months of 1846 had been exaggerated.[119]

Ironically, some of the most incisive critiques of the impact of the policy of allowing food imports and exports to be unrestrained were made by members of the Whig Party – notably the viceroys, Bessborough and Clarendon – rather than nationalist commentators or the Tory opposition. Their comments, however, were confined to the private rather than the public arena. Chapter 4 uses a little consulted source, the Bills of Entry of vessels coming into the major British ports, to compute the amount of food leaving Ireland at the height of the Famine.[120] These records list the cargo of all ships from Ireland to the ports of Liverpool, London, Glasgow and Bristol. The results demonstrate that not only large amounts of grain, but also immense quantities of other foodstuffs, cattle and alcohol continued to leave the country. Moreover, substantial amounts of exports were originating in the west of the country, from areas such as Westport, Ballina and even Skibbereen. They reveal that sufficient food was being produced in the country to feed the people, corroborating Amartya Sen's contention that famines cannot be explained by a shortage of food only, with famine-stricken areas sometimes exporting food.[121]

Many modern famines occur in the midst of war. Despite the absence of war in Ireland in the 1840s, crime rates were high and the country had a reputation for lawlessness. Also, the high military and constabulary presence meant that this was effectively an occupied country. Chapter 5 looks at crime and popular unrest during the Famine. In the wake of the potato failures crime rates rose sharply although they were overwhelmingly directed against property rather than people. In spite of the fact that many of the crimes appeared to be hunger-driven, they lessened sympathy for the Irish poor and confirmed them as lawless and undeserving, especially by those who felt that their property or lives were under threat. In the first two years of shortages, also, popular protests increased, some of them having their roots in a form of moral economy which demanded that staple foods be sold at fair prices, making them affordable to the people employed on the public works.[122] The protests rarely resulted in violence, usually due to the dual interventions of the local priests and constabulary. Other more violent crimes were a reminder that in extreme situations people were willing to resort to desperate measures. The fact that the crimes were perpetrated mostly against the wealthier classes gave them newsworthiness and motivated the authorities to resolve to end them quickly. Fear of crimes, especially violent attacks on landlords, served to increase existing social and economic divisions. Overall, the high instance of crime was a further indication that the fabric of society was breaking down.

Chapter 6 addresses the role of the churches and organized religion during the Famine. At the time, many people, including influential officials in Britain, believed that the Famine was a judgement from God; a way of teaching Irish people to be independent, modern and good British subjects (all of which was generally associated with Protestant-ism). The themes of salvation and regeneration were frequently invoked both to explain what had happened and to justify some of the more callous responses to it.[123] This interpretation clearly influenced the approach of Charles Trevelyan who was convinced that an opportunity had been provided by God to remove 'the inveterate root of social evil' in the country, explaining that 'the cure has been applied by the stroke of an all-wise Providence in a manner as unexpected and unthought of as it is likely to be effectual. God grant that we may rightly perform our part and not turn into a curse what was intended for a blessing'.[124]

One of the long-term legacies of the Famine was that in the late nine-teenth-century divisions between the Catholic Church and the two main Protestant Churches became more polarized, reinforcing a political split along denominational lines. The commemorations forced some of the Protestant Churches to confront uncomfortable aspects of their past. In 1995, the *Church of Ireland Gazette* acknowledged that whilst the British government and Irish landlords had been widely blamed for suffering during the Famine:

the Church of Ireland itself is the third major recipient of severe criticism in traditional assessments of the Famine. *Souperism* may have been practiced by other Protestants too but it was the established church which was most active in the proselytizing campaigns which

rewarded starving converts with soup and other me~~~~
...No attempt should be made to minimize their pe~~~~
particularly the lasting suspicion of Protestant good fai~~~~
the Roman Catholic population.[125]

Just as the Famine served to polarize existing divisions betwe~~n the main churches, it also exacerbated political tensions both within Ireland and between Ireland and Britain. A backdrop to the Famine was the increased revolutionary conflicts in Europe that came to a head with the February revolution in France in 1848. Chapter 7 examines the political context of the Famine and political developments during the crisis. The late 1840s coincided with political fragmentation in Ireland within the ranks of repealers, that is Young and Old Ireland, and between nationalists and loyalists (generally Protestants who supported the Union). Whilst the repeal movement outwardly appealed to all religions Old Ireland, under the leadership of both Daniel O'Connell and his son John, had become indelibly linked with the Catholic Church. In contrast, the Young Ireland leaders, who were drawn from mixed religious and geographical backgrounds, made winning support in the north of the country a vital part of their campaign.[126] Ironically, the revival of nationalism in Ireland coincided with the emergence of a revitalized Orange Order, which viewed itself as the defender of Protestantism and loyal to the Union against the encroachment of Catholic disloyalty.

O'Connell's section of the movement was also committed to constitutional methods and rejected physical force. Initially, also, they had welcomed the new Whig government as the party who was committed to justice for Ireland, but this sympathy was hard to sustain as the Famine progressed. The revolution in France in February 1848 also forced a realignment within the repeal movement between those who supported an uprising and those who continued to favour constitutional tactics. William Smith O'Brien, the leader of the Young Irelanders, reluctantly led a small insurrection in County Tipperary in July 1848, in the midst of a famine. It lacked mass support and was opposed by constitutional nationalists, the government, the Orange Order and the Catholic Church. For the poor, the basic need to survive made them unlikely foot soldiers in an uprising. The attempted uprising failed, but the events of these years proved to be pivotal in the subsequent political development of Ireland. The uprising not only damaged the nationalist movement, but it polarized existing tensions between nationalists and supporters of the Union. In a similar manner to the United Irishmen in 1798, the

Young Irelanders had looked outwards, seeking inspiration and practical support from France. Significantly, the latter came from the United States, at a time when the massive movement of people from Ireland to North America was forging a powerful new bond between the two countries. After 1848, Irish nationalism increasingly looked westward across the Atlantic rather than eastward to France for practical support.

The final section looks briefly at how those who survived the Famine coped with the changed circumstances in which they lived. The recovery from famine was slow. In the course of a six-year period, the Irish population had decreased by 25 per cent. A large portion of those who died had been poor, Catholic and Irish speakers, but no section of Irish society and no part of the country were untouched by the catastrophe. The Famine's legacy and reverberations lasted far longer. By 1851, Ireland was only just beginning to emerge from a sustained period of mass mortality and emigration, and political and revolutionary turmoil. The legacy of Young Ireland was apparent in the political discourse of nationalists in the late nineteenth century, but without their idealism or non-sectarian vision. Instead, Irish politics evolved into a bitter struggle between Unionism and Nationalism. A geographic divide also emerged which had its roots in the Famine as Protestant Ulster began to view itself as different from, and superior to, the rest of the country. The consequence of this approach became apparent in 1920 when 26 counties were allowed to leave the United Kingdom, but the six predominantly Protestant counties in the north-east remained as part of the Union. Moreover, Ireland never recovered demographically from the shock of the Famine and, uniquely, at the end of the twentieth century it was the only country in Europe with a smaller population than it had possessed 150 years earlier.

As the recent commemorations have shown, the Irish population, both within Ireland and elsewhere, took a long time to come to terms with their grief and the enormity of the tragedy. There has also been a reluctance, both at the popular and the academic level, to engage with the more unpleasant side of the Famine – corruption, hoarding, suicide, prostitution, theft (from those equally as poor) and cannibalism – incidents which took place in Ireland as they have done in all famines. The stigma attached means that they are under-recorded and so are particularly tragic when noted in official records. Yet famine was obscene and acute hunger could lead to desperate measures. From Partree in Mayo it was reported that Bryan Sharkey 'concealed his dead child in a dunghill for a fortnight, until the dogs carried it in quarters through the village'. His concealment was 'that he might have the three and a half pounds of relief Indian meal allowed the child'.[127] A number of deaths appeared especially gratuitous. At the assizes in Galway in March 1848, the death of a young woman was recorded. She had drowned herself in a bog, both her husband and sister having recently died. Her children were described as being 'ill with extreme destitution'. The verdict on her suicide was of 'temporary insanity'.[128] In 1849, two years after the Famine was officially over, the *Times* reported alleged cases of cannibalism in Clifden in County Mayo.[129] Were such incidences of suffering necessary or inevitable in the affluent United Kingdom, which lay at the hub of the British Empire?

The economist Amartya Sen has pointed out that even in Third World countries famine mortality could be averted if good will existed.[130] Unlike in many famine-affected countries today, in the 1840s even the poor in Ireland had access to a healthy and substantial diet. Ireland prior to the Famine was producing a large agricultural surplus and the potato diet was highly nutritious. Moreover, the Irish economy was diverse with potatoes only accounting for 20 per cent of all agricultural output.[131] Food exports throughout the Famine continued to be buoyant and the quantity of some exports, such as cattle, increased. The administrative capability of the British government was demonstrated in the summer of 1847 when over three million people were fed daily, at a cost far below that of the public works. Nevertheless, one of the most lethal subsistence crises in modern history occurred within the jurisdiction of, and in close proximity to, the epicentre of what was the richest empire in the world.

Palpably, much of the suffering, mortality and devastation, physical and psychological pain which resulted from the potato failure, was avoidable. The heated debates within parliament and elsewhere demonstrated that the official response to the catastrophe was not inevitable – alternative visions were offered and contemporary criticism of relief policies was compelling. Good will did exist but its proponents were overwhelmed by a lethal cocktail of commercial greed, parsimony, providentialism and political economy. Decisions made in London were frequently contrary to the recommendations of the local relief officials and the advice of administrators in Dublin Castle. Clearly, those officials who controlled relief provision after 1846 possessed little good will towards Ireland. Instead, in the words of a contemporary novelist, Maria Edgeworth, they had 'hearts of iron – natures from which the natural instinct of sympathy or pity have been destroyed'.[132]

Finally, the Famine demonstrated the limitations and deficiencies of the Act of Union. Despite the existence of the United Kingdom – and the determination that it should not be broken up – Ireland in the eyes of many politicians represented the unknown 'other' which had been rendered more burdensome by years of distress and political strife. In Ireland, however, radicals and nationalists believed that the real burden was British rule. In a passionate editorial at the beginning of 1847, the *Belfast Vindicator* informed the people of Ulster that they were being 'ruled, fleeced, taxed, neglected and despised by haughty Englishmen' adding that 'the real blight of this country has been the blight of foreign legislation'.[133] One hundred and fifty years later, the Prime Minister of the United Kingdom admitted that 'those who governed in London at the time failed their people'.[134] One day revisionists and unionists may reach the same conclusion.

2

THE GOVERNMENT'S RESPONSE
TO THE CRISIS

In 1843 an unfamiliar blight was observed on the potato crop in America. Within two years it had spread to Europe, appearing in Belgium, France, Germany, Switzerland, England, and eventually Scotland and Ireland. The new disease was first noticed in Dublin at the end of August 1845 and within a few days isolated instances were being reported throughout the country, especially in the east. The high dependence of the Irish poor on potatoes meant that its appearance in the country was regarded with alarm. The September issue of the *Gardener's Chronicle* posed the question: 'Where will Ireland be in the event of a universal potato rot?'[1]

Potatoes had been introduced into Ireland in the late sixteenth century and by the early nineteenth century they were established as the staple diet of approximately two-thirds of the population. As the population increased rapidly after 1800 dependence on potatoes grew, because they allowed a subsistence survival on land which was either subdivided or of poor quality. Although high dependence on potatoes was generally associated with the west of the country, dependence in the north had increased in the decades preceding the Famine. The contraction of the domestic linen industry after 1815 and its gradual replacement by the industrial process of wet-spinning meant that people who had previously combined weaving with potato or oat cultivation returned to potatoes to provide a staple diet. The Poor Inquiry Commissioners reporting in the 1830s found that even in areas associated with linen production, such as County Armagh, the diet of the poor was exclusively potatoes.[2] In addition to providing a subsistence diet for the Irish poor, potatoes were consumed by other social groups. They were also eaten by pigs and other farm animals, with as much as 30 per cent of the annual crop being so utilized. In years of shortages, therefore, animals acted as a buffer for human consumption, they being the first to feel the impact of the deficiency. Although corn was cultivated throughout the country, it was mostly grown as a cash crop for paying rent and for eventual export. Potatoes, moreover, despite playing such an important role in Irish life and in shaping perceptions of Ireland, accounted for only 20 per cent of all agricultural produce.[3]

A Temporary Calamity

As a subsistence crop, potatoes had a good record of reliability. The potato diet, especially when supplemented with buttermilk, was highly nutritious and the Irish poor were amongst the tallest, healthiest and most fertile population in Europe.[4] They also had access to domestic fuel in the form of peat or turf which, on the eve of the Famine, supplied about one million of the rural population with fuel.[5] Rich fertilizer, in the form of seaweed or pig manure, was readily available, as was basic but cheap accommodation in mud cabins. Yet the life-style of the Irish poor, which was underpinned by the potato economy, was frequently condemned by both foreign visitors and British commentators such as Arthur Young, who viewed a potato diet and inhabiting a mud cabin as indicators of a low level of civilization.[6] Nonetheless, as the economic historian Cormac Ó Gráda has pointed out, 'a wholesome diet and plentiful, inexpensive fuel in the form of turf compensated for the tattered clothing and rudimentary housing of the Irish poor'.[7]

Crop failures had occurred periodically in Ireland in 1740, 1766, 1782–4, 1795–6, 1880–1, 1816–17 and 1822. They generally did not last for more than one season, although an exception was the 1740 failure which had been caused by a mini ice-age and had resulted in high excess mortality.[8] Since the late eighteenth century, the role of the state in alleviating such periods of food shortages had been highly interventionist. At the time of the shortages in 1782–4, the Corn Law was temporarily suspended and the Lord Lieutenant provided £100 000 bounty as an incentive to merchants to import additional oats and wheat.[9] During the shortages of 1816–17 and those of 1821–2 the British government imported corn into the west of the country.[10] In the 1820s and 1830s the responsibility of government to intervene in poor relief was strenuously debated, resulting in the introduction of a 'new', more draconian Poor Law in England and Wales in 1834. The increasingly punitive attitude towards poverty and relief was also evident in the introduction of Ireland's first Poor Law in 1838. By the time of the Irish Famine, therefore, attitudes towards the poor were harsher and more ideologically constrained than they had been during earlier subsistence crises.

The failure of the potato crop in 1845, although widespread, was not regarded with particular alarm, with the main impact of the shortages expected in the months preceding the next harvest. The fact that the blight appeared relatively late in the harvest period in 1845 insulated much of the crop from its impact. Also, as in previous years of failure, the disease was not expected to continue for more than one year. In a number of ways, Ireland was better prepared to deal with food shortages than on former occasions: the development of steam shipping in the 1820s provided faster transport between Britain and Ireland; in 1831 a Board of Works had been set up for the purpose of promoting the economic improvement of Ireland through public works projects; and most significantly, in 1838 a Poor Law had been established which had divided Ireland into 130 Poor Law Unions, each with its own workhouse and elected board of guardians. As a consequence, by 1845 an important administrative network had been established throughout the country. Between 1825 and 1841, a detailed county-by-county ordnance survey was carried out, which mapped every road, house and field, and which included eclectic information on the lives of the population.[11] Various official enquiries had also provided the government with detailed knowledge of both the local people and conditions in which they lived. Additionally, Sir Robert Peel, the Prime Minister at the time of the first appearance of the blight, was unusual for an English politician in that he had lived in Ireland for six years when Chief Secretary in the Dublin Castle Executive. As Home Secretary he had also been in charge of relief provision during the subsistence crisis of 1822.[12]

Peel's response to news of the blight was tempered by his views on the Irish character. In October, he acknowledged that accounts of the crop 'are becoming very alarming', but added 'there is such a tendency to exaggeration and inaccuracy in Irish reports that delay in acting upon them is only desirable'. Peel decided to appoint a Scientific Commission to ascertain the true extent of crop loss. However, the report of the Scientific Commission at the end of October confirmed the seriousness of the crop failure, describing the situation as 'melancholy' and warning that 'it cannot be looked upon in other than a most serious light. We are confident that the reports are underrated rather than exaggerated.'[13] Nevertheless, the belief that reports from Ireland were exaggerated was a recurrent theme which generally worked to the disadvantage of the Irish poor.[14]

In November, Peel established a Temporary Relief Commission which was to operate in parallel with, but distinct from, the Poor Law. The Commission was to oversee the establishment of local relief committees whose main functions were to provide food to the local poor and to establish a limited system of public works. At the same time, Peel secretly arranged for £100 000 worth of Indian corn to be purchased in America.[15] Because the impact of the shortages was not expected to be felt until the following spring and summer, there was sufficient time for Peel's policies to be set in place. Indian corn was chosen as the replacement food as it was cheap and regarded as a useful tool in steering the Irish palate away from the traditional potato diet. Additionally, it would contribute to the decline of the systems of subdivision and conacre (the grant of a small plot for potato growing in return for labour) which were particularly prevalent in the west of the country. Sir Randolph Routh, who was in charge of the Relief Commission, contended that a positive outcome could be expected from weaning the poor off potatoes on the grounds that 'The little industry called for to rear the potato, and its prolific growth, leave the people to indolence and all kinds of vice, which habitual labour and a higher order of food would prevent. I think it very probable that we may derive much advantage from this present calamity.'[16]

Despite a network of workhouses covering the country, the government decided not to make use of these, but to keep temporary and permanent relief separate. The Poor Law was limited by the fact that only indoor relief was permitted and the workhouses could accommodate only 120 000 paupers. In February 1846, the radical MP Sharman Crawford suggested that outdoor relief be permitted in order to cope with the rise in distress in the ensuing months. Yet the government, even in an emergency, was bound by ideological constraints regarding the nature and relief of poverty in Ireland. Instead of utilizing the workhouses or the administrative machinery of the Poor Law, they preferred to rely on a specially introduced system of relief based on public works; the Home Secretary, Sir James Graham, justifying this on the grounds that 'As the evil is likely to be temporary, it [is] better to meet the emergency by extraordinary means, rather than introduce a mischievous system of administration into Ireland.'[17]

Although Peel's policies were generally praised, from the outset they contained flaws which became more critical as famine persisted and intensified. The financial constraints were particularly ominous. After 1845, the relief committees were financed by local funds which were matched by the government. This system worked against areas with inert, absentee or miserly landlords, whilst putting a disproportionate amount of the financial burden on poor districts. The decision to import Indian corn in an effort to retrain the Irish palate, not only meant availability was subject to the vagaries of importers, it also exposed Irish people to a greatly inferior diet. Furthermore, an arduous process had to be followed – steeping, followed by a period of vigorous boiling – to make the corn edible if not palatable. Widespread ignorance of this procedure resulted in dysentery and other stomach problems which, in turn, increased mortality. Nevertheless, when Peel was forced out of office in the summer of 1846, he was commended for his handling of the situation, no deaths having resulted from the first year of shortages. Even the nationalist *Freeman's Journal* praised his policies and commented that 'no man died of famine during his administration'.[18] Ironically, his success had been helped by the fact that the Scientific Commission had overestimated the extent of potato crop loss – in total about 35 per cent was destroyed – and the greatest losses had occurred in the more diverse economies of the east of the country rather than in the subsistence economy of parts of the west. Moreover, an excellent corn harvest, especially oats, had ensured that many of the poor were still able to pay their rent.[19]

From the outset, Peel's policies for relief were made subservient to his longer-term plans for Ireland and Britain. In the former, the desired aim of modernization necessitated ending both dependence on potatoes and the subdivision of land; in the latter case, it meant moving closer to a programme of free trade through a repeal of the Corn Laws. Peel gave a clear indication of the direction of his policies when he stated in October 1845: 'I have no confidence in such remedies as the prohibition of exports, or the stoppage of the distilleries. The removal of impediments to import is the only effectual remedy.'[20] But Peel's commitment to a free trade programme was disliked by many members of the Tory Party and so Peel's premiership during the first year of shortages was precarious. In addition to repealing the Corn Laws, Peel had resolved to introduce a new coercion bill in Ireland, known as the Protection of Life Bill. The bill had the support of the majority of his party, who believed that remedial measures could only be successful if agrarian crimes were reduced.[21] Peel's determination to link Irish relief with repeal of the Corn Laws contributed to his political downfall in June 1846 when the proposed Protection of Life Bill for Ireland was used by an alliance of Whigs, Irish representatives and members of the Tory Party led by Bentinck as a vehicle for defeating the Prime Minister.

The defeat of Peel, due to an improbable alliance of diverse political groupings, resulted in a Whig administration acquiring power. The Whig government remained in office until 1852 and consequently was responsible for policy formulation during the most severe period of the Famine. The fall of the Tories – regardless of the short-term success of their relief policies – was welcomed by Daniel O'Connell and the Repeal Party. O'Connell made it clear that he was willing to re-establish his alliance with the Whigs and to promote their programme of 'justice for Ireland'. Lord John Russell, the new Prime Minister, like his predecessor, was anxious to modernize the Irish economy. He believed such a transition would only be possible by getting rid of potato dependence and subdivision at the bottom of the social scale, and replacing inert or indebted landlords at the upper end. Similar to Peel, therefore, Russell's relief policies were underpinned by longer-term aspirations for Ireland's development.

On a personal level Russell was not a strong party leader. He had a reputation for vacillating and the way in which he came to power probably increased his political insecurities. In December 1845, when Peel had initially resigned over the Corn Law crisis, Russell had agreed to form a replacement government, but he changed his mind a day later.[22] He informed the Queen that he had done so because he was afraid of leading a government with only a minority in the House of Commons.[23] Russell finally came to power by default in the summer of 1846, helped by the Protectionist group of the Tory Party and Irish Repealers. He was, however, at the head of a minority government and depended on Peelites for support. In one of his first speeches in the House of Commons, Russell outlined his commitment to furthering a programme of justice for Ireland, declaring that

> we consider the social grievances of Ireland are those which are most prominent, and to which it is most likely to be in our power to afford, not a complete and immediate remedy, but some remedy, some kind of improvement, so that some kind of hope may be entertained that some ten or twelve years hence the country will, by the measures we undertake, be in a far better state with respect to the frightful destitution and misery which now prevail in the country.[24]

Although the Whig Party won the General Election in 1847, one of the outcomes was an increase in the mercantile interest and a call for financial retrenchment. Whig 'radicals', who now numbered over 80, effectively held the balance of power in parliament and, as one of their leaders John Bright made clear, land reform was crucial to the future well-being not only of Ireland, but of the rest of the United Kingdom. 'Clearing away the fetters under which land is now held' was, therefore, to be a political priority.[25] Managing this process of change, rather than responding to the needs of the destitute became a key concern of the new parliament. All of these factors militated against providing a comprehensive and practical relief programme for Ireland, regardless of the fact that one of Russell's ostensible aims had been justice for Ireland.

Almost immediately upon the Whigs taking office, reports were being received from Ireland of the reappearance of the blight – far earlier and more virulent than in the previous year. On 12 August, Daniel O'Connell, who was the parliamentary representative for Cork, informed Russell of 'the frightful state of famine by which the people of this country are not merely menaced, but actually engulfed'. He asked for public works to be commenced '*without any delay*' and concluded by saying, 'Nothing but the fearful state of my country could justify this urgency.'[26] On the same day in Fermanagh, at the opposite end of the country, Lord Enniskillen was repeating the same message to the Irish government informing them that 'last year the rot was bad but not so much as to make us fear starvation, which I regret to say is the case now'.[27]

The scale of the shortages facing Russell's government was far greater than in the previous year with over 90 per cent of the potato crop being destroyed and the corn crop being far smaller than usual. The programme of relief introduced by Russell's administration, was substantially different from Peel's measures and, despite the indications of a greater shortfall in food supplies, provision was contracted and access was made more restrictive. Public works were made the corner-stone of relief provision but, unlike the measures of the previous season, they were to be made unproductive. Conditions governing them were also to be more stringent. Regardless of the greater food deficiency, the new government decided not to import food into Ireland on the same scale as during Peel's administration, but to leave imports and exports to the free working of the market. Russell also determined that more use should be made of the Poor Law than in the previous year and that alternative relief should not be offered until the workhouses were full.[28] Local relief committees were to be reconstituted but they were to play a less important role in the distribution of food than in the previous year, reflecting the shift in emphasis in relief provision. The involvement of local landlords in relief committees occasionally resulted in a misapplication of resources, with a number of landlords being accused of giving outdoor relief to their own tenants who were not in need.[29] From the outset, the funding of relief placed the heaviest burden on those areas which were the poorest. The 100 per cent matched funding, provided under Peel, was to be reduced to 50 per cent under Russell. No special provision was made for areas which lacked a resident gentry to organize a local committee or to raise funds. A further feature of relief provision which remained constant was that the Treasury was given overall administrative responsibility, which included overseeing the distribution of government funds. Consequently, the two key figures in charge of relief provision were Sir Charles Wood, the Chancellor of the Exchequer, and Charles Trevelyan, the Permanent Secretary at the Treasury.

The change to public works, particularly in the restrictive form envisaged, filled some people with alarm, especially as the scale of demand was far greater than it had been in the previous year. O'Connell, whilst assuring the government that he appreciated that they were doing their utmost for Ireland, simultaneously warned that any attempt to persevere in the plans proposed 'must fail'.[30] The Viceroy, Lord Bessborough, was similarly pessimistic. He believed that the reliance on relief works could only be successful if affordable food was also available. He cautioned that unless the government could take measures to keep down the price of meal, 'the wages that we contemplate will not support the people'.[31] Yet, in spite of the early warning signals about the limitations of the public works, the policy was upheld during the worst subsistence crisis in memory. Plans for relief also took into account the fact that the distress might increase unrest in some areas and Russell told the Viceroy to ensure that there was 'a sufficiency of troops and police in any county that seems growing in disturbance'.[32]

The decision to make public works unproductive divided members of the Whig Party and caused a rift between the Irish Executive and the Treasury, a division that developed as the Famine progressed. The moderate viewpoint of Russell and Bessborough was opposed by the Home Secretary, George Grey, by Charles Wood, the Chancellor of the Exchequer, and by Charles Trevelyan, the Permanent Secretary to the Treasury, all of whom were unsympathetic to Irish landlords and – sharing an evangelical interpretation of the crisis – believed that the salvation of Ireland required punitive measures. The two leading Treasury officials also considered it ideologically unsound to allow relief works to be useful as they would unfairly reward landlords. Public works, therefore, were regarded as a vital tool in the moral regeneration of Ireland rather than simply an apparatus for providing relief. Wood argued that it was essential that they should contain a punitive element, allowing them to appear as 'a sort of test like the workhouse here – I mean for the proprietors ... the time has come when the Irish proprietor must learn to depend upon himself. Hitherto we have oppressed the people and bribed the land-lords. We have given up the first and ought also to give up the latter.'[33] The support for minimal relief of an unproductive nature was also upheld by the *Times*, which was an important mirror of British middle- and upper-class opinion.[34]

Accordingly, after 1846 the formulation of relief policy was under-pinned by the belief that government intervention was to be sparing, on the grounds that 'a continuous and indiscriminate almsgiving by the state tends more to deteriorate than to elevate the people'.[35] Yet the poor were not the only source of concern to the government. Exasperation with Irish landlords also shaped relief measures, particularly the belief that they had to be forced to do their duty rather than be allowed to de-pend on the government. The main proponents of these views held powerful positions in the Treasury and Home Office. Charles Wood claimed that the inertia of the gentry and proprietors had prevented a social transformation of the country. Comparing Irish landlords with those in other parts of the United Kingdom, he asked: 'Why cannot Irish gentlemen do as English gentlemen do and borrow their money from private lenders? It seems to me to be the misfortune of Ireland that every man comes to the government.'[36] Particularly unfavourable com-parisons were made between the response of landlords in Ireland and that of landlords in the Scottish Highlands, where the potato had also failed. Charles Trevelyan, the Permanent Secretary at the Treasury, when praising the latter group added, 'it is a source of positive pleasure to turn from the Irish to the Scotch case – in the former, everything both with regard to the people and proprietors is sickening and disgusting'.[37] Significantly, these attitudes appeared to influence policy. In autumn 1846, the Treasury decided that a portion of the modest amount of grain imported by the government should be sent in the first place to Scotland, despite the greater destitution in Ireland. This action caused considerable alarm amongst relief officials in Ireland.[38] It was also an early example of decisions being made in London which ignored ad-vice from relief officials on the ground. Instead, some members of the government increasingly viewed the crop failure as an opportunity to bring about the much-desired regeneration of Ireland, the objective of saving lives being of secondary importance.

Relief Works

In addition to imposing restrictions on relief provision, the Whig government made the conditions governing the public works far harsher than they had been formerly. Workers were to attend from 6 a.m. to 6 p.m. and if they were late for the morning roll call, they lost a quarter of a day's pay. Because of the Byzantine complexity of the public works bureaucracy, local provision often took as long as six weeks to establish, making it defective as a system of emergency relief.[39] The slowness in providing the works was sometimes blamed on the intervention of the Treasury, which increasingly interfered in the day-to-day administration of all aspects of relief.[40] In contrast with the previous year, after 1846 the wages on the public works were based on piece-work, which often served to depress wages further as the destitute fell into the cycle of hunger and exhaustion. A ceiling was also placed on earnings. The Treasury had insisted that wages should not be above the usual rates of pay in the district and, where possible, should be paid in food. By the end of 1846 the average wage paid on the public works was eight or ten pence a day, although in a number of areas the change-over to task work had reduced it to three pence a day.[41] One of the main weaknesses of the relief works, therefore, was the low level of wages paid, especially in a period of artificially inflated food prices. The complicated system of supervision also contributed to frequent delays in the payment of wages.[42]

Despite daily reports to Trevelyan recounting instances of death from starvation of people dependent on the relief works, the Treasury insisted that the wages paid were adequate.[43] The lowness of the wages contrasted with the high level of administrative expenses for the public works. By the beginning of 1847 a total of 15 978 persons had been employed: consisting of ten inspecting officers, 74 engineers, 558 assistant engineers, 9817 overseers, 4085 check clerks , 429 office clerks, 174 headquarter clerks, one valuator, 181 assistant valuators, 50 inspectors of drainage, 131 sub-inspectors of drainage, 37 inspectors of accounts and 521 pay clerks. The cost of these was £410 000.[44] In total, the public works scheme – which was operative for little more than six months – cost over four and a half million pounds, half of which was advanced as a loan to Ireland. The amount of paperwork generated was also considerable. The *Limerick Chronicle* observed that the relief commissioners were 'wondrously extravagant' with directives and pamphlets having sent three sets of instructions to the Glin relief committee 'teaching the poor how to cook food they do not possess'.[45]

By the end of 1846 doctors were reporting an increase in mortality, one of the main causes being dysentery, the symptoms of which were pains in the legs, arms and head, swollen limbs and an inability to keep anything in the stomach. The dispensary doctor in Skibbereen, which was to achieve international notoriety for the suffering of its population, reported that in regard to the deaths, 'all talk of exaggeration is at an end. The people are dying – not in twos or threes – but by dozens; the ordinary forms of decent burial are dispensed with.'[46] Apart from not saving lives and being expensive, the public works failed in a further way. While people were so employed, they were unable to pursue their usual agricultural pursuits, which had serious repercussions for the following harvest.

In the winter of 1846–7 excess mortality increased sharply although, as Bentinck protested in parliament, accurate estimates were not kept by the government. The cause of deaths was more often disease than hunger. The reliance by the government on Indian corn as a substitute for potatoes also contributed to the death toll. In April 1847 the Lord Lieutenant estimated that half of the deaths were due to bad food or food that had been inadequately cooked.[47] At the beginning of 1847, in recognition of the failure of the public works, the government decided to abandon them and replace them with a new relief measure based on the provision of free food in a number of specially established soup kitchens. The legislation, known as the Temporary Relief Act or 'soup kitchen act', opposed current orthodoxy which viewed the provision of gratuitous relief as both ideologically flawed and expensive. Consequently, it was intended only as a short-term expedient until more permanent changes could be made to the existing Poor Law, thus making it responsible for both permanent and emergency relief. The transition from public works to soup kitchens was sudden, with the Treasury ordering a 20 per cent reduction in the number employed on the relief works in March 1847 to be followed by further large reductions.[48] At that time there were 740 000 employed in this way, with a far higher number dependent upon their wages.[49] The outcome was a sudden rise in mortality, leading Russell to recommend that reductions should be more gradual. Trevelyan, who was increasingly assuming control of all aspects of relief, continued to impose drastic reductions even in areas where soup kitchens were not operative.[50] By 1847 it was evident that the Treasury had taken command of Irish relief operations.

Ironically, despite the fact that public works were expensive and failed in the basic objective of saving lives, they were regarded by the poor as superior to other forms of relief – employment and independence being preferred to the loss of status attached to receiving gratuitous relief in the soup kitchens or to being categorized as paupers by the Poor Law. In terms of relief provision, however, the Temporary Relief Act was undoubtedly the most successful policy introduced by the Whig government. At its peak in July 1847, over three million people were being provided with free rations of food daily, clearly demonstrating the logistical ability of the government to manage a system of large-scale relief. It was also the cheapest system. The government had estimated that it would cost four million pounds, but it actually cost less than two million, which included the cost of grants to fever hospitals. Yet, because the idea of giving gratuitous relief was ideologically unacceptable, it was only ever intended to be a short-term expedient. Paradoxically, it aroused considerable opposition: from the destitute who preferred to work, but for adequate wages; and from landowners and other tax-payers who believed that gratuitous relief was both ideologically and economically lethal.[51] Bessborough, before his premature death, admitted that he felt 'alarmed' at throwing the burden on the tenants, but like most British ministers was determined that landlords should be forced to play a greater role.[52]

Advances under the Temporary Relief Act were to end on 30 September, but the Treasury decided that they should cease in the first two weeks of August when harvest activities commenced. From that period, the support of destitute persons became the responsibility of the Poor Law. Loans for the temporary fever hospitals continued until 30 September when they were closed.[53] Following that date, responsibility for both poor relief and medical assistance transfered to the Poor Law, financed by local ratepayers.

In the summer of 1847, as the number of soup kitchens and the numbers dependent on them peaked, the government started to review the repayment of loans made in the first two years of the crisis. The Recovery of Public Monies Act meant that the money advanced for relief was to be repaid equally by the British government and by Irish taxpayers over the next five to ten years. This legislation was not popular with Irish

MPs but the justification was that, as Ireland paid no income tax, such extraordinary measures were necessary.[54] Consequently, not only were local ratepayers financing ordinary and famine relief, they were also repaying the cost of extraordinary relief since the first appearance of blight.

Irish Responsibility

In the summer of 1847 a new Viceroy, Lord Clarendon, arrived in Ireland as a result of the premature death of Bessborough. Clarendon's initial description of the state of the country was optimistic, reporting it to be 'better than I expected'. This impression was due largely to the fact that soup kitchens had been established all over the country and were providing over three million people daily with free rations of soup, making it the most extensive system of relief at any time during the Famine.[55] Furthermore, during its period of operation, the number of recorded crimes fell, largely due to a reduction in cattle stealing and plundering.[56] Clarendon was able to report that the country was largely 'tranquil' and he maintained that 'if it were not for the harassing duty of escorting provisions, the troops would have little to do'.[57]

Like many other British politicians, Clarendon accepted that landlords had to be forced – through poor law taxation – to carry the financial burden of relief, asserting: 'It will give the upper classes an interest that they never yet felt in preventing the lower from falling.' He was optimistic that long-needed social changes were taking place within the country as a result of the crisis – 'conacre is no more and the middleman is no more, and the squireen is becoming extinct'.[58] Furthermore, he regarded the failure of the potatoes and the introduction of the Poor Law as 'the salvation of the country' as together, they had 'prevented land being used as it hitherto had been'.[59] The government's determination to make relief a local responsibility was made clear in July when the Poor Law Commissioner, Edward Twistleton, sent a circular to all relief officials informing them that financial support from the government was about to cease. Notwithstanding this warning, a few days later Twistleton provided the Ballina Union with a loan of £100, as they had no food for the paupers. Clarendon, who was determined that the government should not deviate from its policy, demonstrated his disregard for Twistleton's judgment by sending an official to the Union to ascertain if this measure had been necessary.[60] Nevertheless, Clarendon's initially confident assessment of the situation in Ireland rapidly dissipated, as the crop proved to be small and the demand for relief showed little signs of abating. His main concern was that many Poor Law unions were already deeply in debt and those with least resources were generally the unions where demand for relief was highest. At the beginning of July, only eight of the 130 unions had any money in hand and that totalled only £36 000, whereas the combined debts of the unions was £250 000.[61]

The poor harvest in 1847 also worried landlords in Ireland in relation to the prospects for the poor and the level of local taxation under a system of Poor Law relief. The Marquis of Sligo, who had a reputation as a humane and liberal landlord, informed Clarendon that if the policy were pursued, officials in Dublin and London would be to blame for the resultant thousands of deaths. He also accused the government of trying to shift responsibility for the previous year's mortality on to the relief committees in Ireland when the real culprit had been the policies under which they were forced to operate.[62] The moderate Whig supporter, the Marquis of Clanricarde, viewed a dogmatic adherence to the new relief measures as ultimately damaging to the Union between Britain and Ireland. He warned that unless more was done to help the people, 'the demand will not just be for repeal, but one more fatal which will await its solution only until England is involved in a European war'.[63] Both of these men were 'improving' landlords who, even before the Famine, had wanted to consolidate and modernize their estates.

Despite viewing the government's policies after 1847 as harsh and misguided, a diverse collection of landlords took advantage of the opportunity available for land clearances. A small number claimed that they were doing so reluctantly. Lord Sligo, who felt he was being squeezed financially by high taxes and low rent, justified clearing his estate in the autumn of 1848 on the grounds that he felt 'under the necessity of ejecting or being ejected'.[64] The incentive to evict was a further harsh by-product of the transfer to Poor Law relief. In 1847 evictions rose sharply and kept rising until they peaked in 1850, reaching 100 000 persons.[65] Many more were illegally evicted or voluntarily surrendered their holdings in an effort to become eligible for relief, forced to do so by the harsh regulations of the new Quarter-Acre Clause which deemed that anybody occupying more than this quantity of land was not eligible to receive relief. Homelessness and social dislocation, therefore, became a major source of distress and death in the latter years of famine.

In 1847, there was relatively little blight in the country, but the potato and corn crops were small. Relief policies following the harvest marked a shift from British to Irish responsibility, reflecting the belief that all relief had to be financed from Irish resources. For the destitute, it also marked a decline in their status as special relief measures were ended and they changed from being a casualty of famine to paupers. Policy changes were also underpinned by a changing perception of the problem as leading officials declared that the Famine was over.[66] The debates regarding the introduction of new relief provision for Ireland took place against a backdrop of industrial recession and a monetary crisis in Britain, which impacted most severely on merchants and traders in London, Lancashire and Yorkshire.[67]

The most fierce opponents of the proposed new Poor Law were the Irish landlords who would carry much of the financial burden in the form of poor rates. However, there were divisions within this class as absentees were widely judged – both by fellow landlords and relief administrators – to be irresponsible and blamed for throwing an even heavier burden on proprietors who were resident. Many landlords also believed that the new system of relief was ideologically flawed; out-door relief had been deliberately excluded from the 1838 legislation because it was regarded as unsuited to a country with such extensive poverty and would swamp the resources of the Poor Law, and the case against outdoor relief was even stronger during a famine.[68] Opposition to the new Poor Law provided Irish politicians in Westminster with a rare display of unity as they formed a deputation to Russell and 'protested violently against the proposal of affording out-door relief to able-bodied Irish paupers'.[69] The most damming condemnation of the move to Poor Law relief was from George Nicholls, a former English Poor Law Commissioner who had been responsible for introducing the workhouse system to Ireland. He believed that it lay beyond the ability of a Poor Law to cope with a period of extraordinary distress or famine because, 'where the land has ceased to be productive, the necessary means of relief cannot be obtained from it, and a Poor Law will no longer be operative to the extent adequate to meet such an emergency as then existed in Ireland'. In such circumstances, he considered it to be the duty of the Empire to come to the assistance of Ireland.[70]

The Poor Law required all occupiers of land to pay rates, with the exception of tenants valued at under £4. This regulation meant that proprietors whose land was greatly subdivided were responsible for a higher portion of the rates. It also increased the financial incentive to evict small tenants. Some landlords ignored the legislation. In County

Mayo, for example, Lord Lucan refused to pay rates for any property valued at under £4.[71] Clarendon again advocated that the government should stand firm against all defaulters believing there would be 'a great deal of money concealed in the country', especially by farmers who had received exceptionally high prices for the sale of cattle and corn.[72] But only two weeks later, he warned Russell that if the new law was rigorously insisted upon in the west, and the Guardians were forced to depend on income from local poor rates, 'unions *must be closed* and nothing will save the inmates who cannot work from starvation . . . we must prepare and take upon ourselves the responsibility of those consequences which in some places will be utter destitution, mortality and popular disturbance'.[73] In recognition that a number of unions could not continue to provide relief without some outside assistance, 22 unions in the west were officially designated 'distressed' and they could receive small grants and loans from the government.

A geographic shift in the impact of the food shortages was apparent; the harvest had been good in some parts of the north and east where dependence on relief works and the soup kitchens had been smaller, whilst the trade depression was starting to improve. The situation in parts of the west, in contrast, gave rise to foreboding. Clarendon reported that in counties Mayo, Galway and Donegal, large tracts of land were entirely uncultivated and overgrown with weeds, adding, 'the whole country looks as if it had been ravaged by an enemy'.[74] The transfer to Poor Law relief, therefore, coincided with a small harvest that yielded little food or employment in many parts of the country. Although the corn harvest was good, corn was for export or was expensive and consequently not available to the poor.[75] Following August 1847, the workhouses were also made responsible for all famine sick as the temporary fever hospitals were to close at the end of September and all special funding was to end. The increased pressure on the workhouses was immediate. In spite of being full, these institutions remained unpopular with the poor. A number of people who were found dead on the roadside following the transfer to the Poor Law were deemed as preferring begging to seeking relief from the Poor Law.[76] In the early months of 1848, there were frequent reports of beggars dying from a combination of exposure and starvation as the very poorest people appeared to slip through the relief safety net.[77] Smallholders of land who were excluded from Poor Law relief could no longer seek assistance from other sources. There were also reports of people on outdoor relief dying due to insufficient food.[78]

By October 1847, as the condition of many parts of the country deteriorated, even the usually phlegmatic Clarendon was alarmed, informing Russell:

> There is one thing I must beg of you to take into serious and immediate consideration which is, that whatever may be the anger of the people or parliament in England, or whatever may be the state of trade or credit, Ireland cannot *be left to her own resources*. They are manifestly insufficient. We are not to let the people die of starvation.[79]

To the Chancellor of the Exchequer, Clarendon divulged:

> I hope Lord John will not persist in his notion that Irish evils must find Irish remedies only, for it is *impossible* that this country get through the next eight months without aid in some shape or another from England – it may be very difficult – very disagreeable. Irish ingratitude may have extinguished English sympathy, and the poverty of England may be urged against further succour to Ireland, but none of these reasons will be valid against helpless starvation.[80]

But once more, advice from Ireland, even from high-ranking Whig officials, did not impact on the decisions being made in London, especially as it appeared that the long-desired social revolution was taking place.

Parliament and Opposition

Despite the apparent cohesion amongst British politicians in Westminster regarding relief measures in Ireland, the limitations of the various policies pursued by the Whigs were widely acknowledged and debated at the time, especially in Westminster, demonstrating that ideological conformity regarding policy formulation did not exist. The parliamentary debates were an embarrassment to the minority Whig administration and the situation did not improve following the General Election in the summer of 1847, when the new House of Commons was described by Lord Clarendon as based on 'ignorance, prejudice, spite, protection, radicalism, railroad and repeal'. He was doubtful that Russell could exert any control over it.[81] Again, Russell was forced to depend on the support of the Peelites in order to have a working majority.[82]

Within Westminster much of the criticism of the policies pursued by the Whig administration came not from Irish MPs or the Repeal Party, but from a handful of English MPs, in particular Lord George Bentinck, the leader of the Protectionist section of the Tory Party, who had led the revolt against Sir Robert Peel.[83] Peel, in contrast, publicly supported the measures of the Whig administration. William Smith O'Brien also made sustained attacks on the government, but his involvement with the radical Young Ireland group ensured he remained isolated within parliament. Other notable critics of government policy included Sharman Crawford – radical MP for Rochdale, a landlord in County Down and supporter of tenant rights – and George Poulett Scrope, the English economist.[84] Scrope was opposed to the dependence by successive governments on coercion, believing that it served only to 'make the people more desperate, encourage the landlords to exterminate them still faster, and aggravate the existing social evils'.[85] His indefatigable attacks on Whig policy, especially the government's unwillingness to put humanitarian concerns before ideological ones, meant that he was widely respected in Ireland.[86]

Whilst Lord George Bentinck's attacks on government policy may have been partly motivated by his position as the leader of the main opposition party, his criticisms, couched in a number of incisive and sustained attacks, nevertheless, revealed flaws in the government's handling of the situation. He repeatedly drew comparisons between Peel's skilful policy 'in the way of introducing supplies of food into Ireland' and Russell's inept handling of food supply, particularly the refusal to interfere with 'the operations of private speculators'.[87] In 1847 he argued that Public Works should not be closed, but extended and made really useful. Bentinck attributed such short-sightedness to ideological considerations rather than to practical or humanitarian ones, opining that:

> The British government, reined, curbed and ridden by political economists, stands alone in its unnatural, unwise, impolitic and disastrous resolves, rather to grant lavishly for useless and unproductive works and for Soyer's Soup Kitchens, than to make loans on a private and efficient scale and on ample security, and to stimulate private enterprise.[88]

A similar point was made by Benjamin Disraeli, an ally of Bentinck, who in a tribute to O'Connell in the House of Commons, following his death, said that the real question that the House should ask was 'should parliament appeal to any pedantic application of the principles of political economy to Ireland, or should Ireland be governed justly and according to the dictates of sound policy and good sense?'[89] A similar accusation was made by the Irish MP, Anthony Lefroy, who observed that 'there are some men in this House, whose natural kindness has been overcome by their austere political economy'.[90]

By the beginning of 1847, as disease and mortality escalated, Bentinck began detailing the high levels of death under the misguided policies of the Whig administration compared with those under the former government. One of his main criticisms was of the government's inability to provide accurate returns of famine deaths. When he raised the question in the House of Commons, the Secretary for Ireland, Henry Labouchere, stated that no such returns were kept, even by religious ministers. Nonetheless, a few days later, Bentinck raised the issue again. He challenged Labouchere's earlier assertion, having ascertained in the interim that it was a requirement of canon law for all Anglican clergy to keep such records. He had also been informed that medical officers of dispensaries were keeping registers of mortality. He concluded that the failure to disclose such information indicated that the government did not want the level of mortality to be made public.[91] Labouchere was forced to admit that such a canon law did exist, but doubted that it was observed. Again, he was challenged on the accuracy of his statement, the Recorder of the city of Dublin having provided evidence that such records were accurately and comprehensively maintained. Labouchere responded that because such records were only kept for deaths of members of the Anglican Church, they would provide an incomplete record.[92]

A few days later, Bentinck again returned to the issue of mortality in Ireland, asking if the Secretary for Ireland had 'made any serious and energetic efforts to obtain a comparative return of the number of deaths which had occurred this year with those which had occurred in the previous year?'[93] Bentinck had been informed by John MacHale, the Archbishop of Tuam, that the Catholic clergy also kept records of deaths and could supply the government with the necessary information if so required. Again, Labouchere demurred, alleging that such information would be 'of such a vague and conjectural character, the accuracy of the information could not be relied on'. Lord John Russell also entered the debate pointing out that, as the administrative duties of public officers in Ireland had increased substantially, it had become impracticable for all statistics to be provided. Disraeli, however, suggested that if a return had been asked for specifying the number of pigs and poultry, it would have been supplied, yet 'the difficulties placed in the way of obtaining the number of deaths appeared to be insuperable'.[94] The Irish Secretary closed the debate by assuring the House that a census of destitute persons would be compiled, but conceded that it would not provide information on deaths.[95]

A constant source of concern was the amount of relief provided. Both Bentinck and Disraeli – but not Peel himself – accused the Whigs of having provided less relief than had been provided in the far less severe shortages of the previous year. In the parliamentary debates, this point was fiercely denied by the government who argued that they had merely streamlined provision. Nevertheless, in their private correspondence, the Executive in Dublin Castle acknowledged that far less had been done by them than by the late government.[96] Up to 2 January 1847, £12 000 had been provided by the government; Peel's administration at that stage had given £75 000.[97] Labouchere admitted in a confidential report to Russell that the consequence of their parsimony had been 'misery' that was 'impossible to relate', whereas the situation under Peel had been by comparison one of 'comfort and abundance'.[98] In March 1847, Bentinck pointed out to the House that rations given to the destitute had been covertly reduced from one pound of bread a day to half a pound. The defence made by the Irish Secretary was that their decision had been based on 'what manner of food could be distributed so as to be mostly conducive to their health, and go furthest'. Moreover, the reduced quantity had been approved by the Board of Health, whom Labouchere considered 'better judges' of the subject than Bentinck.[99] Despite Labouchere's robust public defence of relief policies, in private he was less sanguine. Increasingly, he and other senior officials in Dublin believed that even the small amount of relief sanctioned was being deliberately restricted by the principal official at the Treasury, Trevelyan. By the beginning of 1847, faith in the ability of official channels to provide adequate relief had disappeared. Instead, the Dublin Castle Executive was placing its faith in charitable contributions as a way of avoiding making further demands on the Treasury.[100]

Bentinck was also the main advocate of a scheme to extend railway building in Ireland, financed by a government loan.[101] One of his criticisms of the public works had been that they brought no long-term benefit to Ireland. Not only would building railways provide immediate employment and alleviate the distress in the country, it would also bring long-terms benefits to the Irish economy and facilitate better commercial links with Britain. Improved transport links would also enable Ireland to have access to cheap fuel and Britain to cheaper food. Bentinck also believed that such a measure was justified on the grounds that 'we have misgoverned Ireland for centuries'.[102] Railways, he suggested, would help indirectly to transform the government of Ireland, due to the fact that 'capital, bringing industry, employment, wealth, and contentment in its train, will effectually drive agitation from the shores of Ireland'.[103] Whilst Russell was personally sympathetic to the idea and had viewed the development of railways as an integral part of his programme of bringing improvement in Ireland, he was nervous of committing large amounts of English money, even as a loan, when so much had been expended on relief works and at a time when England was in the midst of an industrial recession and confidence in railway building had collapsed. Retrenchment, therefore, appeared to be more expedient. Consequently, Russell, despite his earlier support for Irish railways, opposed Bentinck's comprehensive scheme on the grounds that it was not advisable for a government 'to step out of their usual functions and interfere with the application of capital by financing some railways to the detriment of others'.[104] Again, Russell's reply demonstrated that even in the midst of famine, he was unwilling to support Ireland being given special treatment.

Russell's caution was possibly heightened by the approaching General Election in the summer of 1847 and the need to transform his parliamentary minority into a majority One of the most outspoken opponents of the railways bill was J. A. Roebuck, the Member for Bath. He opposed the scheme on the grounds that such government intervention would violate the laws of political economy. Moreover, it would 'take money from the hardworking, industrious people of England' in order to 'feed the rapacity of the Irish nation'.[105] Within Ireland, however, Bentinck's proposal was commended, even by the radical Irish Confederation.[106] The Mayor of Cork thanked him on behalf of the citizens for his 'practical effort to relieve the distress of this country'. Bentinck's response was fulsome, averring that as a consequence of 'the warm-hearted thanks I daily receive from the Irish people, I am a hundred-fold repaid for my feeble and alas, I fear, futile efforts to serve the Irish nation'.[107] In 1849, when the House of Commons debated providing a smaller railway loan for a line to Galway, it was again opposed by Roebuck, both on financial grounds and for the reason that 'he could not see how Irish railways could be made without an importation of the more skilled labour of England'. Another MP, who had been responsible for building the Houses of Parliament, pointed out that the best 'navvies' were Irish.[108] A loan was made for building railways, but on a scale far smaller than the original plan of Bentinck and too late for the alleviation of distress, which Bentinck had viewed as a key objective of his scheme.

Black '49

In 1848 the potato blight returned to Ireland and, in the west of the country, was as virulent as in 1846. The character of destitution also changed, reflecting the cumulative effect of food shortages combined with the impact of eviction and homelessness. Response to the continued devastation was shaped by a number of factors which were unfavourable to Ireland: politicians and administrators in London continued to accept that the Famine was over; private charity had virtually vanished; and famine fatigue was evident among the public, amplified by anger with the attempted uprising a few weeks earlier.[109] The *Times* even suggested that the time for 'conciliating Paddy' was over and that harsh measures were required instead.[110] Russell and Clarendon, fearing that the repeated potato failure meant further starvation in Ireland, advocated a system of loans to provide public works and promoted emigration. But their suggestions were rejected; the Treasury demonstrated its continued dominance in relief provision by refusing either to deviate from agreed policy or to increase expenditure when the overwhelming consensus was for retrenchment. Instead, the powerful group centred around Grey, Wood and Trevelyan, decided that the situation in Ireland would have to run its course with a minimum of intervention from the government.[111]

Throughout 1849 the condition of Ireland continued to divide opinion in parliament, although, possibly as a result of the uprising in the previous year, less sympathy was expressed for the poor. There was also a belief that accounts of the suffering had been distorted. The hardening of attitudes towards Ireland, including by Irish landlords, hampered the ability of moderate Whigs to provide even a minimum amount of additional relief. During a parliamentary debate at the beginning of the year, when Lord Wharncliffe claimed that 'such misery had never before existed in any country on the face of the globe', Lord Lansdowne cautioned him that some accounts were untrue or exaggerated.[112] The most bitter divisions over Irish policy, however, took place within the Whig party itself and amongst the officials administering the relief. The Whigs were sharply divided between those who continued to follow a policy of minimal intervention – a group which included George Grey and Charles Wood supported by Charles Trevelyan – and the supporters of a more moderate and flexible approach advocated by Russell, Lord Clarendon and Edward Twistleton, the Chief Poor Law Commissioner. The collapse of a number of Poor Law unions in the west of the country forced the government to provide a small, inadequate grant of £50 000. It was agreed to largely because Russell threatened to resign if it was refused. Opposition to the grant in parliament and in the British press was intense, with even Disraeli, who had previously displayed sympathy to Ireland, insisting that it had to be the last.[113] It was made clear that all subsequent relief had to come from Irish resources. This objective was to be achieved through the introduction of the Rate-in-Aid bill, which provided for a transfer of funds from solvent Poor Law unions to indebted workhouses in the west.

In 1849, cholera appeared in the country and had a short-term, but sharp impact on mortality. The first isolated case had appeared in Ireland in October 1847 in a military hospital and Clarendon had suggested that precautions should be taken against an epidemic.[114] This suggestion was not heeded and when the epidemic appeared, it placed a further strain on already over-stretched relief and medical provision. No additional funding was made available to cope with the spread of the disease. Clarendon's frustration with the parsimony of his party, and the tight control of funds being exercised by the Treasury, had been increasing throughout 1848. The refusal to intervene, despite the reappearance of blight in 1848 and the appearance of cholera, increased his frustration and, in December in that same year, he warned that 'wholesale starvation' was likely in a number of unions which would 'not only be shocking but bring deep disgrace on the government'.[115] Clarendon ascribed the draconian way in which relief was being administered to 'the doctrinaire policy of Trevelyan, reflected through C. Wood and supported by Grey'.[116] More acrimoniously, he added that 'C. Wood, backed by Grey and relying upon arguments (or rather Trevelyanisms) that are no more applicable to Ireland than to Loo Choo, affirmed that the right thing to do was to do nothing – they have prevailed and you see what a fix we are in.'[117]

The Rate-in-Aid tax was viewed as the solution to the need to provide limited relief, but to finance it from Irish resources. The proposed tax was unpopular in Ireland especially amongst ratepayers in the north-east who viewed it as divisive, believing that they were being unfairly burdened for the irresponsibility of people in the south of the country. Joseph Napier MP argued that the outcome of the bill if it were passed would be 'keeping up an army of beggars fed out of the industry of Ulster'.[118] An editorial in the *Armagh Guardian* demanded to know why people in the north (an area never clearly defined) should pay the tax when 'we have no connection whatever with Connaught'.[119] Significantly, the ratepayers in Ulster used the debate concerning the Rate-in-Aid tax to perpetuate a myth that the Famine had little impact on Ulster and that they were somehow different from, and superior to, the rest of the country. The differences were constantly repeated at various meetings held to protest at the new tax. Another Ulster newspaper expressed its objections in thinly veiled sectarian language:

> It is true that the potato has failed in Connaught and Munster; but it has failed just as much in Ulster; therefore, if the failure of the potato has produced all the distress in the South and West, why has it not caused the same misery here? It is because we are a painstaking and industrious people who desire to work and pay our just debts, and the blessing of the Almighty is upon our labour. If the people of the South had been equally industrious with those of the North, they would not have had so much misery among them.[120]

These claims had little basis in reality with the province of Ulster suffering an average population loss of 17 per cent, which was higher than that experienced by Leinster. It also denied the intensity of the suffering at the height of the Famine. In 1847, mortality in a number of Ulster workhouses, including those in Belfast and Lurgan, had been amongst the highest in the country, whilst the general destitution led a Quaker who visited County Down fresh from providing relief in the south of the country to liken the area to Skibbereen.[121]

The proposed Rate-in-Aid tax was also unpopular with moderate politicians and some relief administrators. One of their main criticisms was that the bill was unconstitutional in that it violated the Act of Union. Lord Clarendon argued that it negated the idea of a *United* Kingdom and thus would serve to promote ideas of rebellion and separatism.[122] Sharman Crawford, who had frequently argued for more liberal relief measures to be introduced, reasoned that as all taxes were paid into an Imperial Treasury 'and placed at the disposal of an Imperial Legislature for the general purposes of the United Kingdom', expenditure by the Treasury should similarly be used for all portions of the United Kingdom.[123] One of the most vociferous opponents of the Rate-in-Aid tax was the Chief Poor Law Commissioner, Edward Twistleton. He had nominally assumed charge of relief operations following the change over to Poor Law relief in 1847 but, like many other administrators in Dublin, he felt that his efforts were repeatedly undermined by the officials at the Treasury. The consequence of this interference, he contended, had been unnecessary deaths. He suggested that this course had been pursued because 'It seemed to be a less evil to the Empire to encounter the risk [of mortality] than to continue the system of advances from the public purse.'[124]

For Twistleton the introduction of the Rate-in-Aid was a final straw in the abandonment of Ireland and he resigned in protest. Before he left office, he informed Trevelyan that as he had been deprived of all funding, he considered that he and his colleagues were 'absolved from any responsibility on account of deaths which may take place in consequence of those privations'.[125] In the same year, Twistleton informed a parliamentary committee that the government could have intervened to prevent deaths in the poorest unions 'by the advance of a few hundred pounds'.[126] The Rate-in-Aid bill passed through the House of Commons with ease – with 206 votes supporting it and only 34 against. The introduction of the Act was significant in demonstrating that – despite the existence of the United Kingdom – at a time of crisis, Ireland was to be left to her own resources. It also demonstrated that within Ireland a division was emerging in the memory and understanding of the Famine – a myth was being created that some parts of Ireland had emerged unscathed from the Famine, it being a judgment of God on Catholics in the south and west of the country.

Apart from the social revolution that was taking place at the bottom of the economic scale, the system of land ownership was also being transformed as large estates were sold or broken up. This process – which had been desired by successive British governments – was facilitated by the passing of two 'encumbered' estates acts which were intended to simplify the administration of property sales. Despite the introduction of legislation to facilitate the sale of indebted land, the years of shortages had greatly depressed land values. In the poorest districts of Mayo and Galway, large tracts of land were left vacant because poor rates and county cess (a local tax which included repayment of monies loaned for the public works) exceeded the value of the land. Even in areas which

possessed rich grazing land, taxation and a decline in the price of cattle
had depreciated the value by an estimated 35 per cent. The letting value
had also dropped; in County Limerick land, which had been let at £3 an
acre prior to 1846, was being let for £1.[127] In these conditions, the hoped
for regeneration and modernization of the country looked improbable
in the short term.

A visit by Queen Victoria to Ireland had been long anticipated but
frequently delayed. It was finally arranged for August 1849. Rumours
abounded in the nationalist press that her visit would result in an amnesty
for those men who had been involved in the rebellion in 1848, with their
sentences being reduced from transportation to Australia to voluntary
exile in Europe. Instead, the men were hastily sent out of the country,
almost a year after the rebellion, but only a few weeks before Victoria
took her first steps in the country.[128] Victoria's visit was brief and care-
fully choreographed. Her arrival in Ireland was due to coincide with the
harvest, which was expected to be a good one with few isolated instances
of blight.[129] She visited only Cork, Dublin and Belfast, travelling by yacht
between her destinations. Controversy was avoided wherever possible.
Victoria had been scheduled to visit the Deaf and Dumb Institute in
Belfast, but only passed by its gates due to the sectarian nature of the
school.[130] Yet, possibly as an act of defiance, the Ulster landlords chose
the Earl of Roden, who only a few weeks earlier had been disgraced in
the sectarian clash at Dolly's Brae, as their representative to the Royal
party. The British press viewed her visit favourably, especially the fact
that it was taking place so soon after the rebellion. The *Liverpool Mercury*
believed that the visit would reconcile the Irish people to the political
union, opining 'Irish men must awaken from the wild dream of separation from the British Empire before they can hope for better things for
themselves or their children. Human nature, and especially Irish human
nature, is more powerfully acted on through imagination and sentiments than through the intellect and reason.'[131]

Because of the continued distress in Ireland, Victoria's visit was a private rather than a state one, but preparations were elaborate, especially
in Dublin. Some of the nationalist press was critical of the high expenditure, especially for decorations, contrasting it with the parsimony evident
in relief provision. The *Freeman's Journal* describing it as being a choice
between 'Starvation versus Illumination'. They were particularly angry
when the Lord Mayor issued a proclamation that the population of the
city should light up their homes for the visit, but he quickly retracted to
say that those who could afford to do so, should. One Dublin inhabitant

suggested that rather than lighting up their households, they should place a placard in front of their houses saying that instead of spending the money on illuminations, it was being given to the General Relief Committee.[132]

In July 1849, whilst preparations were being made for Victoria's visit, the condition of the poor in many districts was regarded as being the worst at any stage during the Famine, as the pre-harvest period was always the poorest time of the year but in 1849 it was also the culmination of four years of shortages. Evictions too were more widespread than before. Cases were still being reported of destitute people being found dead by the roadside, some of whom were identified but the majority remaining nameless.[133] As no further relief provision had been made by the government, private charity was regarded as essential, with only a shilling making the difference between life and death.[134]

One of the key purposes of Victoria's visit was to demonstrate a return to normality, in the hope of attracting foreign capital into the country, but the Famine was still far from over. In a number of districts the Poor Law was unable to cope with the demands being placed upon it, whilst the punitive Quarter Acre clause effectively disbarred small farmers from receiving relief. At the beginning of 1849 an attempt had been made in the House of Commons to suspend the clause, but without success. In July 1849, a deputation from the Royal Exchange Relief Committee in Dublin met with Russell. The delegation was accompanied by some English MPs, including Poulett Scrope and John Bright, leader of the Free Trade group within parliament. The *Freeman's Journal*, whose proprietor was one of the delegation, regarded such support as crucial to ensure that their request was 'not pooh-poohed by vipers of the Roebuck school as merely a new form of what some are pleased to term Irish mendicancy'. The aim was to impress on Russell the need to give prompt relief to small tenant farmers (which they defined as occupying between one-quarter of an acre and six acres) who had been excluded from relief under the Poor Law. They had tried to raise the money through private charity, but knew that in the current climate of antagonism towards Ireland they could not raise more than £500. The deputation therefore requested that a small advance be made to alleviate the suffering of this group until the harvest was ready.

They estimated that 30 shillings, or even a pound, given in food would, in nearly all instances, be adequate to provide for a family – in total, it was calculated that a grant of £25 000 would be sufficient to save this class of occupier from extinction. The delegation also pointed out that, in the long run, such a grant would prove to be economical as it would enable the smallholders and their families to remain independent rather than force them to become reluctant dependants on the Poor Law. If they did not receive assistance, 'they must either die of starvation or give up those crops for which they suffered so much'. Russell acknowledged that this class of small farmers had suffered greatly. He had hoped that charity would have raised sufficient funds to assist them, but this had not proved to be the case, 'for reasons on which it would not perhaps be well to enter'. Russell did not make any promises at the meeting, but he promised to give the request his 'full consideration'. The delegation were optimistic, believing that the Premier's reply 'very nearly amounted to a promise of assistance'. Russell, however, declined the request for special assistance.[135]

The End of Famine?

The 1849 harvest was good in many parts of the country and trade, especially the linen trade in the north-east, had revived.[136] Yet demands on a number of Poor Law Unions in parts of the west and south-west were as high as at any time during the Famine, with mortality in some of the unions in County Clare being higher than at any stage since 1845. Evictions and emigration, two of the by-products of the Famine, were also continuing to increase.[137] For those who had the resources and energy, emigration provided an option to remaining in Ireland. Emigration from Ireland had always been relatively high but during the Famine years it escalated, with approximately one and a half million people leaving between 1846 and 1852. Moreover, once the process had been set in train, the high level continued into the post-Famine decades. A unique feature of famine emigration was that it was self-financed with only a small portion – approximately 5 per cent – being paid for by either the government or landlords.[138] Consequently, it tended to be the better-off groups who were able to leave.

The horrors of famine did not end on leaving Ireland as disease and mortality were rampant on board the ships, especially during the long journeys to America or Australia. Moreover, on arrival, the survivors were frequently subjected to degrading periods of quarantine or anti-Irish prejudice.[139] Because the demand to leave Ireland was so high, vessels which had previously been considered unseaworthy were utilized, leading to the sobriquet 'coffin ships'. Although the vast majority of emigrants did arrive at their destinations, their health was irrecoverably damaged by the ordeals of the journey, contributing to high mortality amongst the first generation of migrants. Even letters published in newspapers outlining these horrors were not a deterrent. One letter published in a Dublin newspaper in July 1849 was from on board the *Aeolus*, a ship which arrived in New York after a journey of 49 days. During the journey, 33 deaths had taken place from cholera, and the dead bodies were thrown overboard at a rate of up to five a day. Because all of the sick passengers had died on route, quarantine (of 14 days) was not required. Unlike some published accounts, the writer was full of praise for the crew. 'To the first mate who was the captain's brother, we gave a testimonial for his skill and humanity in attending on the poor creatures who were dangerously ill', adding, 'The crew were the most civil and obliging set of fellows I ever met.'[140]

A particularly tragic incident occurred on a vessel sailing from Sligo to Liverpool, carrying a mixture of cattle and 174 steerage passengers, with the passengers then travelling onward to America. A storm started a few hours out at sea and they had to stay below deck in a space suitable for 55 passengers. When they asked the crew for water and for more air, they were refused and the crew covered the area with a tarpaulin and fastened them in. As a result 72 people suffocated. When the storm had passed the ship docked in Derry to get rid of the dead bodies. The findings of the inquest in Derry was uncompromising, stating that the deaths had occurred due to 'gross negligence and the total want of the usual necessary cautions'. The officers of the ship were found guilty of manslaughter, and the inquest concluded by pronouncing that 'we consider it our duty to express in the strongest terms an abhorrence of the inhuman conduct of the rest of the seamen on board, on the melancholy occasion, and the jury beg to call the attention of the proprietors of steam boats to the urgent necessity of introducing some more effectual mode of ventilation in the steerage, and also of affording better accommodation to the poorer class of passengers.'[141] The government, who had repeatedly refused to intervene to regulate such passages, were exonerated and, instead, emigration was allowed to be subject to the vagaries and avarice of free market forces.

The majority of famine emigrants went to North America, especially Canada, although substantial numbers also migrated to Britain and Australia. In the ports and cities which were their new homes, their arrival was often regarded with dismay as they usually lacked capital and skills and were unwitting carriers of disease. Some of the most vehement opposition came from Britain, where the new arrivals were viewed as a double burden on British taxpayers, as money was being given to Ireland anyway – and there were pleas for this emigration to be restricted. The Select Vestry in Liverpool asked the Home Secretary to intervene to stop Irish people from emigrating to Britain and to provide the local authorities with a grant to meet 'the enormous outlay made by the parish for the relief of the Irish poor'.[142] Both requests were refused, although the Home Office assured them subsequently that they 'regretted the inconvenience to which Liverpool is subjected'.[143] When the government proved reluctant to intervene in emigration, the local relief authorities carried out their own programmes of expulsion under the terms of the Laws of Removal which were embodied in the English and Scottish, but not the Irish Poor Law.

The social and psychological dislocation attached to the process of emigration – especially for emigrants from the west who were predominantly illiterate, Irish speakers, Catholics and skilled only in potato cultivation – undoubtedly added to the horrors. Yet, for those who were able to do so, emigration provided an outlet from the Famine. However, a number of emigrants took with them an image of Ireland and the circumstances which had led to their leaving which was able to be moulded into anti-British sentiment. Moreover, they and their descendants believed that they were exiles or economic refugees rather than emigrants.[144] The memory of the Famine, therefore, was carried far beyond the shores of Ireland and its legacy gave rise to a new form of Irish nationalism that looked to America for inspiration and support.

3
PHILANTHROPY AND PRIVATE DONATIONS

A feature of famine relief that has received relatively little attention is the role of private charity. Yet public and private assistance coexisted and they frequently complemented each other. In England, despite the existence of a long-established Poor Law, organized philanthropy continued to be important; by the 1840s, for example, the expenditure of the various philanthropic bodies exceeded state expenditure on poor relief.[1] A common feature of state and private aid was that the administrators of both systems viewed religious and social welfare as being closely linked.[2] Charity was an integral part of all Christian denominations, and private benevolence was usually attended by the desire to promote thrift, frugality and self-help amongst the poor. These values also underpinned both the British and the Irish Poor Laws.

Although a system of poor relief had not been introduced into Ireland until 1838, organized philanthropy was less developed than in Britain. Nonetheless, during the Famine private charity played an essential role in alleviating the distress. The politicians and administrators, who viewed charitable endeavour as more acceptable than government intervention, for the most part welcomed the involvement of private philanthropy. Hence, many politicians were publicly associated with various charities, whilst having a royal patron was regarded as particularly beneficial in helping to raise funds.[3] Apart from direct involvement, private charity could facilitate state intervention in a variety of less-conventional ways. For example, in 1847 the government agreed to pay freight charges on food sent to Ireland from America and the Treasury provided the main relief bodies with screw steamers to allow them to distribute food around the coast of Ireland.[4]

The growth of private philanthropy from the end of the eighteenth century coincided with an evangelical revival and Protestant evangelicals were prominent in many charities, especially ones associated with Bible and scripture reading.[5] Many evangelical charities were also xenophobic and anti-Catholic.[6] The outbreak of the French Revolution in 1789 also gave an impetus to charitable activities, possibly as a way of undermining any threat of popular revolution. Nevertheless, even after the French wars were over, private charity continued to be politically and socially conservative.[7] A feature of many charitable bodies was that they appealed to people of all social groups, although administrative control was in the hands of the higher classes. Women, also, were particularly active in such organizations.[8]

Despite the fact that private philanthropy was well established in the United Kingdom by the 1840s, the Irish Famine was the first national disaster to attract sustained international sympathy on such a large scale. Aid was provided in a variety of forms from a diverse group of people who transcended geographic, religious, political, economic and ideological divisions. Many of the donors to famine relief were nameless and anonymous, but eminent benefactors included Queen Victoria, Pius IX, the President of the United States and the Sultan of Turkey, whose motives were more likely to have been political rather than personal. The size of their donations was less important that the fact that their public support for the victims of famine encouraged, for a short-lived period at least, contributions from people who had little direct association with Ireland.

The idea that private charity in addition to public relief should play a part in alleviating the consequences of the crisis was outlined as early as October 1845 by the Home Secretary, who stated that the Irish peasants should be relieved 'both by public and by private charity. And, that this charity may go as far as possible'.[9] Nonetheless, Peel was not optimistic about the capability of private relief efforts, conjecturing that 'There will be no hope of contributions from England for the mitigation of the calamity. Monster meetings, the ungrateful return for past kindness, the subscriptions in Ireland to Repeal rent and the O'Connell tribute, will have disinclined the charitable here to make any great exertions for Irish relief.'[10] But Peel was proved to be incorrect. In the wake of the second failure of the potato crops, massive amounts of contributions – in money, food and clothing – flooded into Ireland from all parts of the world, including England. Some of the money raised was for the Highlands of

Scotland, where the loss of the potato crop was also having a devastating impact on the population. Official approval and encouragement for private relief by the Whig government was evident when, in November 1846, Russell gave £200 to a Relief Fund in India, where the first famine relief organisation had been established.[11]

By January 1847 a frenzy of fund-raising had commenced which cut across all social groups and religious divisions, and which extended far beyond Britain. However, some sectarian dimensions were also evident. For example, the Church Education Society in Ireland, which promoted scriptural education, advertised in the *Times* for funds on behalf of their teachers who, because of the distress, were not receiving their usual income. They appealed to 'the bounty of Englishmen' to ensure that the work of their schools could continue.[12] The same papers that carried appeals for public contributions simultaneously called into question the reason for British assistance. One letter from an Anglican minister accused the 'Irish masses' of 'perpetually looking for charity to that England whom they are as perpetually denouncing with all the scorn of bigots and all the hate of rebels'. The divisions within the United Kingdom were also apparent when the letter averred that the claims of the poor in Scotland and England were just as compelling, thus, 'we ought fairly to postpone our subscriptions for a neighbouring race until we have somewhat adequately relieved our own'.[13]

Most of the charitable aid to Ireland was provided in 1847, which was the worst single year of famine in terms of mortality and disease. Without the intervention of private aid, the suffering would probably have been far higher. The fund-raising activities for Ireland were, therefore, short-lived. The relatively blight-free crop in 1847 (regardless of its smallness) lent credibility to the government's assertion that the Famine was over. Also, once the momentum gained by the charitable bodies had disappeared, it was hard to revive despite the reappearance of blight in 1848 and 1849 and the continuing suffering of the Irish poor. Sympathy had also diminished as Irish paupers started to arrive in the countries that had so generously raised money, leaving doubts as to the efficacy of their endeavours. Reports in the British press also, most notably the influential *Times*, were suggesting that aid to Ireland had been wasted or was not needed, one letter by an Anglican minister suggesting that sending any more money would be 'about as ineffectual as to throw a sack of gold into one of their plentiful bogs'.[14]

For the most part, fund-raising cut across religious divisions, although inevitably the Catholic Church became a main channel for raising funds.

Occasionally such activities could become divisive, for example, at the beginning of 1847 the *Freeman's Journal* reported on rumours that Protestant clergymen were going to raise money exclusively for Protestants.[15] More damaging, however, was the fact that the emergence of private philanthropy was accompanied by the appearance of a number of English proselytizing groups, such as the Exeter Hall Society, which viewed the distress as an opportunity to increase their involvement with the Irish poor.[16] Some of the proselytizing bodies already had bases within Ireland. One Catholic priest in Ballycastle in County Mayo described how in his impoverished parish: 'There were last year waste lands – the Presbyterian minister and many others connected with the Belfast Societies have bought a great part of the said land and intend to form a colony here. They have money in abundance and many hearers on Sundays for the sake of getting meal and money.' He pleaded with Archbishop Murray in Dublin for funds to help him to counteract the attempts to convert his parishioners.[17] Moreover, even after the flush of fund-raising for Ireland had disappeared, the proselytizing activities of a number of evangelicals continued, they sometimes being the only source of relief available.

Landlords and Irish Relief

The involvement of individuals within Ireland in private charity was important, especially by local landlords and clergy who had influence and the ability to access funds either from local or external sources. Landlords, especially resident landlords, played an important role both in the raising of private charity and in its distribution, although their role varied enormously and after the harvest of 1847, when relief was made the responsibility of the Poor Law, their involvement became less significant. The payment of poor rates was clearly a heavy burden for many landlords, especially after 1847.[18] Between 1845 and 1850 over £10m was paid in poor rates by Irish taxpayers, thus equalling the contribution of the British government to poor relief, half of which was a loan.[19]

Most of the charitable endeavours by Irish landlords were concentrated in the early months of 1847. The Marquis of Sligo, who had a reputation as a liberal landlord, was chairman of a committee that set up a private soup kitchen in Westport in January 1847. He made an initial donation of £100, with a promise of a further £5 as a weekly subscription. Other local gentry and Anglican clergy also contributed and the opening donation reached £255.[20] In County Down, Lord Roden, a landlord who was notorious for his evangelical views and involvement with the Orange Order, opened a soup shop on his estate in which soup – comprising of rice and meal porridge, was sold at the cost price of a penny for a quart, and 12oz of potato cake for a penny. He recommended that other resident gentry in Ireland should do the same.[21] Landlords could also play an important role in bringing corn into an area. A number of landlords, such as the Earl of Shannon, also resold it at less than the cost price.[22] Soup, because it was cheap and easy to produce, was the favourite form of relief by private relief bodies. Even before the Temporary Relief Act was introduced in the spring of 1847, a network of privately funded soup kitchens was operative, many of which had received their initial funding from the Society of Friends. In Skibbereen – which has achieved notoriety for the suffering of the local population – the Anglican minister, the Rev. Caulfield, was giving 1149 people one free pint of soup each day.[23] In Belfast, a privately funded relief committee in Ballymacarrett was providing soup to over 12 000 people daily, which was approximately 60 per cent of the local population.[24]

On a number of estates rent reductions were made or employment provided.[25] Daniel O'Connell, who owned land in County Kerry, gave his tenants a 50 per cent reduction in rent.[26] Lord and Lady Waterford financed a soup kitchen on their estate and Maria Edgeworth in Edgeworthstown provided free seed to her tenants.[27] The Earl of Devon sent £2000 and the Duke of Devonshire, £100 for the relief of the tenantry on their Irish estates.[28] A number of Irish newspapers, including the *Nation*, called attention to landlords who were helping their tenants. Sir Robert and Lady Gore Booth in County Sligo, for example, were singled out as good landlords.[29] Lord Lurgan in County Armagh was also praised for his regular and generous donations to his tenants.[30] But not all landlords behaved well and absentee landlords were widely criticized. In January, the Poor Law Guardians in the Waterford Union, issued a public condemnation of local absentee landlords.[31] The Rev. Saurin established a soup kitchen in Seagoe in county Down in December 1846. He had written to all local absentee landlords appealing for financial support, including to the wealthy Duke of Manchester, but only one replied, Mr James Robinson, and he donated £1 for the soup kitchen.

Saurin publicly condemned the indifference and parsimony of the local landlords, especially that of Manchester. The Duke responded to accusations of meanness in the columns of the *Times* newspaper, where he claimed that his dispute with Saurin was long standing.[32] Manchester, however, was actively involved in providing relief through his membership of the Irish Relief Association, a body which had been linked with souperism. His participation led the *Northern Whig* to comment, 'the Duke was too much taken up with the spiritual concerns of the famished poor to have time or inclination to look to their physical condition'.[33] Lord Londonderry, one of the ten richest men in the United Kingdom, who owned land in counties Down, Derry, Donegal and Antrim, in addition to property in Britain, was also criticized for his selective parsimony; he and his wife contributing £30 to the local relief committee, but £150 000 on renovating one of their houses. A series of articles in the *Londonderry Standard* disclosed Londonderry's contribution to famine relief, which elicited the response that 'My conscience acquits me of ever having wrongly acted as a proprietor, a landlord or a Christian', to which the editor of the newspaper responded: 'His Lordship is then in a most enviable state of inward blessedness for we imagine that some of the Apostles themselves could scarcely have made such a declaration.'[34]

Within Ireland a number of groups and individuals became involved in fund-raising, especially in Belfast and Dublin. The Irish Art Union organized an exhibition of Old Masters, the proceeds of which were distributed to various relief organizations.[35] The Irish Benchers gave £1000 to the General Relief Fund and the Irish Coast Guards raised £429.[36] The brewer Arthur Guinness also made two separate donations of £60 and £100.[37] The Belfast Ladies' Association and the Belfast Ladies' Association for Relief in Connaught raised over £7000, which was apportioned between the poor in Belfast and those in Connaught, the latter organisation providing relief through scriptural schools.[38]

Relief in Ireland

In the wake of the second crop failure, a number of committees were formed for the purpose of providing relief to Ireland. They raised large amounts of money, food and clothing for the poor in Ireland that provided an invaluable supplement to government relief. In some instances, they filled a vacuum when official relief was deficient, delayed or so circumscribed as to be ineffectual. A further important function of private relief committees was their role as pressure groups, especially in keeping the crisis in the public eye. The Quakers were particularly effective in informing newspapers in Dublin and Britain of the true situation in the west of Ireland, emphasizing the extent of suffering in the country.

The second appearance of blight resulted in the formation of a number of private relief committees in Dublin. One of the first relief committees to be established was the General Central Relief Committee in December 1846. The Marquis of Kildare was chairman and other influential members included the Marquis of Abercorn, Archbishops Murray and Whately and Lord Charlemont. Daniel O'Connell, his son John and the Young Irelander William Smith O'Brien were also involved. The provision of relief was to be interdenominational, and given regardless of class and creed and 'in the distribution of relief there shall be no Religious distinction whatever'.[39] At the beginning of 1847, the Committee warned that unless more food was made available millions of lives would be lost, adding, 'those who are guilty of neglect in these particulars will be responsible before man, and we venture to add, before an all-just Providence'.[40] Its donations amounted to over £83 000 and they came from a wide-reaching group of people and places, including from Grahamstown in South Africa (£470), Buenos Aires in Argentina (£441), Delhi in India (£296) and Toronto in Canada (£3472). The British Relief Association also gave a grant of £20 000 to the committee. During its 12 months of existence the Association distributed almost 2000 individual grants ranging from £10 to £400, mostly through the medium of Protestant and Catholic clergymen. The highest portion of its grants – over £20 000 – was distributed in Connaught, although over £11 000 was donated to Ulster, principally in counties Cavan and Donegal.

At the end of 1847, as donations dried up, the committee wound down its activities. The committee did not accept, as had been suggested by the government, that the Famine was over but felt that the charitable impulse towards Ireland had dried up. They were pessimistic about the ability of the Poor Law to meet the distress, warning that 'in some respects the condition of the peasantry is this year more lamentable than it was during the past season'.[41] In response to the deepening distress following the harvest failure in 1848, the committee reconvened in May 1849. The revived committee raised and distributed over £4000 within two months. All of the money was allocated to clergymen in the south and west only, reflecting the geographical shift in the demand for relief. In July they appealed in a number of newspapers, including the *Times*, for financial support to enable them to respond to the 200 outstanding applications. The committee estimated that only 2s 6d. would keep a family of five alive until the harvest was ready in four to six weeks' time.[42]

The Society of Friends also became involved in providing private relief at the end of 1846. Of all the private relief bodies, their work was probably the best known, largely because they provided eyewitness accounts of their involvement which were published in the British and Irish newspapers, and which were also reprinted further afield. Also, the Quakers left a detailed account of their involvement and individual Friends published accounts of their work.[43] Although the Quakers were associated with various social issues, including the reform of prisons and the ending of slavery, before the Famine they had little direct involvement with poor relief in Ireland. They had acquired a reputation, however, for not using their social activities as a platform for proselytizing, although in Britain evangelical Quakers had been involved in philanthropic activities.[44] The involvement of the Quakers in famine relief was formalized in November 1846 when, at the suggestion of Joseph Bewley, they founded a relief committee in Dublin. A similar organization was established in London. Female Quakers also founded a Ladies' Irish Clothing Society and a Ladies' Relief Association in London and Dublin respectively. There was a close cooperation between the various bodies. Before the end of the year, the Irish Relief Committee had contacted Friends in the United States where Jacob Harvey agreed to coordinate contributions. From the outset they did not limit their fund raising to fellow Quakers, but appealed to people throughout Britain and Ireland, and increasingly the United States, to provide assistance.[45] They also raised money from other Friends in England.[46] The banker Samuel Gurney, for example, raised £2000 from his family.[47] By May 1847 Quakers in Ireland had raised £4800 and Quakers in England, £35 000.[48] Nevertheless, they did not accept all of the money offered to them. The Quakers refused a donation from a theatre company in London on the grounds that such entertainment was 'inconsistent with the gravity and sobriety required of professors of Christianity'.[49]

The way in which the Society of Friends distributed aid was unique, with a number of their members travelling to the south and west of Ireland establishing relief, usually based on a network of soup kitchens managed by local clergymen. From their headquarters in Dublin they also processed claims from all parts of Ireland, responding with money, seed, clothing or bedding. They described their role as acting as a 'suitable channel' for receiving and distributing contributions for Ireland, but acknowledged that for every 100 people they were able to help, 900 more would remain unrelieved.[50] This approach provided them with a first-hand knowledge of the actual situation and the publication of their letters, in British newspapers especially, provided a valuable balance to reports which were suggesting that the distress had been exaggerated.[51] In their private correspondence, their descriptions were even more forthright. William Forster, describing children in a work-house, reported 'their flesh hanging so loose from their little bones, that the physician took it in his hand and wrapped it round their legs'. He added that looking upon such scenes 'takes too much possession of me, and almost disqualifies me for exertion'.[52] Moreover, the Quakers were not afraid to attribute blame; seeing the disaster not as a providentialist judgment on the Irish people, but as a largely man-made disaster, exacerbated by the inadequate response of both absentee landlords and the British government.[53]

At the end of 1847, the Quakers withdrew from providing direct relief to the poor although they continued to provide aid, which would bring long-term benefits to Ireland, such as seeds, fishing tackle and farm implements. One of the reasons given was that their colleagues were exhausted. The personal toll on the Quakers involved in providing relief had been high: Jonathan Pim had collapsed from overwork, and the premature deaths of Joseph Bewley, Jacob Harvey and William Todhunter had also been attributed to exhaustion. Fifteen other Quakers also died from diseases caught whilst working with the famine sick.[54] In a period of 12 months they had distributed approximately £200 000 in aid. Although they had only been involved in famine relief for a year, their involvement was particularly important because it was direct, was based in the communities where it was most required, and did not carry any ideological or religious constraints. Moreover, the Quakers had frequently intervened when no other assistance was available. For example, in April 1847 the Ballymacarrett Relief Committee near Belfast, having been turned down by both the government and the Belfast authorities for aid, appealed to the Quakers for help. The Quakers, recognizing that the situation was desperate, arranged for two tons of Indian Corn to be immediately provided to the committee.[55] In the spring of 1847, when the public works were closed and replaced by government soup kitchens, it was the Society of Friends who undertook the practical task of purchasing and distributing large cauldrons to the west and south of the country in which the soup could be made.[56] The value of their work was also apparent in 1848 when they were secretly approached by the Treasury and asked if they would again become involved in providing private relief. They were offered £100 to do so. But they refused, their focus having changed to longer-term help for Ireland.[57]

Women played an important role in a number of charitable organizations. In both Dublin and Belfast, Ladies' Relief Associations were formed which raised money not only in those areas but also in Britain.[58] Asenath Nicholson, an American evangelist who set up her own one-woman relief organization in Dublin, was full of praise for the Belfast women, whom she avowed were: 'Not in the least like the women of Dublin, who sheltered themselves behind their old societies – most of them excusing themselves from personal labour, feeling that a few visits to the abodes of the poor were too shocking for female delicacy to sustain.' Although she praised the overall generosity of the people of Dublin, she added '*giving* and *doing* are antipodes in her who has never been trained to domestic duties'.[59] The Belfast Ladies' Relief Association, which was formed on 1 January 1847, attracted support from women of all denominations. The Belfast Ladies' Society for Relief of the Poor in Connaught, however, was a proselytizing organization, which was under the control of the Rev. Dr Edgar of the Presbyterian Church.[60]

For the most part, the various relief organizations wound up their activities at the end of 1847. But whilst more money was raised in the early part of the Famine, in the latter years, as government finance dried up, charitable donations became more important as a tool for saving lives. This was especially true after the autumn of 1847 when a number of poor people were excluded from obtaining relief under the strict provisions of the Poor Law. The need for more private relief was recognized when Trevelyan secretly – but unsuccessfully – attempted to persuade the Quakers to resume their operations.

Private Charity in Britain

The success of the relief committees in raising funds was made possible by the swift response of people throughout Britain. A number of government officials were apprehensive regarding the ability of charities to raise money for Ireland in parts of Britain. At the beginning of 1847, Trevelyan warned the British Relief Association that 'Feeling is so strong against the Irish that I doubt if much progress will be made in subscription until further horrifying accounts are received.'[61] Yet his concerns proved to be largely unfounded; within days of the Association being inaugurated, London had raised almost £14 000, a small part of which was for Scotland.[62] This initial support was maintained throughout 1847 as, towards the end of the year, one day's collection in London still amounted to £2701 6s. 10d.[63] Collections were not confined to the Catholic community; Anglican churches throughout Britain responded generously to the Queen's appeal in January 1847; a Baptist Church in Cambridge contributed £500; in Norwich the Octagon Chapel gave £87 and the Unitarian Church, £100; in Neath in South Wales the Somerfield Independent Chapel raised £7 on behalf of the British Relief Association.[64]

The largest body involved in famine relief was the British Relief Association which was constituted in London on 1 January 1847 by a number of wealthy businessmen, notably Lionel de Rothschild, the Jewish banker and philanthropist, and Samuel Gurney, the Quaker banker. Each of its founders provided an initial donation of £1000. Unlike other bodies, the British Association also provided relief in the Highlands of Scotland, dividing its income between Ireland and Scotland in the proportion of five to one. To oversee the local distribution of its Scottish donations, the Association worked through the Central Committee, which had been established in Scotland to assist the distressed districts.[65] In Ireland, the British Relief Association appointed a full-time official to oversee the distribution of relief, Count Paul Strzelecki, a Polish nobleman. As far as possible, its relief was to be donated in the form of food, fuel or clothing, rather than in money. The Association also decided to work through the relief network already established by the British government.[66] Consequently, their work became associated with official relief and they had little contact with groups who were excluded from receiving it. Strzelecki, however, increasingly became disillusioned with government relief, especially the way in which Charles Trevelyan managed its distribution.[67]

Having the support or patronage of royalty was important to any charitable endeavour. The British Relief Association was able to name as their first donor Queen Victoria, who donated £2000, the largest single donation. Her donation, however, was the subject of a private controversy. In the first instance, the Queen had sent a donation of £1000. The Irish Secretary of the Association, Stephen Spring Rice, was not impressed by the donation, saying: 'Receiving this, I refused to place or abstained from placing the subscription on the list and went to G. Grey, Secretary of State, to say that it wasn't enough. It was increased to £2000.'[68] This episode was kept out of the public domain. Other royals followed Victoria's example and contributed to the British Relief Association, including: Prince Albert (£500), the Dowager Queen (£1000), the King of Hanover (£1000), the Duke of Cambridge (£500), the Duchess of Gloucester (£200) and the Princess Sophia (£100).[69] Royalty from outside Britain also made donations to the Association. The most publicized international donation came from the Sultan of Turkey, Abdulmecid.[70] He donated £1000 to Irish relief, although it was rumoured in the Irish press that he had offered to give a far larger sum, but had been persuaded from doing so by a British official who had suggested that it would offend royal protocol to give more money than the British monarch.[71]

The British Relief Association, helped by the patronage of the Queen, was the favoured charity of the rich and distinguished members of British society. The first donation list of the Association included Lord John Russell (£300), the Right Honourable George Grey (£200), Sir Charles Wood (£200), Sir Robert Peel (£200) and Charles Trevelyan (£50). The desire to give was evident amongst commercial classes, with some of the largest banking houses including Barings Brothers, Jones, Lloyd and Co, Rothschilds and Co, Overend, Gurney and Co each contributing £1000.[72] The diversity of donors to the Association was evident in the second subscription list which included donations from the Singapore Irish Relief Fund (£31), Earl Grey (£200), Lord Brougham (£100) and the *Observer* newspaper (£50).[73] Money was also donated by the East India Company (£1000), members of the Royal Household (£247), the president and scholars of Magdalene College Oxford (£200), officers of the First Battalion Rifle Brigade (£23), non-commissioned officers and men of the same (£18), and non-commissioned officers of the 69th Regiment (£75).[74]

Apart from providing a personal donation to the British Relief Association, the involvement of Queen Victoria was important in fund-raising, especially through the publication of two Queen's Letters, appealing for collections and prayers on behalf of Ireland and, to a lesser extent, Scotland. The first Letter, of 13 January 1847, which was sent to the Archbishops of Canterbury and York, asked for an appeal to be read in every church on behalf of famine relief.[75] A Proclamation also announced that 24 March 1847 would be designated a day of 'General Fast and Humiliation before Almighty God', a further purpose of which was to raise money for Ireland and Scotland.[76] The second Queen's Letter, which appeared in October, demonstrated that much of the charitable spirit within England had, within the space of a few months, dissipated. Angry letters opposing the Queen's 'ill-advised letter' appeared daily in the *Times* one suggesting that any money donated in this way would provide 'a direct premium to the people of that country to again commence a reckless waste'.[77] Another letter in the same vein, referring to the Irish as 'thankless and worthless people', asked: 'What commiseration can we have for these people, and why should we be called on to support them? To do so is, in effect, a premium for recklessness and improvidence.' A further letter from London suggested that 'by private charity, public subscriptions, or Government grants, we shall only perpetuate the habit she has acquired of depending on extraneous and chance contributions'.[78] Significantly, the second Queen's Letter raised only £30 000.[79]

Of all of the relief bodies, the British Relief Association was the most effective in raising funds, their contributions reaching almost £500 000. The British Relief Association officially closed its operations in the summer of 1848 and in September Strzelecki left Ireland, refusing to accept any payment for his work. The vast majority of the funds of the British Relief Association were expended in the provinces of Munster and Connaught, which totalled £105 152, whilst £6360 was given to County Donegal. Following the harvest of 1847 and the transfer to Poor Law relief, the funds of the Association had kept many of the workhouses in the distressed unions open through their subventions.[80] A further initiative by Strzelecki was the provision of relief to schoolchildren financed by the Association. Trevelyan had attempted to prevent this scheme being established, warning Strzelecki that it would 'produce the impression that the lavish charitable system of last season was intended to be renewed'.[81] When the Association closed its operations, they were feeding over 200 000 schoolchildren daily in some of the poorest western unions. Russell had promised Strzelecki that the government would continue to fund this project, but this promise was not kept. Trevelyan, who had earlier objected to this form of relief, used Strzelecki's departure as a pretext for ending it.[82]

Money for Ireland was also raised in a number of more unusual ways. A benefit performance was held for Scotland and Ireland in Drury Lane Theatre, its low attendance being attributed to bad weather.[83] A selection of the British press also made donations, including £50 from the *Observer*, £100 from the *Morning Herald*, £37 from the *Daily News* and £50 from the journalists from *Punch* – a journal renowned for its acerbic attacks on Ireland.[84] Contributions were also provided by members of the British army, one of the largest of which was £3000 given by soldiers in the Regent's Park Barracks in London to the Ladies' Relief Committee in Belfast.[85] The same organization also received a donation from Lady Byron, widow of the poet.[86] Subscriptions were raised even amongst the poorest and most marginalized groups in society. Convicts on board a prison ship in Woolwich, hearing of famine in Ireland, raised a sum of 17s. from their own meagre resources in pennies and halfpennies.[87]

Provincial towns played an important role in fund-raising and local committees were established in a number of them. In Birmingham a meeting convened by the mayor to raise subscriptions for Ireland was held in the Town Hall, which included merchants, Catholic priests, Anglican clergy and a number of dissenting ministers: £800 being raised at the meeting including donations from workers in Messrs Chance Bros., glassmakers, and Messrs Molliet and Son, engineers. A separate collection in the town raised over £3000 and the local Society of Friends raised £1000.[88] Other towns organized large collections: Manchester and Salford raised almost £8000; Newcastle and Gateshead, £3902; Hull, £3800; Leeds, £2500; Huddersfield, £2103; Wolverhampton, £1838; and York £1700. A large number of smaller donations were also made which included grants from Birkenhead, Bristol, Cardiff, Chester, Glasgow, Neath and Rugby. A number of subscriptions were also made in Liverpool but, due to the religious divisions within the town, it was decided not to organize a formal relief committee.[89] By the end of 1847, the same towns which had given relief so generously only a few months earlier were growing exasperated by the fact that paupers were arriving in Britain in massive numbers, and usually without capital, skills, or even health. The Irish poor were regarded as a double burden, expecting relief both in Ireland and in Britain. Consequently, by the end of 1847, a campaign was under way to prevent the Irish poor from coming to Britain, whilst the efficacy of the charitable efforts of a few months earlier was doubted.[90]

Aid from Overseas

The Famine not only brought Irish affairs to the centre of British political discourse, it also brought them to the attention of an international audience. The Catholic Church was a major conduit for fund-raising for the Famine, as was Ireland's membership of the British Empire. The news of the distress in Ireland travelled quickly despite the slowness of communications. Apart from newspaper accounts, members of the British army, religious ministers and letters carried descriptions of the suffering, as did eyewitness reports by emigrants. Overseas observers were primarily dependent on newspaper reports, but by the end of 1847 reports from Ireland were frequently conflicting – tales of indolence, crime, firearm purchase and rebellion often eclipsing accounts of suffering.[91]

The first donation for Irish relief was raised in India at the end of 1845 and was an initiative of British troops serving in Calcutta. It was followed by the formation of the Indian Relief Fund in January 1846 that appealed to British people living in India to initiate similar collections. Their appeal also raised money for Ireland not just within India, but also from Ceylon (£718), Hong Kong (£82) and Toronto (£300), and in total raised almost £14 000. The Indian Fund appointed a committee of Trustees in Dublin to oversee the distribution of their collection. The committee, which included both Archbishop Whately and Archbishop Murray, received over 2000 applications for a grant. By December 1846, its funds were exhausted and the committee folded, just at the point when many new relief committees were being established.[92] The Indian Fund played an important role in providing assistance in the months before the main philanthropic organizations were operative. However, it was not just British soldiers and the Indian Fund who raised money. Sepoys serving in the army and a number of native princes also made donations.[93] The Freemasons of India contributed £5000 to Ireland. A number of Hindoos (*sic*) of high caste promised to make a large dona-tion, they also having recently been admitted into the Freemason Lodge of England.[94] A contribution of £3000 was also raised in Bombay in the space of just one week.[95]

The largest overseas donations came from America where, as early as November 1845, newspapers on the east coast were carrying reports of the failure of the potato crop. However, the first failure elicited little reaction, with the exception of Boston where a relief committee was established. The committee was largely an initiative of the Boston Repeal Association and so fund-raising became tied in with opposition to the Act of Union. At a relief meeting at the beginning of December, which was attended by over 3000 people, the Rev. Doctor O'Flaherty claimed that 'by the fatal connection of Ireland with England, the rich grain har-vests of the former country are carried off to pay an absentee government and an absentee propriety, and the potato, which is at best a wretched material of subsistence, now appears to be totally destroyed'. He called on his fellow citizens to provide relief to Ireland and 'the dormant Repeal Associations throughout America to revive their activity in the cause of Ireland'. In total, $750 (£160) was raised at the meeting on behalf of the Irish poor.[96] Within a few weeks the Boston committee had raised several thousand dollars, largely due to the involvement of local Catholic priests and supporters of repeal. But its overt political approach alienated some members of the Boston community. A number of members of the Repeal

Association also feared that the fund-raising activities were detracting from their political activities. News from Ireland also suggested that the impact of the blight would not be as serious as had first been anticipated, and the Corn Law debate, rather than food shortages in Ireland, dominated newspaper reports from Britain. Consequently, by the beginning of 1846, donations to the committee had fallen off sharply.[97] Despite its short-lived existence, the Boston Relief Committee was the first relief committee to be established in the United States.

But although the first failure due to blight led to the formation of few relief committees, large amounts of money were raised through individual donations, especially from recent immigrants. Jacob Harvey, who coordinated relief donations in New York, estimated that in January and February 1846, Irish labourers and servants had sent $326 410 to Ireland in small bank drafts.[98] By January 1847 they totalled over one million dollars, including $808 000 from New York, $120 150 from Philadelphia, and $23 500 from Baltimore. He described the money as 'part of the earnings of the poor Irish emigrants...all done quietly, regularly and systematically, without any parade of public meetings or committees'.[99]

The second failure of the potato crop produced a more widespread response, helped by the fact that America had enjoyed a bumper harvest in all crops.[100] A meeting in Washington in November 1846, chaired by the Mayor, appointed a committee of four citizens to organize house-to-house visits to solicit donations for Ireland. Newspaper coverage of the meeting linked Ireland's distress to the fact that 'for centuries she has been groaning under all the evils that a tyrannical government could inflict upon her'.[101] In New York, it was also decided to make door-to-door collections and to ask all the churches in the city to hold special collections for Ireland.[102] A few weeks later, a Ladies' Relief Association was established in Brooklyn.[103] Again, people with few resources themselves played a significant part in raising money for Ireland. The workmen in the Bay State Corporation in Massachusetts gave one day's labour on behalf of Ireland, which amounted to $410.[104] In Boston, the policemen made a donation of $100.[105] Children in a pauper orphanage in New York raised two dollars, which was used to purchase meal.[106]

Occasionally, the relief efforts were tangled with anti-British sentiments. At a large meeting in Rutland, Vermont, the blame for the hunger was firmly placed in the hands of England which was 'disgracing herself in the estimation of all nations, by suffering tens of thousands of her subjects to die for want of food'. The meeting also agreed that 'as England boasts of her power and wealth, and continued to extend her empire in every quarter of the world, she should be held responsible by all nations, for the degradation, suffering and starvation of her subjects'.[107] In New York, relief meetings occasionally became platforms for voicing criticisms of the policies of the British government. John Hughes, the Tyrone-born Catholic Bishop of the city, gave a lecture in March 1847 entitled 'Antecedent Causes of the Irish Famine', in which he ascribed much of its origins to 'bad government'. He rejected the Whig government's faith in political economy, arguing that more, rather than less, government intervention was necessary. He was particularly scathing about Russell's determination not to interfere with trade, despite the human costs of following such a policy.[108]

Fund-raising in the States received an impressive backing on 9 February 1847 when the Vice-President, George Mifflin Dallas, chaired a meeting in Washington on behalf of Irish relief. It was attended by a number of influential citizens, including members of the Houses of Congress, representing each State and territory. Letters were read from Ireland, following which the meeting agreed that 'such unexampled calamity and suffering ought to overcome in their regard all considerations of distance, foreign birth and residence'. The Mayors and Collectors of Customs of all cities were asked to receive and forward donations.[109] A more ambitious plan to assist Ireland was made by Senator Crittenden of Kentucky, who proposed that the federal government give $500 000 to Ireland and Scotland to help alleviate the distress. The Ways and Means Committee announced that the proposal was unconstitutional and threw it out.[110] The President, James Polk, was accused by one Boston newspaper of not supporting the measure and criticized personally for only contributing $50, which was 'squeezed' out of him.[111] A few days after throwing the proposal out, Congress demonstrated a willingness to assist Ireland in some way by agreeing to the request of the Boston relief committee for a sloop of war, the *Jamestown*, to be sent to Ireland and a smaller one to be sent to Scotland carrying relief provisions.[112] The fact that the United States was in the midst of war with Mexico made the granting of permission even more noteworthy. In response to criticisms of the government for permitting a warship to be used for the benefit of another country, Captain Forbes of the *Jamestown*, justified it on the grounds that 'it is not an everyday matter to see a nation starving'.[113]

The sanction by the government to allow the *Jamestown* to bring a cargo of supplies to Cork in March 1847 was one of the most publicized and praised interventions from America. One Boston newspaper commented that 'every paper in this country has noticed most enthusiastically the mission of the *Jamestown*, and all concur that it is one of the most sublime transactions in a nation's history'.[114] The supplies were provided by voluntary subscriptions raised by the Boston Relief Committee which had amounted to over $100 000. The cargo included over 7000 barrels of flour, 400 barrels of pork and 353 barrels of beans. Volunteers who had at least a year's experience at sea manned the *Jamestown*. They were warned by the commander Robert Bennett Forbes that, in return, they would receive 'room to swing a hammock on the gun deck, plenty of bread and small stores, plenty of hard work under strict discipline, and a return to Boston in about two months'.[115] The men chosen were described as being 'substantial citizens of great respectability'. A second American vessel of war, the *Macedonian,* was also sent with a cargo to be shared between Ireland and Scotland.[116]

The loading of foodstuffs on to the *Jamestown* commenced on St Patrick's Day, 17 March 1847. It left Boston 11 days later and took only 15 days and three hours to reach Cobh, just outside Cork. Amongst those people who met it was William Rathbone of Liverpool, a noted philanthropist who had agreed to oversee the impartial distribution of relief.[117] Forbes was embarrassed that he was feted on his arrival in Cork and refused to participate in official welcomes by the British government in Dublin and London. Instead, he was anxious that his relief should reach the poor as quickly as possible. Nevertheless, he did attend a reception organized by the Temperance Institute and was shown around the area by the leader of the Temperance movement, Father Mathew.[118] Forbes likened his visit to some of the poorest streets in Cork City to stepping into 'the Valley of the Shadow of death ... It was the valley of death and pestilence itself.'[119]

The provisions on the *Jamestown* were forwarded by British naval steamers to other ports on the west coast, and were divided between 160 different localities in quantities of five tons. A number of newspapers in Cork used the arrival of the *Jamestown* to contrast the generosity of the people of the United States with the parsimony of the British government. The *Cork Examiner* pronounced that 'a Nation which owes us nothing ... [should] be a model to a Nation that owes to us her pre-eminent greatness'.[120] Another article in the *Cork Advertiser* drew an unfavourable comparison between the swift response of people in America with the response of the British government, pointing out that the Jamestown had arrived in Ireland 'in less time than it would take to get an intelligible answer from the Board of Works, to comprehend the provisions of

one of our bewildering Acts of Parliament, or to take the initiatory steps
towards carrying them into execution'.[121] Letters of thanks written by
Father Mathew were published in a number of American newspapers, in
which he stated that the generosity of people in the United States 'has
inspired every heart in this island with ardent gratitude'. He also pointed
out that a further practical benefit of such relief was that maize prices in
Cork had fallen from £19 to £10 a ton.[122]

The *Jamestown* remained in Cork for just over a week, leaving on
22 April. The journey home was marred by the loss of the third mate
who fell overboard, he having been the only Irish-born member of the
crew.[123] In total, over 100 vessels carried foodstuffs carrying in total
20 000 tons of provisions, from the United States to Ireland in the wake
of the *Jamestown*.[124] This form of relief was also made easier by the lifting
of the Navigation Laws at the beginning of 1847. This aid was welcomed
by the British Government, who agreed to pay the freight charges of all
vessels from the United States carrying food to Ireland, a charge that
amounted to £70 000.[125] In March 1847, Lord John Russell praised
America for giving so much to Irish relief.[126] Whilst the Catholic Church
was important in raising large sums of money throughout the United
States, fund-raising cut across religious divides, especially in New York.
The Protestant Episcopal Church in the west diocese of New York raised
$10 000.[127] The Franklin Street and Crosby Street synagogues in New
York raised $80 and $175 respectively. The Baptist Church in Amity
Street, the Protestant Dutch Church in Franklin Street and a German
Lutheran Church in Walker Street all made collections for Ireland.[128]
Ecumenical collections were also made in other parts of the country. The
Shakers of New Lebanon sent, via the Society of Friends, $700 worth of
clothing.[129] A number of African churches also made collections for
Ireland.[130] The *Boston Pilot* used the donation from black slaves in Rich-
mond, Virginia to attack Britain, pointing out:

> What a forcible rebuke is this to those English bigots who say that no
> slave can live on British soil, and that the Southern slaves would be
> justified in cutting their masters' throats! We see these slaves enjoying
> the necessaries, and many of them even the luxuries, of life, in abun-
> dance, while thousands and tens of thousands of *freemen*, yes *free Britons*,
> are perishing for want of mere sustenance.

The editorial concluded with the admonition: 'Before false British
philanthropy exhausts all her resources and sheds her tears over the

supposed evils imposed on the slave of the South, let her look to her own land to find some object having *more* claims upon her sympathy.'[131]

Unlikely contributors to Irish relief included a number of Native American Indians in Oklahoma. Their government agent, Colonel William Armstrong, informed the Choctaw Indians of the suffering in Ireland, which resulted in a collection being made by 'Red men and white' amongst traders, missionaries and Indians and which raised $170. This money was forwarded to the local committee of the Society of Friends, who referred to it as 'the voice of benevolence from the western wilderness of the western hemisphere'.[132] The local press also commented on the generosity of the Choctaw Nation, suggesting

> What an agreeable reflection it must give to the Christian and the phil-anthropist, to witness this evidence of civilization and Christian spirit existing among our red neighbours. They are repaying the Christian world a consideration for bringing them out from benighted ignorance and heathen barbarism. Not only by contributing a few dollars, but by affording evidence that the labours of the Christian missionary have not been in vain.[133]

The Cherokee Nation also held a meeting to discuss both aid for Ireland and for Scotland. They felt particular empathy for Scotland because many of their ancestors had married Scottish settlers. The meeting referred to the fact that 'the greatest distress is now prevailing in Ireland and Scotland for the want of food, so that thousands are perishing with hunger, and many thousands must perish or subsist on charity – and whereas Providence has bestowed on the Cherokee people an abun-dance for their own subsistence'. A subscription of $172 was raised, the greater portion of which was to be sent to Scotland.[134] Within two weeks this amount had been increased to $245.[135] The local Cherokee news-paper reported that 'Although we may never receive any pecuniary benefit or aid in return, we will be richly repaid by the consciousness of having done a good act, by the moral effect it will produce abroad and by the reflection that we have helped to allay the sorrows of the land rendered illustrious by the deeds of Wallace and Bruce and the songs of Scott and Burns.'[136] The *United States Gazette* described the donation as particularly welcome because 'it comes from those upon whom the white man has but little claim. It teaches us that the Indian, made like as we are, has a humanity common with us.'[137] The Relief Committee in Philadelphia described the Cherokees' donation in religious terms, describing it as an act 'of truly Christian benevolence' which provided evidence of the Cherokees 'having already attained to higher and purer species of civilization derived only from the influence of our holy religion, by which we are taught to view the sufferings of our fellow beings wherever they exist as our own'.[138]

The Quakers used their international network of Friends to encourage fund-raising. Their work in famine relief in Ireland was also brought to the attention of an international audience through the letters that they sent regularly to the newspapers. The Quakers were particularly successful in America, largely due to the indefatigable work of Jacob Harvey, a wealthy merchant and businessman who was based in New York. His premature death was attributed to exhaustion brought about by his involvement in relief.[139] A number of the contributions made to the Quakers caused a moral dilemma, most especially donations raised in Charleston and Baltimore, which were both slave-owning cities. Following discussion, it was agreed to accept these donations.[140]

Large amounts of money were also received from other parts of the British Empire. In the first few months of 1847 an estimated £20 000 was raised in Canada.[141] In April 1847, £2000 had been received from Jamaica and a first instalment of £1200 from British Guiana, both of which were sent to the British Relief Association.[142] Barbados also contributed £2000 in appreciation of money they had received from Ireland when, 65 years earlier, their island had been devastated by a hurricane.[143] Large amounts were also raised in British Canada, which had strong links with both Britain and Ireland, including £3472 from Toronto.[144] The donations included a contribution from Native Americans, the Governor stating that 'several of the Indian tribes have expressed a desire to share in relieving the wants of their suffering White Brethren. The sum donated by them already exceeds £175.'[145] In July 1847, Earl Grey estimated that subscriptions from the North American colonies amounted to £33 000.[146] Significant contributions were made from the British West Indies, including from people who a decade earlier had been slaves. A donation was given by the 'Negroes of Antigua', who raised £144 from 'their own scanty resources'.[147] The contribution from British Guiana, which amounted to over £3000, included donations from 'many coolies' who 'have contributed a day's wages cheerfully'.[148]

Because of the greater distances involved, news took longer to reach Australia, with the first report of the potato failure appearing in national newspapers on 25 February 1846 which, in turn, were based on Irish reports of 18 October 1845.[149] Relief committees were not established in

Melbourne and Sydney until August, the delay partly attributable to the conflicting reports from Ireland. Religious divisions were quickly apparent with a Protestant, pro-empire committee being set up as an alternative to one established by a Catholic priest. For the most part also, the committees attempted to remain apolitical, unlike their counterparts in the United States.[150] In 1847 and 1848, committees in Australia raised over £10 000 which was given to Archbishops Whately and Murray in Dublin and to the British Relief Association. A portion of money was also set aside to assist emigration from Ireland to Australia, but was eventually returned to the donors as the committee disagreed whether the emigrants so helped should be paupers or able-bodied emigrants.[151]

News of the distress in Ireland took even longer to be reported in newspapers in the Cape of Good Hope in South Africa, despite the fact that it was about half of the sailing distance to Australia. Reports of the first blight appeared in February 1846, but it was not until October that the seriousness of the situation was realized. In April 1847, a subscription list for the destitute in the highlands of Scotland was opened in Cape Town. A week later a subscription for the 'starving Irish' was opened and a committee established, which included a number of prominent citizens of both Irish and British extraction. Again, the subscribers to the collection were diverse, ranging from members of a Lutheran congregation and of a number of Dutch reformed congregations, wealthy merchants, and a donation from the Malay population.[152] Within a few weeks donations of £70 from Grahamstown and £550 were forwarded to the British Relief Association.[153] By the end of July almost £3000 had been donated but fundraising activities appeared to cease as the new harvest approached.[154]

Contributions to the alleviation of Irish distress also came from places that had little direct contact with Ireland. An Irish Relief Fund was established in Florence that raised £500, largely from English residents.[155] A Society Ball was also organized by the Prince de Demidoff, which raised £892. The servants of the English nobility in Florence also held a separate collection, raising almost £10.[156] The British residents in Mexico contributed £652;[157] £2644 was raised in St Petersburg; £620 in Amsterdam; and £620 from Constantinople. The islands of Malta and Gozo sent £720 to Ireland and the inhabitants of the islands of Seychelles and Rodrigues, who themselves were described as poor, sent £111 and £16 respectively.[158] The geographic range of contributions on behalf of the poor in Ireland demonstrated that interest in the Famine had spread far beyond Ireland and the United Kingdom, such that it had become an event of international significance.

The Catholic Church

The Catholic Church in Ireland, despite having no formal relief organization, was one of the most effective channels for raising and distributing relief in Ireland. The two bishops who were particularly involved
were Archbishop Murray in Dublin (who was aged 80 in 1847) and
Archbishop MacHale of Tuam. An unusual feature of aid given to the
Catholic Church was that it continued beyond 1847, when many other
forms of private relief had dried up. Due to the fragmentary nature of
the donations and because no official organization was established for
receiving funds, the amount collected is hard to quantity but was probably in excess of £400 000.[159] Most of this money was in turn redistributed amongst local priests in the distressed areas, thus avoiding much of
the expense and delay which had become a feature of government
relief.[160] Nevertheless, there was discord amongst the bishops as to how
the money forwarded to them from overseas priests and bishops should
be distributed. Murray and Archbishop Crolly of Armagh were in favour
of giving the money to the ecumenical General Central Relief Committee, whereas the Archbishops of Tuam (MacHale) and Cashel (Slattery)
were adamant that it should remain in the hands of the Catholic Church.
The latter won and the money was divided amongst the four bishops.[161]
The disputes between the bishops were also evident in 1848 when,
despite extensive suffering in his diocese, Archbishop MacHale spent
seven months in Rome lobbying for papal condemnation of the Queen's
university colleges.[162]

As a result of its overseas network, the Irish Church was able to attract
a considerable amount of financial support. The name of Daniel O'Connell was also well known by liberals and nationalists throughout Europe.
Even before the Famine, the Irish diaspora was far ranging, and Irish
Catholic communities had been established in all parts of the world.
Some of the largest amounts of money were raised by the Catholic
churches in Britain and the United States. At the beginning of 1847, the
Roman Catholic bishop of London asked all clergy in the metropolis to
devote sermons to the suffering in Ireland and the poor of London, and
collections raised were to be divided equally between the two, the latter
part to be sent to Archbishop Murray.[163] The *Tablet*, the leading Catholic
newspaper in England, offered to act as a channel for English Catholics
to send money to Ireland.[164] By March 1847 Bishop Fitzpatrick in Boston had raised almost $20 000, mostly from local Catholics, although it
was for distribution to all creeds in Ireland. The bishop decided to send

money rather than use it to purchase food on the grounds that money would arrive more quickly in Ireland than cargoes of food.[165] Apart from donations from outside Ireland, priests in Ireland donated money for the famine poor. James Maher, the rector of the Irish College in Rome, sold his horse and gig for this purpose.[166] The staff and students of Maynooth College made a donation of over £200.[167] Local priests and other religious ministers also played a vital role in the distribution of relief on behalf of other charities such as the Society of Friends.

The involvement of the Catholic clergy was helped by the early and public involvement of Pope Pius IX. A committee for the Irish poor had been established in Rome on 13 January. The Pope donated 1000 Roman Crowns from his Privy Purse.[168] Students and staff of the Irish College in Rome missed a meal and also gave the proceeds to the committee.[169] In May 1847, English Catholics asked the Pope if he would provide an autograph to be auctioned at a bazaar to raise money for Ireland. Pius not only consented to this request, he also provided a set of agate rosary beads and a carnelian medallion, together with a handwritten letter, *Scritta di sua mea*, all of which were to be auctioned and the proceeds sent to Ireland.[170]

In addition to personal financial assistance to Ireland, Pius also offered spiritual and practical support. In March 1847, he took the unprecedented step of issuing a papal encyclical to the international Catholic community, which appealed for support for the victims of the Famine. Catholic bishops were asked to set aside a day of prayer for the poor in Ireland, who were 'oppressed by the most terrible and awful distress from lack of food' and whose devotion to the 'Apostolic See' made them particularly worthy of such support. Spiritual compensation was offered in return. Three days of prayers for the Irish poor could lead to a seven-year indulgence, and if it was combined with receiving communion, a plenary indulgence was offered.[171] Three days of prayer were offered in Rome; in Italian, English and French. Dr Paul Cullen, who was Irish-born and rector of the Irish College in Rome, held the prayers on the second day.[172]

The example of the Pope was potent, with bishops in all corners of the world reproducing copies of the Pope's appeal. In the wake of the appeal, large amounts of money were raised by Catholic congregations and clergy: the Vincent de Paul Society in France raised £5000; the diocese of Strasbourg collected 23 365 francs; two priests in Caracas in Venezuela contributed £177; Father Fahy in Argentina sent over £600; £70 was sent by a priest in Grahamstown in South Africa; and over £1500 from the Catholic community in Sydney in New South Wales. Most of this money was sent to Archbishop Murray in Dublin, who redistributed it to Catholic priests in the west of Ireland.[173] Regardless of the unprecedented intervention by the Pope, the Irish bishops failed to thank him for his donation or for the encyclical letter until coerced into doing so by Paul Cullen. Cardinal Fransoni, an adviser to the Pope, was also angry at the inactivity of the Irish bishops in raising funds on behalf of the Irish poor, although he had given them official permission to take whatever steps were necessary. The apparent ingratitude of the Irish bishops and their internal wrangling lost them further vital support in Rome.[174] The Pope's concern and support for Ireland came to an abrupt end in 1848 when the revolutionary struggle within Italy forced him to flee Rome. Nevertheless, his brief interest proved to be a powerful inducement to the international community of Catholics to provide support to Ireland.

Famine Fatigue?

After the end of 1847 much of the private relief to Ireland had dried up with the exception of small donations being made to the Catholic Church. Most of this money was sent to either Murray in Dublin or to MacHale in Tuam. Yet the need for private relief in many unions was as great as it had been in 1847. Furthermore, the money was generally in small amounts, Irish suffering no longer proving capable of attracting the rich and prestigious donors it had in 1847. Consequently the small contributions of the poorer classes acquired a new significance. In July 1849, the inhabitants of Upper and Lower Liffey Street in Dublin made their eleventh donation, which totalled £18 4s. 3d. The *Freeman's Journal* commented: 'would that others had followed the noble example set by these high-minded men, and the poor streets from which they obtained such creditable contribution'.[175]

In 1849, as the government contribution disappeared, private charity became a vital lifeline for the poor. At the same time, there was some anger that those with money in Ireland were not doing more. A donor to Archbishop MacHale asked: 'What are the bishops of the established church doing with their several thousands a year, or where are those very reverend gentlemen; do they think it beneath them to attend to the affairs of charity?' The executive in Dublin Castle were also criticized, it being pointed out that the Lord Lieutenant's income was £20 000 a year; Sir William Somerville, the Chief Secretary, earned £5500 a year and owned a large estate in Meath; and Thomas Redington, the Under Secretary, received £2000 and had a large estate in Galway.[176] Responses to the Famine were continuing to divide Irish society.

In 1849, MacHale, whilst thanking subscribers, informed them that the misery of the people was being aggravated by 'the most sweeping and cruel evictions which this devoted land has ever witnessed'.[177] Paradoxically, as money was being raised for the poor in Ireland, Catholics in the country were also being asked to give money for the Pope, 'in his struggle against the Roman republic'.[178] Collections for the Pope were made at Catholic churches throughout Ireland.[179] Some of the money raised for the Pope was large, at a time when private aid to the poor had virtually dried up. In August 1849, Roman Catholics in the town of Limerick raised £560 on his behalf.[180] The *Times* regarded this fund-raising as inappropriate, pointing out that the Pope was 'living in the palace at Gaeta, courted by the king of two Sicilies, and attended by ambassadors from most of the European sovereigns'.[181] By 1849 also, a number of proselytizing groups were finding it difficult to maintain their activities due to diminishing income. Michael Brannigan, a proselytizer on behalf of the Presbyterian Church, who himself was a convert from Catholicism and a native Irish speaker, appealed to Protestant churches in Britain and Ireland for additional funds for his scriptural schools in counties Mayo and Sligo. His ability to raise further contributions for proselytizing was in stark contrast to the difficulties experienced by other groups in raising money for relief.[182] The Famine, and the private fund-raising in the early part of it, clearly had a further consequence for Irish society as the repercussions of proselytism continued to divide local communities and left a trail of bitterness.

The continuation of distress and lack of intervention by the government resulted in the revival of the General Relief Committee on 3 May 1849. Recognizing the long-term consequences of the Famine for Ireland, one of the main purposes of the reconstituted committee was to stimulate industrial development. In the short term, it wanted to provide support to impoverished small tenants who were excluded from receiving any form of relief under the Poor Law. Its main target was the poor in counties Mayo, Galway and Roscommon, where the crop had failed for four consecutive years. It anticipated that the summer months would 'witness scenes of even greater privation than those at present in existence, and unless private benevolence interpose, the year 1849 is likely to be the most memorable epoch in the annals of Irish misery'. The Committee decided to send a deputation to the Prime Minister in London and, in order that he could be informed of the situation, asked clergy of all denominations to complete a questionnaire about their locality.[183] The editor of the *Freeman's Journal*, Dr John Gray, who was a member of the new committee, was part of the delegation to the Prime Minister seeking to get assistance for these small farmers who were excluded from relief under the terms of the amended Poor Law of 1847. The Rev. Dr Spratt, a Dublin Carmelite, was also a member of the committee. The committee found that it was far more difficult to raise money in 1849 than it had been two years earlier, and therefore decided to appeal directly to the Prime Minister for assistance.[184] In July 1849, the deputation travelled to London in order to raise money for those groups excluded from receiving Poor Law relief. They also hoped to persuade Russell to adopt a more flexible approach to relief. In particular, they wanted the government to make provision for smallholders of land who were ineligible to receive relief under the Irish Poor Law.

The delegation had little success. They were unable to raise funds for Ireland because 'a very strong prejudice, even in the most influential and enlightened quarters, existed against the making of any effort by voluntary contributions for the relief of Irish distress'.[185] A general belief also existed that the money which had been given both by the government and by private subscriptions had not reached the starving peasantry, but had been used to provide assistance to ratepayers. Additionally, one of the closing statements which had been made by the Society of Friends when they withdrew from providing direct relief was used against the delegation, the Quakers having admitted the 'hopeless of any good effects from giving', the destitution being so endemic that it was beyond the capabilities of private relief.[186] The General Relief Committee did win the support of a number of eminent British politicians, notably John Bright and George Poulett Scrope. The Irish delegation held a number of public meetings presided over by Bright, but in total only raised £250 for Irish distress. Despite appearing sympathetic to the request of the committee, Russell rejected their suggestions. Nevertheless, shortly after the deputation arrived in London, the government started a subscription for the distressed districts in Ireland under the patronage of Queen Victoria, who donated £500. The money was to be entrusted to Count Strzelecki, who had returned to Ireland and offered his services in a voluntary capacity. He promised to use it in such a way as not to interfere with the administration of the Poor Law. Other contributors included

Lord John Russell, Henry Labouchere, Charles Wood and Baron de Rothschild, who each contributed £100; the Archbishop of Canterbury, £50; and Sir Charles Trevelyan, who gave £25.[187]

By the end of 1849 both official and private assistance to Ireland had ended. Much of the good will and generosity evident only two years earlier had disappeared and Irish poverty had unequivocally become the responsibility of Irish property. Russell acknowledged that public opinion towards the suffering in Ireland had changed, informing Clarendon that:

> The great difficulty this year respecting Ireland is one which does not spring from Trevelyan or Charles Wood but lies deep in the breasts of the British people. It is this – we have granted, lent, subscribed, worked, visited, clothed the Irish; millions of pounds worth of money, years of debate etc. – the only return is calumny and rebellion – let us not grant, clothe etc. any more and see what they will do.[188]

For a short period in 1847, however, one of the worst years of the Famine, the suffering in Ireland had attracted the attention of people throughout the world and the response had transcended differences in religion, nationality, social position and income. The donations had not merely supplemented official relief, they had provided a vital means of sustenance, which frequently made the difference between survival and death.

The total amount of aid given through private charity was difficult to quantify, partly as a consequence of the high number of donations. The General Central Relief Committee, for example, estimated that they had received over 70 000 donations, whilst the British Relief Association calculated that over 15 000 individual contributions had been made to their committee. The greatest amount of relief came from the United States: it was estimated by a Boston newspaper that during the seven-month period between January and July 1847, over one million dollars was given to the major relief organizations.[189] Private remittances from Irish people in the States were also considerable, and in the 12 months after November 1846 probably reached a further half a million dollars.[190] Overall, the contribution from the States, which was concentrated in 1847, was in the region of two million dollars (approximately £380 000). The cash contributions made to the main relief organizations were in excess of one million pounds, whilst contributions in food, clothing and the like meant that the real value of the assistance was far higher. In total, therefore, private donations were probably in the region of two million pounds. In comparison, the financial contribution of the British government between 1845 and 1849 was just over ten million pounds (0.3 per cent of the Gross National Product), over half of which was provided as a loan.[191] Clearly, private aid accounted for a large portion of famine relief. Its effectiveness was helped by the fact that its overheads were low (most of the work being done by volunteers), its bureaucracy was minimal, and it could be provided without the practical or ideological constraints that accompanied so much official relief. However, a further significance lay in the fact that, in contrast with the frugality and resentment evident in so much of the official response, it provided evidence of a humane response to a massive human tragedy.

4

FOOD SUPPLY AND TRADE

One of the most polarized and controversial aspects of Famine historiography relates to the issue of food production, export and distribution.
The popular understanding has tended to believe that large amounts of
food left Ireland whilst the people starved. This interpretation has its
roots in the writing of the radical John Mitchel. In his *Jail Journal*, published in 1854, he presented the Famine as starvation in the midst of
plenty, the blame for which he unequivocally attributed to 'English'
rule.[1] Mitchell further developed this theme in *The Last Conquest of Ireland*,
published six years later which included the much-quoted phrase, 'The
Almighty, indeed, sent the potato blight, but the English created the
Famine.'[2] Mitchel's interpretation has been frequently criticized for being
simplistic and politically motivated.[3] One historian has suggested that as
a consequence of Mitchel's accounts, 'by a masterly stroke of propaganda,
the tragedy became harnessed to the bandwagon of Irish nationalism'.
Moreover, those who have supported the idea that the Famine was
neither inevitable nor caused simply by food shortages have similarly
been tainted with political or nationalist motivations.[4] But over-reliance
on Mitchel as a source (significantly by his detractors) has served to
obfuscate the complexity of the issue of food supply. Before Mitchel had
put pen to paper, it was being argued in parliament, in the press and by
a diverse range of politicians that policies rather than food shortages
were causing famine. This chapter reappraises policy formulation with
regard to food supply and food export through an examination of little-
used sources. It also moves the debate from the narrow parameters of
the Mitchel thesis to assess how such policies were viewed at the time. It
concludes that Ireland was producing enough food to feed its people

after 1846.[5] Clearly, food shortages alone were not responsible for the excess mortality in Ireland.

The most common perception of the pre-Famine economy was that it was poor and underdeveloped. This view was confirmed by foreign visitors to the country and by various government enquiries. Comparisons were commonly made with the more commercialized economy of Britain, and they were inevitably unfavourable to Ireland. Irish farming techniques were generally regarded as primitive and potatoes˜as ubiquitous.[6] Indolence was both a cause and a consequence of a life-style where people lacked any incentive to improve their condition. The ridged field systems in which the potatoes were grown were significantly referred to as 'lazy beds' because the period of cultivation was estimated at being less than four weeks.[7] Ironically, regardless of the disdain with which potato cultivation was viewed, its nutritional value was acknowledged; the Halls, who toured around Ireland in 1840–1 maintaining that 'It is universally admitted that a finer or hardier race of peasantry cannot be found in the world.'[8] The alleged laziness of Irish labourers was mirrored by the apathy of many landlords who had allowed a system of subdivision to proliferate. Their repudiation of tenant rights and lack of capital investment were also held responsible for the backwardness of agriculture and the hostile relationships between landlords and tenants. Yet the perceptions of Ireland were largely derived from people who were using Britain – or more accurately England – as a cultural and social benchmark and who showed little sensitivity to Ireland's unique system of agriculture and the historical circumstances which had given rise to it.

Despite the persistence of such perceptions, Irish agriculture was dynamic in a variety of ways. Irish crop yields exceeding those of a number of other European countries, including those of France and Scotland.[9] Ireland was a significant exporter of agricultural produce and proved able to adjust to the demands of external markets. Grain exports grew in keeping with the demands of both protective legislation and of the British markets. In the late eighteenth century, the Irish parliament had passed a series of measures to encourage a change to tillage, including the provision of travel subsidies on the internal movement of grain. Grain production was regarded by the parliament as a way of giving Ireland a stronghold in Anglo-Irish trading relations. Between 1792 and 1819 (during most of which Britain was at war with France) food exports from Ireland to Britain rose dramatically, the largest growth being in the export of wheat which expanded twentyfold.[10] A number of Irish MPs were anxious that Ireland was vulnerable within the trading relationship and in 1784 John Foster introduced a bill which intended to protect Irish corn from English demands during periods of shortages.[11] Britain's dependence on Irish corn was obvious: in the 1790s Ireland had supplied Britain with 16.5 per cent of corn imports; by 1810 this had risen to 57 per cent; and by 1830 80 per cent of British corn imports came from Ireland.[12] After 1815 produce from Ireland filled a gap in markets in Britain resulting from rapid population growth and the shift to industrialization and urbanization.[13]

Developments in steam shipping and the spread of the railway network in Britain also facilitated a growth in the export of livestock to Britain. However, processed meat continued to be important, with many of the poorest paid workers in towns such as Manchester consuming large quantities of Irish bacon.[14] There was also rapid expansion in the export of Irish provisions, notably butter. Liverpool was the major port of entry and by 1841, 198 490 cwt. was imported annually. This amount had increased to 262 677 cwt. by 1845 and only fell slightly over the next three years. In 1848, 223 040 cwt. of butter was imported into the port and in the following year it reached its highest level of 280 200 cwt.[15] Irish agricultural output also grew to meet the fast-growing demands of the rapidly increasing domestic population, which in the 40 years following the Act of Union grew from approximately five million to eight and a half million. This level of productivity was made possible by a massive increase in agricultural output, which grew by an estimated 80 per cent during the same period.[16] On the eve of the Famine, therefore, Ireland was not only feeding her own large population, but also exporting large amounts of foodstuffs to Britain, producing in total enough food to feed over 11 million people.

Although potatoes were regarded as synonymous with Irish agriculture, they accounted for only approximately 20 per cent of production, with tillage representing over 60 per cent.[17] Also, the division between the east and west of Ireland was less marked than traditionally depicted.[18] A buoyant export sector existed in each of the coastal districts of Ireland, even close to areas traditionally associated with subsistence potato cultivation. Developments in cross-channel shipping after the 1820s facilitated the movement of people and goods to Britain – coastal communication being more advanced than the internal transport infrastructure, although, following the establishment of the Board of Public Works in 1831, road access did improve.

Even before the Act of Union, trade links between Ireland and Britain had been strong and they increased after 1800. In 1801, the value of exports from England to Ireland had been £3 270 350; in 1821, £5 338 898; and in 1825, £7 048 936. After that year, complete returns of exports to Ireland had not been kept, as from 1824 custom duties between Ireland and Britain had been abolished and the United Kingdom became a free trade zone. However, according to an estimate based on the tonnage of ships travelling to Ireland, made at the time of the appearance of the potato blight, the value of exports had grown to £10 000 000 annually. The value of exports to Britain was far higher. The strong trading links led Anthony Lefroy, MP for Longford, to argue in 1847 that Ireland should not be treated as a separate identity during the Famine, as the commerce of Ireland and Britain was inextricably linked. Lefroy suggested that rather than British interests being regarded habitually as separate from those of Ireland, they were interdependent. Apart from being important as a supplier of food, Ireland also provided an excellent outlet for British goods because it was 'vast, a near and a safe market'. Moreover, he suggested that if the resources of Ireland were developed, the consumption of British produce could increase.[19] British prosperity, therefore, was contingent on the concurrent development of Ireland.

Corn and Repeal

The appearance of potato blight in Ireland precipitated a crisis within British parliamentary politics that was to have an immediate impact in that it brought the Whig Party to power in 1846, at a time when the food crisis intensified; in the long term, it split the Tory Party and thus altered the direction of British politics in the late nineteenth century. The main reason for these changes was Peel's decision to tie in the food shortages in Ireland with the essentially British question of the repeal of the Corn Laws. A number of famine historians have attributed Peel's decision to repeal the Corn Laws to his desire 'to allow the immediate importation of corn into Ireland'.[20] Peel, however, had been moving towards a policy of free trade since his return as Prime Minster in 1841, and the potato blight provided an opportunity to remove one of the last remaining barriers to free trade – the Corn Laws. By doing so, he offended many in his own party whilst stealing from the Whigs one of their policies. From the outset, Peel tied in repeal with food shortages in Ireland, although he believed that by the time repeal was in place, the subsistence crisis would be over and that, in the longer term, it would be damaging to Ireland's corn trade.[21] The injury to Ireland's economy was acknowledged during the debate. George Poulett Scrope, the economist and radical MP, predicted that the impact would be to 'increase the desire to lay down arable into pasture and thus deprive the people still further of their only means of subsistence'.[22]

A more conservative commentator, Lord Northland, pointed out that the repeal of the Corn Laws would 'make the condition of Ireland even worse than it was now' because Ireland was so heavily dependent on her agricultural sector and had few industries. These concerns were echoed in Ireland, even in Belfast, the most industrialized part of Ireland.[23] The food shortages in Ireland coincided with poor corn harvests throughout Europe, which increased the optimism of free traders throughout the United Kingdom that the Corn Laws would be repealed. The *Belfast News-Letter* suggested that 'the most gloomy accounts of the potato failure have been recklessly exaggerated in order to give colour for the agitation for Free Trade'.[24] Peel's decision to make the removal gradual, based on a three-year sliding scale, also indicated that he was less concerned with the immediate problem of easing food supply in Ireland than with completing his free trade programme. Richard Cobden, the leading apostle of free trade in Britain, admitted that the impact of the repeal on the Irish economy was of very little interest to the English public.[25]

Following his initial attempt to introduce repeal, for which he had the support of only three members of his Cabinet, Peel tendered his resignation as Prime Minister in December 1845. He explained his drastic behaviour and willingness to break up the government as being due to 'that great mysterious calamity which had destroyed the article of food on which so many of the poor in this and the sister kingdom depended for their subsistence'. But whilst the potato blight may have provided a trigger for his action, he also admitted that 'he would not deny that his opinions on the subject of protections had undergone a change'.[26] Nevertheless, Peel remained in office and the Tory Party in government as Russell was unable to form a ministry. Back in power, Peel introduced a modified version of his corn bill. The prolonged debate regarding repeal also had an immediate detrimental impact on Ireland's agriculture as the corn trade throughout the United Kingdom had suffered as a consequence of the uncertainties regarding the future of the protective legislation. Within Ireland, this doubt resulted in 'uncertainty as to how long the existing laws regulating the duties on corn may remain in force, or if altered, the nature of the change likely to be proposed'.[27]

Anger at large quantities of food leaving the country and the deployment of a military escort for this purpose was noted in the first year of
shortages. In April 1846, in the wake of a number of food riots in
Ireland, Smith O'Brien sought to bring the situation to the notice of the
House of Commons saying: 'The circumstance which appeared most
aggravating was that the people were starving in the midst of plenty, and
that every tide carried from the Irish ports corn sufficient for the maintenance of thousands of the Irish people. Was it not, then, surprising
that there should not, under such circumstances, be more attacks on
property.'[28] Yet the response of the hungry people was not always passive.[29] In Dungarvan in County Waterford, which was a major area of
grain production and export, tensions were evident in the wake of the
first potato failure. As a consequence, a local merchant, Patrick Howley,
decided to halt corn exports in the spring of 1846. This decision was
clearly pragmatic as he also requested that Dublin Castle send marines
and dragoons to the area to enable future supplies to leave the harbour.
The authorities alerted the troops in Youghal to the possible need for
their intervention.[30] Anger at the export of food was exacerbated by the
inadequacy of the revised public works in the autumn of 1846. Despite
a high troop presence and 18 additional constables being sent to the
area, there was unrest throughout the summer. Again, one of the targets
of the local population was the export of food, groups assembling on the
quayside to prevent transportation. The local fishermen and their wives
also blockaded ships carrying grain from the port. On 1 October two local
corn merchants sent a petition to the Lord Lieutenant saying:

> That from the present state of mob excitement in this town, petitioners
> are not allowed to ship their corn, though fully protected by the mili-
> tary and police that the intimidation is so high that the men employed
> permanently and usually for this purpose have refused to work
> thereby leaving the petitioners without the means of shipping their
> corn.[31]

During Peel's ministry, therefore, a pattern of protest had been established which illustrated the popular antagonism to food being exported
during times of shortages – even if it was believed that the shortage
would be a short-term one. The response of Peel's government and the
local merchants, however, demonstrated that they were willing to rely
on force and legislation to ensure the free movement of food out of the
country.

Food Supply and Price Increases

Whilst the debate raged over the repeal of the Corn Laws, Peel's government had put in place a series of short-term measures to meet the shortages expected in the spring and summer of 1846. The question of food supply was central to these measures, with the government acting as an importer and distributor of imported corn. One of the primary aims of the decision to import corn was as a way of both stabilizing prices and keeping provisions as cheap as possible.[32] His position on the Corn Laws meant that he alienated support in his party which would have made it difficult to introduce radical measures to alleviate Irish distress. The relief measures introduced, however, demonstrated that, with the exception of the Corn Laws, Peel was determined to keep interference in trade to a minimum. In October 1845, the Irish Viceroy Lord Heytesbury suggested that Irish ports should be opened immediately to encourage the import of corn. Both Peel and the Home Secretary James Graham were opposed to the measure on the grounds that it would be iniquitous to show Ireland preferential treatment even during a period of food shortages.[33] Requests for the ports to be opened were also made by many corporations including those of Belfast, Cork and Derry.[34] In Belfast, also, some of the local press appealed for all impediments to imports to be removed, the *Belfast* Vindicator suggesting that not to do so 'may be dangerous indeed'.[35] In Dublin, the reconstituted Mansion House Committee, whose members included Daniel O'Connell, Lord Cloncurry and the Duke of Leinster, met with the Viceroy in November 1845 and suggested a comprehensive package of relief measures for 'prompt, universal and efficacious measures for procuring food and employment for the people'. The proposals included providing works of 'national utility', establishing public granaries and banning the use of grain in distilleries. The committee also passed a resolution condemning 'the culpable conduct of the present administration' for not taking sufficient measures to alleviate the calamity, in particular 'the positive and unequivocal crime of keeping the ports closed against the importation of foreign provisions'.[36]

Various other ways were suggested for food supply to be increased, including a variety of unusual ways to make the diseased potatoes edible. In November 1845, for example, thousands of leaflets were distributed around Belfast entitled 'Plain Directions for making Good Bread from Unsound Potatoes'.[37] The disease was so degenerative, however, that the propositions were not successful. A traditional way of preserving grain supplies was for distillation to be suspended. This measure was suggested by Lord Heytesbury; in October 1845, he informed Peel that 'this be demanded on all sides'.[38] One Belfast newspaper, the *Vindicator*, suggested the opening of ports and the closure of every distillery in the country.[39] This suggestion was adopted at a meeting convened by the Mayor of Belfast, and was strongly supported by advocates of temperance within the town. The MP Sharman Crawford, who attended the meeting, called on the government to do everything possible to make provisions inexpensive. The town meeting adopted a memorial to the Lord Lieutenant, proposing the immediate closure of the distilleries and the opening of the ports.[40] All of this advice was rejected by Peel, demonstrating at an early stage that policy formulation in London did not follow the guidance of the Dublin Castle Executive, or of locally elected government or their parliamentary representatives. A sharp condemnation of Peel's food policies was made by the *Banner of Ulster* in April 1846. The paper argued that 'the harvest was sufficiently abundant to give food for man and beast. The famine – if there be a famine – is man made. We have malted and distilled the famine. That fact must never be forgotten – unless we would lose the lessons that this judgement should teach.'[41]

Following the second failure, appeals were repeated for distillation to be ended, but Russell's government was even more determined not to intervene in trade. At the end of 1846, the Mayor of Belfast convened a meeting asking for the government to suspend the distillation of alcohol from grain.[42] The meeting considered that such a measure was even more necessary than it had been 12 months earlier. It was also pointed out that former governments had preserved grain supplies in this way. Sharman Crawford made the point that in such circumstances, 'individual interests must give way to public good'.[43] One speaker explained why the government was unlikely to respond to their demand: 'As long as England is unvisited by the appalling distress that unhappily exists in this country, it will never consent to the proposal of prohibiting the use of grain in distilleries and breweries.'[44] Nevertheless, the meeting also appointed a deputation, which included Sharman Crawford, to meet the Executive in Dublin Castle and request that grain distillation be halted. But this appeal did not have universal support. The *Northern Whig*, which supported the non-interventionist policies of the government, accused the deputation of being 'innocent of any knowledge of the principles of trade and the tendency of demand and supply'. Moreover, Sharman Crawford was charged with 'running away with his judgement'.[45]

Table 4.1   Spirits (in gallons) Charged with Duty for Home Consumption

1845	1846	1847	1848	1849	1850
7 605 196	7 952 076	6 037 383	7 072 933	6 973 333	7 408 086

Source: *Report of the House of Lords, to consider extending the functions of the Constabulary to suppressing Illicit Distilling*, PP 1854, x, p. 4.

Within the United Kingdom Ireland was a major supplier of spirits, by the 1840s producing about three times as much spirits as were produced in Scotland.[46] Moreover, Irish spirits were produced entirely from grain. Even after the laws were relaxed at the beginning of 1847, allowing sugar to replace grain in distillation, Irish spirits continued to be produced entirely from corn.[47] At the beginning of January 1847, the Waterford distillery stopped working for want of corn, but the crop failure had little impact on the industry elsewhere.[48] Overall, the production of spirits showed no signs of strain, Table 4.1 shows the quantity of spirits being produced in Ireland.

Significantly, in the late 1840s illicit distilling almost disappeared.[49] The stoppage in illicit distillation was not only due to the repeated bad harvests, but the local constabulary attributed it to massive emigration and the fact that 'those left behind who are disposed to illicit distillation are so crippled, not even having the means of emigration, that they have not the means of carrying out private distillation'.[50] At the beginning of 1847, the leading mercantile journal in England, the *Mark Lane Express and Agricultural Journal*, published a series of suggestions for increasing food supply throughout the whole of the United Kingdom in an article entitled: 'It is in the power of the government to prevent a lamentable crisis in the nation'. The suggestions were that they could stop distillation from corn; remove the import duty from corn and flour; let spare shipping be used by merchants to bring food into the country; stop fine flour being produced; make it illegal to give corn to horses and other beasts of burden; and allow sugar to be used in distilleries and breweries if they were unwilling to stop distillation. They argued that it was necessary for the government to intervene to prevent the situation deteriorating further throughout the whole of the United Kingdom, asking: 'What will become of the poor inhabitants of Ireland, when England cannot assist? The probability is starvation to death.' The paper also added that government in England, 'the richest and ablest nation', had a duty to 'exercise the power the Almighty has given it' in order to prevent starvation.[51]

Many of these suggestions were incorporated into a bill introduced into parliament two week later.

Food supply was also constrained by the small size of the crop sown. The impact was particularly devastating following the massive potato and corn failures in 1846 when less than one-sixth of the usual potato crop was sown.[52] The shortage of seed potatoes was intensified by the inability of labourers to attend to the crops because they were employed on the public works. After 1846 the increase in food prices was exacerbated both by Russell's refusal to import large amounts of food and also, urged by Trevelyan, his refusal to use the depots, as Peel had done, to regulate food prices. The amount of food that was available to the poor was highlighted in a heated parliamentary exchange in March 1847. Disraeli, a member of the Protectionists group, revealed that in November and December 1846, only 638 932 lb of meal had been distributed, whereas under Peel, 23 257 000 lb had been distributed. Furthermore, whilst in the previous year there had been 93 food depots operative, under the Whigs there were only 24.[53] Ironically, also, the imported Indian corn was not only alien to the Irish palate, but it was difficult to cook and was frequently eaten only half-cooked. In April 1847, Bessborough estimated that half of the deaths had been due to food that had been inadequately prepared and badly cooked.[54] It was not only the price of food that increased. Even the cost of emigration increased at the beginning of 1847: the passage from Cork to America in the forecastle increased from £4 to £5, thus making it more difficult for the poorest groups to escape from famine.[55]

The second harvest failure was quickly followed by a sharp increase in the price of provisions, which allowed those in possession of stocks to make large profits. The *Banner of Ulster* observed that in the north of the country: 'Farmers are asking and holding out for the most exorbitant prices and their terms are accepted.'[56] The poor grain harvest had also pushed up the price of all corn and between the end of August and mid-December, oatmeal had doubled in price, reaching 21s. a cwt.[57] The sharp price increase put some basic provisions out of the reach of the poor, which meant that 'several of the retail grocers declare that they find it impossible to find purchasers among the poor at the present high prices'.[58] The Belfast company of Richardson Bros., which was the largest importer of Indian corn into Ireland, ascribed their inability to import large amounts of the grain to 'either lack of vessels or the extravagant rates of freight demanded'. They petitioned the government suggesting that the situation could be eased by allowing official vessels to be made available to bring grain into Ireland. But the government refused their request.[59]

In the early weeks of 1847, prices demonstrated an upward trend which kept food purchase out of the reach of those employed on the public works; in Mohill in County Donegal, for example, oatmeal rose from 22s. a cwt. to 24s., and in Boyle from 23s. to 24s., in the same week.[60] The price rises did not just affect the poor. Even people in employment or who were not traditionally dependent on potatoes found it difficult to pay the inflated prices. From County Mayo it was reported that 'the markets are so exorbitantly high that it is next to an impossibility for anyone to buy food . . . beef, mutton, butter, milk, bread, eggs, and everything bearing the name of human food is now gone beyond the purchase of tradesmen or of poor housekeepers'.[61] Many of the soldiers in the garrison in Westmeath were suffering from dysentery, which was attributed to the fact that they could not afford to buy adequate food as their wages were insufficient to afford the 'famine prices'.[62] Even Indian corn, which had been intended as an inexpensive substitute for potatoes, was selling for 2s. per cwt., double its cost 12 months earlier. Parliament was informed that the price of wheat had risen from 47s. a quarter in the first week of August, to 49s. A month later it had risen to 64s. and to over 70s. on 16 January. The price of barley had shown a similar sharp increase from 31s. in 1846 to 50s. by mid-January 1847. Russell's statement, however, caused some dissent within parliament, one member suggesting that the government had not provided accurate information regarding the price of corn at the beginning of 1847, it being approximately eight shillings a quarter more expensive than had been stated.[63] Despite it being contrary to government regulations, a number of relief committees unilaterally reduced the price of their supplies; the Tralee committee for example, reduced the price of Indian corn from 2s. 5d. to 2s. 2d.[64] In Limerick the relief committee resolved to purchase a stock of corn to resell at a low price, but the Lord Lieutenant refused to sanction this decision as it flouted Treasury regulations.[65]

Hoarding and forestalling were also blamed for the rapid price increases in many parts of the country. The *Roscommon and Leitrim Gazette* reported that by January 1847, the price of basic foodstuffs had become so high that people could not afford to buy them. Oatmeal had risen in the local markets to between 22s. and 23s. a cwt.[66] They attributed this price increase to speculation.[67] In Galway, one of the main market towns and ports in the west, a similar practice was reported. A number of local merchants had made an agreement to keep the price of provisions at 'famine prices'. The only competition was the sale of food from the commissary stores to the relief committees, which were not very extensive anyway. The merchants, however, asked the Relief Commissioners if the government stores could be closed, but the request was refused. Such actions were regarded with anger by the local press, the *Galway Vindicator* threatening to publish the names of the men involved in the 'nefarious transaction'.[68] The opportunities to make high profits through speculation were clear. The *Times* reported that several corn agents based in Ireland had been called back to England by their houses, because higher profits could be made by selling their corn in the English markets.[69]

In the summer of 1847, it was reported that merchants in Clonmel who had realized vast profits from hoarding, were being obliged to destroy large quantities of meal and the like because it had become overheated in storage. The paper concluded 'the River Suir now receives what would have subsisted many who have gone off this stage forever'.[70] The government, whilst acknowledging that food prices had put staple food out of the reach of the poor, feared that any sudden fall in price might result in the Irish merchants selling their corn in France, which had experienced a poor corn harvest the previous year, and where the government and merchants were more proactive in bringing food into the country.[71] Free trade had not kept people from dying, but had increased the wealth of many merchants and farmers who had received unusually high prices for the sale of cattle and corn.[72] The Viceroy Bessborough was particularly critical of the behaviour of the merchants whom he judged to have behaved selfishly. He was convinced that 'the merchants who in last July made promises of all sorts about the stock of meal etc., that they would bring into the country, having failed in making good their promises and have done their best to keep up prices and, as I am assured, have done as little as they could, even if the government had entered the trade'.[73]

It was not only in Ireland where food supply was regarded as a problem. In May 1847, the Earl of Hardwicke raised concerns in the House of Lords about the quantity of corn in Britain. Buyers from France and Belgium had recently purchased large quantities of corn in the south-eastern markets and, as a consequence, in one week corn had risen from 96s. to 120s. a quarter. He believed that there was not enough corn in Britain to feed the people until the next harvest. He felt that measures should be introduced to stop corn leaving the district or being purchased by large dealers who could then charge exorbitant prices. Lord Ashburton

also suggested that 'with great reluctance', he believed they should consider whether they ought to place restrictions on the export of corn.
Lord Lansdowne, on behalf of the government, pointed out that since
January large amounts had come into the United Kingdom, showing the
efficacy of the government's decision not to interfere with trade.[74] The
matter was also raised in the House of Commons, where the Earl of
Winchilsea suggested the expedience of establishing public granaries,
which should be opened if grain prices became high. He also reported
that, within the last few days, the French government had bought large
quantities of flour and wheat in England. Winchilsea believed that the
government needed to reconsider the issue of free trade.[75] A few days
later, the Home Secretary Sir George Grey confirmed that food riots had
taken place in Cornwall and Exeter due to the high price of provisions,
but that order had been restored owing to the prompt intervention of
the local authorities. The question was again raised in the Commons as
to whether the government intended to stop the exportation of wheat –
134 000 quarters having been exported in April alone, but Russell
answered that the government did not intend to interfere.[76]

Trade and Ideology

Because no excess mortality occurred in the first year of shortages, Peel's
handling of the food shortages was generally praised. His decision to
import Indian Corn, although not sufficient to feed the distressed, was
successful in stabilizing the price and distribution of corn. Russell's
administration, in contrast, chose to make public works rather than food
imports the core of their relief policies, leaving food import and distribution to market forces. Despite the apparent variance in policies, overall
both governments took a cautious approach, abandoning traditional
polices in favour of short-term political advantage. The actions of Peel
and Russell were partly due to a belief in the free market, but also
because the merchant class was both economically and politically powerful. Peel carried out the purchase of corn in 1845 secretly and in such
a way as not to undermine or compete with merchants. Indian corn was
chosen not only for its cheapness, but also because little trade in it had
previously existed in the United Kingdom, and therefore corn merchants
'could not complain of interference with a trade which did not exist, nor
could prices be raised against the home consumption on an article of

which no stock was to be found in the home market'.[77] Moreover, the quantity of corn imported 'was not for the purpose of meeting the entire wants of the Irish people, but for the purpose of checking the markets and of preventing the price of corn from being unduly enhanced'.[78]

The policies of both Peel's and Russell's governments in relation to food imports and exports were widely criticized at the time. During Peel's administration there was some concern within the country that more extensive relief measures were required, especially in relation to food supply. Even following the first less extensive failure of the potato crop in 1845, a number of people had suggested that all restrictions should be removed from the import of food into the country. In January 1846, free trade deputations from both Dublin and London met the Queen and asked for the ports to be opened to allow cheap food to be imported.[79] Following the second failure when the shortfall in food supplies was greater, the demands for more government intervention increased. A number of individual corporations, including those of Belfast and Limerick, requested that the ports be opened to allow food to be imported unrestricted. Similar requests were made in London and at the end of November 1846, four deputations from the capital met Lord John Russell to ask that all duties be removed from foreign corn.[80] At a public meeting held in Dublin at the end of the year, the policies of Russell in relation to the purchase and distribution of grain were compared unfavourably with those of Peel's administration. Even the moderate, pro-government, Catholic Archbishop Murray proposed a motion, seconded by a Presbyterian minister, condemning the government, 'who allowed the poor to perish sooner than interfere with the interests of the general trader'.[81]

The market was not, in reality, free nor was competition perfect. The existence of the Navigation Acts meant that food could only be brought into a United Kingdom port if it was carried on a British ship. In effect, these laws placed a ceiling on the amount of food that could be transported to Ireland. The food imported into Ireland to fill the deficit, was also hampered by a sharp increase in freight charges. Trevelyan admitted that the sudden and sharp rise in freight charges in the winter of 1846–7, from the United States to Russia, made it difficult to obtain foreign supplies at 'moderate rates'.[82] Isaac Butt, an Irish political economist who had been a political opponent of O'Connell, described the government's commitment to free trade whilst such restrictions continued as 'the climax of infatuation', pointing out: 'If ministers resolved to trust the lives of the Irish people to private enterprise, was it not common sense and common justice to them that private enterprise should be unencumbered by any restrictions in the execution of the task of supplying, at the notice of a few months, provisions to five million people?' He argued that freight charges and the Navigation Laws should have been temporarily removed if there existed a genuine desire to alleviate the situation. He also argued that by treating Ireland in such a way, the Act of Union was being irreparably damaged.[83] In January 1847, the Navigation Acts and all duties on foreign corn were temporarily suspended, but in the critical months following the harvest of 1846, a starvation gap had undoubtedly existed in Ireland and its consequences had been disease, death and emigration.

The decision to not interfere in food exports was criticized in the Irish nationalist press. The *Nation* frequently made the point that, regardless of the failure in 1846, there was 'within our four seas, food enough growing up to feed all Irishmen next year'. But they warned that 'Already the English are counting on the appearance of our food, as usual, at their tables; and if the ordinary commercial intercourse between the two islands shall be in operation at October next, another million of the Irish must perish.'[84] The *Nation* also pointed out the financial motives which lay behind the decision not to intervene in the food trade, putting it further out of the reach of the poor, especially as some of the food was then reimported to Ireland at vastly inflated prices. They explained to their readers the nonsensical implication of allowing the harvest to leave the country:

> Early in winter it was conveyed, by the thousands of shiploads to England; paying freight it was stored in English stores; paying storage: it was passed from hand to hand among corn-speculators; paying at every remove, commission, merchants' profit, forwarding charges, and so forth: some of it was bought by French or Belgian buyers and carried to Havre, to Antwerp, to Bordeaux – meeting on the way cargoes of other corn coming from Odessa, or Hamburg, or New York, which other corn was also earning for merchants, ship-owners, and other harpies, immense profits, exorbitant freights, huge commissions, in all latitudes and longitudes and whatever corn *you* eventually got to eat, came to you loaded with all those charges to increase the price. In other words, you sent away a quarter of wheat at 50 shillings, and got it back, if you got it at all, at 80 shillings.[85]

Following the harvest failure of 1846–7, Russell was particularly anxious not to offend the merchant or trading classes. The impending

Table 4.2 Total Amounts of Irish-Grown Grain Exports, 1844–6 (in quarts)

	1844	1845	1846
corn	2 801 206	3 251 901	1 825 394
wheat flour	839 567	1 422 879	723 562
oatmeal	1 150 976	1 059 185	553 147

Source: The *Times*, 3 February 1847.

General Election in the summer of 1847 meant that Russell and his party were particularly sensitive to political opinion. But the policy failed in that during the critical winter months of 1846–7, the merchants had failed to bring in sufficient grain. Moreover, far from depressing prices, the merchants had deliberately kept them inflated as a way of increasing their profit margins.[86] Supporters of the government, however, pointed to the success of their trade policies. Charles Trevelyan, who published an anonymous account of the Famine in 1848, asserted that 'prodigious efforts were made by the mercantile community to provide against the approaching scarcity. The whole world was ransacked for supplies'.[87] In parliament also, the Whig members continued to defend the decision not to interfere with food supply, despite repeated onslaughts from Smith O'Brien, Bentinck, Disraeli and a handful of Irish members. The free market, however, failed to provide Ireland with a sufficient supply of cheap food. In the three months ending 27 December 1845, the quantity of oats exported from London to Ireland was 221 817 quarters, but in the same period in 1846 it was only 77 000 quarts.[88]

The export of food from Ireland showed little signs of the deepening subsistence crisis in the country. Although grain exports decreased, the export of other foodstuffs was sustained or increased. The drop in grain exports, however, was largely in response to a poor harvest rather than an indication of the commodity being diverted to home consumption.[89] At the request of Poulett Scrope the total amount of Irish-grown grain exports was put before parliament in January 1847 (see Table 4.2).

Because of the free trade zone created in the wake of the Act of Union, it was difficult to disaggregate exports made from Ireland to other parts of the United Kingdom. The quantities of food imported into Ireland was similarly unreliable. George Bentinck challenged the figures provided by the government on food imported into the country as overestimates.[90] Bentinck, speaking in the House of Commons, cast doubt on the accuracy of the figures. In June, he pointed out that the returns relating to the import of corn by foreign ships since the suspension of the Navigation Laws were inaccurate. This accusation was not denied. The Chancellor of the Exchequer and Russell, nevertheless, defended the returns as being 'generally correct', but admitted that the amount of corn imported had been inflated. He added that even if the number of ships entering Ireland was substantially less than had been stated, a continued suspension of the Navigation Laws was necessary to 'secure a supply of corn for Ireland'. Also, despite the distress in 1846, exports of grain from Ireland and Britain to a number of European countries increased: the combined exports to Holland, Belgium and France for 1844, 1845 and 1846 were 107 777 quarters, 104 045 and 1 066 594 quarters, respectively.[91]

By the beginning of 1847 the relief measures introduced only a few months earlier could clearly be seen to have failed and the government was introducing a series of emergency measures to cope with the crisis, replacing public works with soup kitchens. A further indication of the failure of the government's policy of non-intervention in trade was evident in the decision taken at the first meeting of parliament in January 1847 when it was proposed to remove all duties from foreign corn and to suspend the Navigation Acts, both with immediate effect until 1 September and 1 November respectively. The existence of the laws meant that despite a superficial commitment to free trade, major impediments to the import of food still existed. At the same time, Russell proposed that all duties on the importation of foreign corn were to be removed for the same period. A resolution was also passed permitting the use of sugar in breweries. In his explanation for wishing to suspend corn duties, Russell explained that despite an abundant harvest of wheat and corn in the United States, little had reached the United Kingdom. He believed that, as strong competition continued to exist for corn supplies, it was necessary to remove impediments to import. France, for example, which had already suspended its own Navigation Laws, had been a major recipient of foreign corn. The existence of the Laws had also increased freight charges, because they created an artificial shortage of shipping. Russell quoted the example of the freight charges from London to Cork, which had risen from one shilling to three shillings and three pence. By suspending the Navigation Laws he hoped that freight charges would fall and a larger number of foreign vessels would become available to transport grain to Ireland. In proposing to remit the duties on corn, Russell was following the actions of the governments of France, Belgium and many German states which had already suspended duties on foreign corn. It was also clear that the measures were intended to be beneficial to

England, as some of the mills were already on short time and their work-force depended heavily on imported grain for food.[92]

The relaxation of the Navigation Laws did appear to have a positive impact on food imports that the government was anxious to publicize. Ships from various European ports carrying grain and food began to arrive in Ireland. However, the suspension coincided with the beginning of better weather, which benefited the transport of goods by sea. At the beginning of March the *Cornelia* from Baltimore, carrying 500 barrels of flour, 7000 bushels of Indian corn and 2800 bushels of wheat, arrived in Dublin, making it the only ship to have come to that port directly from the United States for nearly 20 years.[93] The supplies of food were also arriving in time to ensure that the newly established soup kitchens were well supplied with cheap grain. Yet even with the suspension of the Navigation Laws, sufficient vessels could not be found to carry supplies of grain from the United States, which had experienced a bumper harvest in 1846. This apprehension led an American newspaper to warn that unless Britain could send more vessels, they would not be able to export their surplus, which they attributed to a miscalculation by the British government, asserting that 'When Lord John Russell said that there would be ships enough to take over our winter supplies he made a great mistake – he forgot that the tobacco and cotton crops require a large fleet of themselves, and that the Government [American] had abstracted some 50 vessels to send troops to Mexico.'[94]

Poulett Scrope continued to believe that the government needed to do more to bring larger quantities of food into Ireland. He suggested that Navy ships should be used to transport corn on the grounds that 'there was starvation in Ireland – that there was plenty of food available for our population in foreign parts, and especially in the United States where there was 1 700 000 quarters ready for exportation – that there was a great want of ships to remove that corn from the ports where it was warehoused – and that 1 500 000 quarters of corn were required for the supply of Ireland alone'. Russell responded that the government had decided against such a measure on the grounds of cost, time and for other practical reasons.[95] Nevertheless, by summer the government had also realized that the removal of duties and the suspension of the Navigation Acts, introduced as short-term expedients, would need to be extended until the following March if food was to continue to enter Ireland.[96] For nationalists such as William Smith O'Brien the actions of the government were still too little and too late, which was verified by the continuing high levels of mortality and emigration. In April 1847 he announced his decision to withdraw from parliament, believing he could do more good if he remained in Ireland.[97]

In the spring of 1847, due to the increased arrival of foodstuffs, the price of provisions was starting to fall. But many of the supplies were arriving too late for those who had died in the preceding months or whose health had been debilitated during the winter months. Moreover, despite cheap food arriving in the country, the poor still could not afford it as low wages and the closure of the public works meant that the Irish peasantry did not possess any purchasing power.[98] The cautiousness of Irish traders in purchasing the supplies was also evident in the Cork market when 1000 barrels of prime American flour offered for auction at 43s. each only resulted in the sale of 150 barrels.[99] In Dublin, also, where wheat was selling at between 43s. to 50s. a quarter, the grain market was described as being 'exceedingly depressed', with few transactions being made.[100] The arrival of large supplies of food into the country coincided with the onset of a trade depression, which had serious repercussions in the large towns and ports.

In March 1847, the Chief Secretary for Ireland, Henry Labouchere, responding to criticisms from Bentinck and Disraeli, informed the parliament that 'he was daily more and more satisfied that it had been a wise and necessary policy on the part of the government to abstain from interfering with the supply of food by the legitimate means of private enterprise'. He substantiated this assertion by claiming that on that day there were 100 vessels with cargoes of grain in Cork and similar amounts in Galway, Limerick and other Irish ports. In addition, the warehouses and granaries of private merchants were full.[101] Russell reinforced his colleague's explanation. He quoted from a letter received from Cork harbour as proof of the food flooding into the country; adding that such large quantities would not have been imported if the government had interfered with the trade.[102] Disraeli pithily pointed out that food arriving in the country at this late stage was analogous to locking the stable after the horse had bolted. In the hungry months of June and July 1846, despite Peel's intervention in the market place, 23 257 000 lb of meal had been imported into Ireland. In November and December, when food shortages were even more acute, only 68 650 lb had been imported, despite the government's determination to rely on merchants to supply the deficiency. He concluded that 'the Government had trusted to those favourite principles of political economy which might be very efficient but which had only proved to be efficacious when they had reduced the population by a million'.[103] Unwittingly, Disraeli was mirroring the interpretation of the radical nationalist, John Mitchel, that the Irish died of political economy.

Despite public defences of the policy, in private a number of leading Whigs were less sanguine about the outcome. At the beginning of 1847, Bessborough admitted privately to Russell that the policy had failed, observing, 'it is difficult to persuade a starving population that one class should be permitted to make a 50 per cent profit by the sale of provisions which they are dying in want of'.[104] Clarendon made similar criticisms shortly after taking up post as Lord Lieutenant in July 1847. He informed Russell that Lord Cloncurry had communicated to him that 'no one could now venture to dispute the fact that Ireland had been sacrificed to the London corn-dealers because you [Russell] were a member for the City, and that no distress would have occurred if the exportation of Irish grain had been prohibited'. Clarendon discovered that Cloncurry was not alone in attributing the distress and mortality to the export of Irish grain. Clarendon, who was adept at using propaganda for political gain, suggested that they should contrive 'for some articles to be published which say the opposite to this'.[105] He also arranged for accounts to be prepared which would show the extent to which England had assisted Ireland and the positive effects of having allowed trade to remain free. He also considered paying the writer Cooke Taylor to write a number of newspaper articles praising the government's non-intervention.[106] Moreover, Clarendon was aware that such allegations, if widely reported, could be damaging to the Whig Party and he confided to the Chancellor of the Exchequer that he would be 'very glad when you get rid of parliament, for every day now brings with it disaster'. He proposed that something should be done to keep the 'villainous' *Morning Chronicle* quiet, suggesting that it should be banned or the editor given a warning.[107]

The tardiness of the British government in responding to the crisis was also evident when compared to the reaction of other governments. Food shortages were being experienced throughout Europe following the poor corn harvest in 1846 and both local and central authorities showed themselves willing to intervene. The French government responded to their food scarcity by importing large amounts of wheat – over 1 200 000 quarters by the end of the year. They also suspended the Navigation Laws and allowed corn to be imported free of duty by ships of any nation from any port to benefit private traders. Much of the corn imported came from Russia, which was reported as having had 'an abundant harvest'.[108] The Portuguese government had also prohibited the export of corn from the country.[109] At the beginning of February

1847, a Royal Decree was issued in Brussels forbidding the export of bread of every kind until the following 1 October.[110]

The British determination not to interfere with the food trade was commented on beyond the United Kingdom. The *New York Weekly Herald*, which carried frequent reports from Ireland, commented that although 'the wail of famine rises louder and louder ... still the ports are closed and still there is no restriction on exporters'. The public works were criticized also because the wages paid were 'hardly sufficient to keep body and soul together'. Russell's response was described as 'trifling and contemptible' when Ireland needed 'that iron will which should command the ports to be opened, and which should prohibit in breweries and distilleries the use of grain, thus preventing the consumption of the people's food in distillation, and permitting the free importation of every species of food necessary for daily sustenance, indiscriminately, from every country'. Unfortunately for the Irish poor, Russell did not possess either the will or energy to impose such measures.[111]

Exports from Ireland

The issue of food exports during the Famine has, perhaps more than any other issue, tended to polarize recent historical scholarship. For example, the historian Peter Grey has claimed: 'Even if exports had been prohibited, Ireland lacked sufficient food resources to stave off famine in 1846–47'.[112] It has also been suggested that because of the massive crop failure in Ireland after 1846, the Famine represented a 'classic case of food shortage' and that 'during the famine years, food imports dwarfed food exports'.[113] To substantiate this point, it is generally pointed out that by 1847 grain exports had fallen and were being exceeded by imports, but, by their own admission, the government's data was flawed, both underestimating exports from Ireland and exaggerating imports.[114] Furthermore, most of the debate about food availability has centred on corn, ignoring the fact that large amounts of other foodstuffs were being produced in and exported from Ireland, whilst little food apart from grain was being imported. The economist Amartya Sen's point that famine was often not about total food availability but about food distribution, therefore, has particular resonance in the Irish situation.[115] That the mechanisms could be quickly put in place for the distribution of large quantities of food was proven during the successful

Table 4.3 Exports of Cattle and Livestock from Ireland to Great Britain in 1846

	Oxen	Calves	Sheep/Lambs	Swine	Total
Jan.	4 828	68	5 074	43 429	53 399
Feb.	3 235	25	3 245	47 693	54 198
March	6 786	90	2 802	61 709	71 387
April	8 064	60	4 112	54 939	67 175
May	11 490	1 003	15 682	39 815	67 990
June	14 296	860	36 875	30 008	82 039
July	18 197	766	36 804	33 582	89 349
Aug.	20 087	755	43 272	27 821	91 935
Sept.	33 444	1 388	43 296	28 545	106 673
Oct.	23 389	543	26 554	34 626	85 112
Nov.	28 739	654	27 758	46 644	103 795
Dec.	13 918	151	13 783	32 006	59 858
Total	186 473	6 363	259 257	480 817	732 910

Source: William Irving. *An Account of . . . the Number of Cattle, Sheep and Swine imported into Great Britian from Ireland in 1846*, placed before the House of Commons, 19 January 1847.

operation of the government soup kitchens. The point was frequently made in the columns of the *Nation* that, even without the potatoes, sufficient food was being grown on Irish soil to feed the population.[116] Even allowing for a massive shortfall in potatoes and a smaller shortfall in corn production, immense quantities of foodstuffs left Ireland between 1845 and 1850. Yet the fact that such large amounts of provisions were being exported from Ireland was not widely recognized at the time; even the authoritative *Mark Lane Express* pronounced in January 1847: 'With the people starving in many parts of the island shipments of provisions from there to England are, of course, out of the question.'[117]

Whilst it was generally recognized that Ireland before the Famine was the breadbasket of the United Kingdom, exporting enough corn to feed two million people, the export of other foodstuffs was less recognized. By the 1840s the export of cattle to Britain was considerable (see Table 4.3) and following the appearance of blight in 1845, it did not decrease.

Apart from the trade in corn and cattle, large quantities of other provisions left the country including vegetables and pulses, dairy products (in particular, butter and eggs), fish (especially salmon, oysters and herrings), poultry, and a miscellany of rabbits, honey, tongues and lard, and even occasionally potatoes and Indian corn. For example, 3435 poultry were exported to Liverpool and 2375 to Bristol in the first nine months

Table 4.4 Grain Exports from Kilrush to Glasgow in 1847 (in pounds)

	1847
Oats	2 682 932
Barley	110 628

Table 4.5 Grain and Foodstuffs Exported from Kilrush to Liverpool in 1847 and 1848 (in pounds)

	1847	*1848*
Wheat	19 320	88 452
Oats	447 384	1 477 980
Oatmeal	224 000	–
Beans	–	90 300

of 1847. In April 1847, 20 tons of potatoes were exported from Porta-ferry to Liverpool. Another feature of the export trade was that it was not confined to the larger ports, but also took place from small ports in the west of the country which were associated with suffering rather than commerce, towns such as Dingle, Bantry, Killala, Ballina, Tralee and Kil-rush. Even Skibbereen, which had achieved such notoriety at the beginning of 1847, was exporting foodstuffs, including 181 496 lb of oats to Liverpool in June 1847.[118] The town of Sligo, in addition to exporting large amounts of grain to Liverpool, in 1847 also exported 172 barrels and ten hogsheads of bacon, 28 barrels and 42 hogsheads of ham, 17 barrels and one tierce of beef, 57 barrels of pork, 796 376 lb of butter, 238 boxes of eggs, 78 036 lb of lard and 322 680 lb of peas. Whilst Liverpool, London, Bristol and Glasgow were the main ports of entry from Ireland into Britain, smaller ports such as Dundee, Preston, Perth, Runcorn, Plymouth and Leith, were also importing foodstuffs although accurate records were not maintained.

The Kilrush Union in County Clare experienced some of the greatest and most protracted suffering during the Famine. Its population in 1841 had been 82 353 and in the summer of 1847, 62 per cent of the population were receiving government aid under the Temporary Relief Act.[119] In 1848 the Kilrush Union had achieved the same notoriety amongst relief officials as Skibbereen had two years earlier. Whilst other parts of the country were beginning a slow recovery from famine, 25 per cent of the local population were still in receipt of poor relief and an estimated 300 people were being evicted daily.[120] Following the 1849 harvest, the situation in Kilrush did not improve and, at the end of the year, the Poor Law officials had to suspend all relief in the union because the Guardians had no money in hand. At the insistence of Poulett Scrope a select committee was appointed in 1850 to enquire into the local administration of relief. Its conclusions were critical of relief provision and it estimated that the population had fallen in the union by between 25 per cent and 50 per cent.[121] The situation of the poor did not improve and, in 1851, the demand for relief in Kilrush was higher than at any time in the previous six years, with almost 50 per cent of the population still dependent on the Poor Law.[122] Food was, however, exported through the small port throughout the Famine. The amount of grain exported from Kilrush to Glasgow in 1847 and from Kilrush to Liverpool in 1847 and 1848 is shown in Tables 4.4 and 4.5.

The experience of Kilrush was not unique. In the summer of 1847, 79 per cent of the population of Ballina in County Mayo, and 57 per cent of the population of Tralee were dependent on government relief.[123] Tables 4.6 and 4.7 show exports over the same period from these two small ports to Liverpool.

Large amounts of grain were also exported from Westport in County Mayo, although more sporadically. In August 1846, 1 135 680 lb of oats were exported to Liverpool. Grain exports from the town remained high even in the wake of the poor harvest. In the three-month period between October and the end of December 1846, 1 680 368lb of grain left Westport. No exports were recorded between January and March 1847, but grain exports in the following three months, April to June, reached 1 826 552 lb; in July to September, 19 691 481 lb; and October to December, 1 860 945 lb. In total, grain exports from Westport to Liverpool between October 1846 and December 1847 amounted to 25 059 346 lb.[124] This area was one of the poorest throughout the Famine. In the summer of 1847, 86 per cent of the local population were dependent on government soup.[125] In August 1847, it was officially designated as a 'distressed' union by the British government and the locally elected Board of Guardians was replaced by paid officials.[126] Within a few days of taking up office, the new administrators informed the central Commissioners that the poverty of the local ratepayers was so extreme that the union was on the verge of financial collapse.[127] For some of the poor in the union the only relief available was in a local school, established by Count Strzelecki of the British Relief Association, where the children received rations of soup and bread.[128]

Table 4.6 Grain and Foodstuffs Exported from Ballina to
Liverpool in 1847 and 1848 (in pounds)

	1847	*1848*
Wheat	548 268	
Flour	38 360	
Oats	140 000	562 000
Oatmeal	85 120	208 320
Barley	127 120	112 560
Meal	19 320	
Beans	57 680	
Peas	36 120	
Peameal	5 460	
Butter		280

Table 4.7 Grain and Foodstuffs Exported from Tralee to
Liverpool in 1848 (in pounds)

Wheat	28 000
Flour	330 820
Oats	4 375 392
Barley	289 688
Meal	20 580
Wheaten Meal	489 442
Butter	12 656
Beans	31 920
Bread	26 880
Rice	106 680
Biscuits	24 360

How many people could have been fed by the food exported? A
pound was the British government's allowance of corn per day to feed
an adult. According to official statistics – which the government, at the
insistence of Bentinck, admitted were an underestimate – in 1846 and
1847, 430 000 tons of grain were exported, that is 963 200 000 lb. Using
the government's ration allowance, this quantity would have fed two
million people for 16 months of those two years. Much of the exports
were made from areas where the greatest need for food existed, which
would have made redistribution relatively simple and immediate, in
contrast with the slow and cumbersome system of depending on foreign
imports. Taking the single commodity of oats from the port of Limerick
to Bristol and Liverpool in the first six months of 1847 and 1848, the

Table 4.8 Oats Exported from Limerick in 1847 and 1848 (in pounds)

1847	Oats in lb	Possible population fed for a month
Jan.	775 992	25 030
Feb.	3 286 920	117 390
March	2 555 568	81 792
April	540 820	18 027
May	1 863 988	60 129
June	784 588	26 153
1848	*Oats in lb*	*Possible population fed for a month*
Jan.	6 292 888	202 996
Feb.	7 495 068	267 681
Mar.	4 548 964	146 741
April	4 891 376	163 046
May	4 760 000	153 548
June	1 583 148	52 771

exports, if a mechanism had been deployed to divert them to the starving population, would have fed them for that month.

Butter was a significant item of export, although the government did not keep official records of dairy exports. In the first week of 1847, 249 480 lb were exported from Ireland to Liverpool, and by the following week this had increased to 262 692 lb Cork was a major exporter of this commodity and, in 1847, the port exported 3 396 736 lb of butter to Liverpool.[129] The trade in eggs was also massive and remained buoyant throughout the 1840s. By 1850, an estimated 90 million eggs were being imported into Liverpool each year from Ireland.[130]

Alcohol was also a major item of export, mostly in the form of ale, stout, porter and whiskey. Again, the quantities exported were large. In the first nine months of 1847, 874 170 gallons of porter and 183 392 gallons of whiskey were exported to Liverpool alone. During the same nine months, 278 658 gallons of Guinness were imported into Bristol. Much of the whiskey leaving Ireland originated in Cork, yet in January 1847 the local distillers raised the price of whiskey to 7d. a gallon due, they said, to a scarcity in the product.[131] These products were derived from grain or, occasionally, potatoes and therefore represented an averted supply of food. Moreover, stopping the distillation of alcohol had been widely called for both within Ireland and Britain. Clearly, during the course of the Famine Irish markets continued to function well in the commercial sense, and were able to respond to changes in both supply and demand. But because they were transferring foods away

from areas of the greatest poverty, they worked to the disadvantage of
the poor in Ireland. As was recognized, government intervention was
necessary to transfer food resources to those who most needed them.
Instead, the so-called 'free market' diverted food to areas with greater
resources, whilst the poor in Ireland starved. Yet the scale of food being
produced in, and exported from, Ireland was little understood at the
time. Moreover, misinformation and lack of accurate data furnished by
the Whig administration ensured that the scale of food exports was not
fully appreciated. The Irish poor did not starve because there was an
inadequate supply of food within the country, they starved because
political, commercial and individual greed was given priority over the
saving of lives in one part of the United Kingdom.

Economic recovery from successive years of poor harvests, combined
with the changes engendered by the repeal of the Corn Laws, was slug-
gish. In the summer of 1849, the *Freeman's Journal* reported that, despite
prospects of a good harvest, 'there is no disposition to enter into heavy
transactions'. Retail trade in Dublin, however, was unexpectedly but-
tressed by the intended visit of the Queen.[132] By 1849 food prices were
falling and there was less dependence on imported corn. The price of
imported rice had fallen dramatically due to the prospects of a large
crop.[133] The early crop of new potatoes was of good quality and was
selling in the north from 4d. to 9d. per stone, which was cheaper than in
the years preceding the disease.[134] The linen trade in Belfast, which had
been hit by a poor flax crop in 1846 and industrial recession in the British
markets, was recovering. Much of the flax, however, was being imported
from the Baltic rather than being home grown.[135] Shopkeepers who survived the Famine did well. Thomas Carlyle described what he believed
as a typical one in Scarrif in 1849, saying: 'he had got his house new
floored; was prospering, I suppose, by workhouse grocery-and-meal
trade, by secret pawn broking – by eating the slain'.[136] Recovery in other
areas of day-to-day life took longer, reflecting a massive shock not just
to the Irish economy, but also to the psyche of those groups who had
suffered most.

5

RIOT, PROTEST AND POPULAR AGITATION

Throughout the Famine, many reports on the condition of the destitute emphasized the passivity and resignation of the poor.[1] Writing at the end of the nineteenth century, the nationalist Michael Davitt condemned such compliance, describing it as 'the wholesale cowardice of the men who saw food leave the country in shiploads, and turned and saw their wives and little ones sicken and die, and who "bravely paid their rent" before dying themselves'.[2] However, the sustained food shortages between 1845 and 1849 resulted in a period of extraordinary disorder and protest, whilst riot and theft were integral parts of the crisis. The high incidence of agitation was not surprising given the prevalence of rural protest, or 'outrages', in Ireland before 1845 and the longevity of the crisis triggered by the blight. The character of the agitation changed after 1845. Much pre-famine agitation had been local, rather than national, and conservative, in that a primary objective was frequently to resist change or modernization. The pre-famine protests were often associated with Catholic secret societies such as the Whiteboys or Molly Maguires, who were known generically as Ribbon Societies. The growth of Ribbonism and its various offshoots had generally been in response to local grievances, although they increasingly aspired to an independent Ireland. In the north of the country, secret societies tended to be more overtly political and sectarian.[3]

The failure of the potato crop in 1845 exacerbated many of the existing grievances of the rural poor, particularly as it was followed by a cycle of high food prices and widespread evictions. At the same time, the successive

117

potato failures necessitated a high level of bureaucratic interference in a
society that had traditionally resisted intervention and authority at both
local and national levels. Also, as a consequence of the food shortages,
social and economic relationships changed. Popular agitation, in turn,
had an impact on this process. During the Famine, however, agitation
represented immediate need rather than long-term aspirations and
could be regarded as one of a range of survival strategies. Most of the
agitation concerned with food availability occurred during the first two
years of shortages, particularly following the disastrous harvest of 1846.
It was also concentrated in counties Clare, Cork, Kilkenny, Limerick,
Tipperary and Waterford; areas with a tradition of agrarian protest
although they were not the poorest counties. As the Famine progressed,
the nature of disturbances changed, with fewer instances of collective
agitation, but with more individual actions being directed against property
and people. Yet deteriorating conditions rendered the poor increasingly
impotent. For the most part, the collective actions apparent in 1846 and
the early part of 1847 ceased. By the end of the year, prolonged hunger,
disease and fatigue had taken their toll on a population who increasingly
preferred emigration or resignation to protest.

Pre-Famine Agitation

A common perception within Britain was that lawlessness was a particularly Irish characteristic.[4] Catholics, in particular, had a reputation for
being unruly; the evangelist Asenath Nicholson noting that disturbances
were 'all laid at the door of the Papists'.[5] In the decades following the Act
of Union, agrarian unrest was a major concern to the British government
and law and order was a principal political consideration. The fact that
popular agitation could challenge central as well as local authorities was
evident during the 'tithe war' in the 1830s. This widespread campaign was
a protest at the compulsory payment of a tax (tithe) for the upkeep of the
Established Church. In addition to support from the agrarian secret
societies, the protest had the support of larger farmers and the Catholic
Church. Following a number of violent clashes, the government passed
an act in 1838 reforming tithe payments, thus marking an end to the 'war'
and, in effect, tithes.[6]

By the 1840s, recorded crimes in all key categories were far higher in
Ireland than in England and Wales; in particular, crimes against the

person, crimes relating to rioting and breach of the peace, and most strikingly, rescue and refusal to help police officers. In the latter category, in 1845 there were 14 committals in England and Wales compared with 1119 for the same crimes in Ireland. The large discrepancy in this category indicated that attitudes to authority and law enforcement were different within Ireland than in other parts of the United Kingdom.[7] The high level of crimes in Ireland was frequently blamed on Irish poverty, agrarian backwardness, or the peculiarities of the Irish character. But a number of liberal commentators deemed the main cause of agrarian unrest to be the unjust system of landholding in Ireland. Supporters of tenant rights argued that the irresponsible attitude of some landlords had been a major contributor to agrarian outrage and that only a reform of the landholding system – rather than punitive measures – would end it.[8]

After 1801 successive British governments, especially Tory ministries, responded to Irish crime through a combination of permanent and temporary legislation. As Irish Chief Secretary from 1812–18, Robert Peel demonstrated his willingness to use repressive measures to deal with agrarian unrest. In 1814 he was responsible for introducing a Peace Preservation Force in Ireland, an armed force based in Dublin, which was in readiness to be sent to any county deemed to be 'disturbed'. This was the first such force to be created in any part of the United Kingdom. In 1822 a network of constabulary was established and further legislation in 1836 completed the process of providing Ireland with a centralized national police force. The 1836 act also removed much power from the magistracy to the new constabulary body, and forbade the force from membership of secret societies – thus incurring the wrath of both landlords and Orangemen.[9] From 1814, it was clear that the cost of administering the force was regarded as an exclusively Irish responsibility. In 1829, when it was suggested that the state rather than local taxation should pay for the Irish Constabulary, Peel responded 'Why should England pay the charge of civilizing Ireland?'[10] In 1845 the Devon Commission made a similar recommendation but Peel again opposed the change.[11]

In addition to the constabulary force, a high military presence was maintained, especially during periods of political agitation. At the height of the Catholic Emancipation crisis in 1829, out of a regular infantry force in the United Kingdom of 30 000 men, 25 000 were either stationed in Ireland or on the west coast of England with a view to travelling quickly to the country.[12] Even at periods of relative political calm, rural agitation continued to be widespread. Overall, a higher military and police presence was maintained in Ireland than in other parts of the United Kingdom.

In 1844 the Home Secretary, Sir James Graham, admitted that 'we had a military occupation of Ireland, but that in no other sense could it be said to be governed; that it was occupied by troops not governed like England'.[13]

Throughout the early nineteenth-century also, a number of short-term measures were introduced, which were referred to generically as Coercion Acts. In 1833 the Suppression of Disturbances Act provided for the Lord Lieutenant to proclaim a district as disturbed, impose a curfew and to detain without trial for up to three months. Trial was then to be carried out by a military court rather than by a magistrate.[14] This repressive legislation was followed by a more liberal phase when the Whigs were returned to power in 1834. One of the cornerstones of the Whig policies during their administration from 1834 to 1841 was Russell's programme of 'Justice for Ireland', by which he hoped to reconcile Irish Catholics to the Union using conciliation rather than coercion. This programme was facilitated by an alliance with Daniel O'Connell known as the Lichfield House Compact. Reforms in the wake of the agreement included reorganization of the Established Church, reform of the tithes and the introduction of a Poor Law in 1838. The Dublin Castle Executive mirrored the more conciliatory approach of the government in London, most notably under the administration of Lord Mulgrave (later Lord Normanby), Lord Morpeth, the Chief Secretary, and Thomas Drummond, the reforming Under-Secretary. During their administration over 30 per cent of new appointments went to Catholics or to liberal Protestants, whilst symbolic gestures included the stoppage of flying the flag over Dublin Castle on the anniversary of the Battle of the Boyne. A number of leading Whig administrators also recognized that the actions of landlords were a major contributor to Irish agrarian unrest and desired to alleviate some of the grievances of tenants.[15] Mulgrave's liberal administration alarmed both Orange peers and conservative landlords.[16]

Coercion in Ireland had been traditionally tied in with rights of property but this view was challenged in 1838 when Drummond, responding to Tipperary landlords who were demanding extra coercive powers, remarked that 'Property has its duties as well as its rights. To the neglect of those duties in times past is mainly to be ascribed that diseased state of society in which such crimes take their rise.'[17] The success of the Whig approach was evidenced by the fact that they did not have to rely on coercion during their period in office. Unfortunately, Drummond died prematurely in 1840 and his death heralded the end of this more liberal phase in Irish politics. Ultimately, also, the Whig government disappointed a section of Irish repealers who felt that not enough concessions had been made. In 1840, therefore, O'Connell launched the Loyal National Repeal Association, with the primary objective of bringing about a repeal of the Act of Union.

Peel was returned as Prime Minister in 1841. Although he continued to believe that the maintenance of law and order was a crucial precondition of Ireland's modernization, he was increasingly impatient with Irish landlords, acknowledging that their irresponsible behaviour was contributing to rural unrest. Consequently, he admitted that a reform of Ireland's landholding system was necessary in order to reconcile Irish people to the Union. The renewed repeal agitation led by O'Connell, which peaked in 1843, propelled the question of agrarian and political agitation to the forefront of political discourse. Peel responded with the appointment of the Devon Commission in November 1843, to enquire into landlord and tenant relations. He also introduced a new coercion act, an arms bill, in the same year. During the two-year period that the Devon Commission sat, there was a growth in agrarian unrest in Ireland. Additionally, there was a fear that crime might increase further if the report raised expectations amongst the rural population that were not met. The Devon Commission reported at the beginning of 1845 following a long and detailed enquiry. A Tenants' Compensation bill was introduced, based on the report of the Commission, but it was defeated, Scottish and English landlords fearing its introduction as much as Irish proprietors.[18] Moreover, a few months later the report of the Commission was overshadowed by the loss of the potato crop, which meant that its recommendations were submerged beneath new wrangles within parliament. Consequently, it was blight, rather than legislation, which heralded radical changes in the system of Irish landholding and in landlord-tenant relations.[19]

In the aftermath of the first potato failure there was an upsurge in the number of agrarian crimes. The majority of these crimes were concentrated in five counties, whilst elsewhere they had declined. Nevertheless, this increase caused concern in parliament as it coincided both with a renewed phase of repeal agitation and with a revival in the Orange Order. In the autumn of 1845, a revival in 'monster' repeal meetings resulted in a number of Irish landlords, Tory politicians, and sections of the British press, demanding more coercive measures. The Duke of Wellington, who believed it was necessary to use force in Ireland, warned the Prime Minister, Sir Robert Peel, that 'conciliation without coercion will be ridiculous'.[20] Despite the Union, there was widespread consensus that Ireland should not be treated in the same way as the rest of the United Kingdom. *Fraser's Magazine*, for example, claimed that constitutional rights such as trial by jury were 'as little suited to the actual condition of the Irish people as they are to the condition of a horde of Bedouin Arabs or a tribe of Red Indians'.[21] The months following the first appearance of blight, therefore, were dominated not only by debates on relief policies and Corn Law repeal, but also on new coercive measures for Ireland.

In February 1846, a new coercion bill known as the Protection of Life bill was introduced into the House of Lords. Peel had intended it to be a permanent measure but a Whig amendment had limited it to three years. Its supporters argued that a diminution of crime in Ireland was a precondition for investment and modernization.[22] Its opponents suggested that the high military and police presence in the country made a new Coercion bill unnecessary.[23] The unrest peaked in the spring of 1846, before the system of famine relief slowly became available. Despite the decline in crime in the spring of 1846, Peel went ahead with the coercion bill. O'Connell's supporters and a number of Whigs, including, after some hesitation, Lord John Russell, opposed it.[24] But the Whigs were not united on the coercion issue, although many of those who owned property in Ireland supported it, believing that some repressive measures were necessary.[25] The Protectionist group within the Tory Party, led by Lord George Bentinck, were also determined to vote against the bill in an effort to defeat Peel as punishment for his involvement with Corn Law repeal.[26] Their resolve to oppose the bill made the fall of Peel's government inevitable. At the same time, it contributed to a re-alliance between O'Connell and the Whigs with the former declaring that he would be proud to serve under the new Prime Minister, Lord John Russell.[27]

The incoming Whig government was keen to demonstrate that its Irish policies would not depend on coercive measures similar to those proposed by Peel. Instead, a re-alliance between the Whigs and O'Connell heralded a return to a programme in which justice for Ireland appeared to be given precedence over coercion. The more conciliatory approach had the support of some sections of the British press, although not the *Times*.[28] The alliance raised expectations that various social reforms would follow, especially in relation to the rights of tenants. Secretly, however, one of the first actions of the new Prime Minister was to offer the Irish Constabulary an additional 2000 police in order to put down rural outrages.[29] More crucially, however, the reforms expected from the new Whig administration were forced increasingly to take second place to relief provision, the potato blight having reappeared in Ireland earlier and more extensively than in the previous year.[30] In addition, the widespread distress was accompanied by a rise in crimes, which meant that one of the cornerstones of Whig policy – social reform in Ireland – was abandoned.

Food Riots

Even before 1845 a source of discontent amongst the poor had been price rises and food exports during periods of scarcity. The protests in Ireland were similar to the food riots in other parts of Europe, which attempted to impose a 'fair' price on basic foodstuffs, usually grain or bread in Europe, but potatoes in Ireland. In Britain food riots had occurred intermittently throughout the eighteenth century but less frequently in the nineteenth century. A number of localized riots did take place in Cornwall and parts of the south-west in 1847.[31] Food riots were generally structured protests which took place in pre-industrial societies and which were based on an unspoken code of conduct, usually referred to as the moral economy. The moral economy also governed market practices especially during periods of food shortages. Riots occurred when the traditional moral assumptions were ignored and they were usually triggered by sudden increases in food prices.[32] In Ireland prior to 1845, food riots were generally a local response to unfair market practices. Their objective was to lower the selling price of bread and corn – which had replaced potatoes as the staple food – to what was considered to be a reasonable or fair price, rather than the market price.[33] If the request for cheaper food was acceded to, the crowd generally dispersed.[34] The export of food during a period of scarcity was disliked and attacks frequently took place during the transport of goods, especially on small quantities that were too small for an official escort. Women were as active as men were in the food riots and raids.[35]

Although such riots took place in a number of western counties, they were most numerous in counties Clare, Galway and Limerick. They generally occurred following a poor harvest. In the summer of 1842, for example, a sharp rise in potato prices resulted in riots and attacks on food stores in parts of Galway and Clare in an attempt to impose a 'fair price'. The riots were led by women and children, and most of their anger was directed at local merchants and farmers whom they accused of deliberately withholding supplies in order to create an artificial scarcity and thus increase their profits. The rioters also broke into some of the stores and distributed the corn. As had been the case in many food riots in Britain in the previous century, the magistrates agreed to enforce 'the reasonable demands of the people'.[36] The millers also promised that they would sell meal at 15d. a stone.[37] Some fighting did take place and the fear of mob rule was evident in that extra police and troops were dispatched to the area. This and similar incidents demonstrated the power of collective action and the fact that a form of moral economy was in existence in the Irish countryside. Like similar incidents elsewhere, food riots in Ireland displayed elements of organization and they demonstrated an awareness of the market even by people employed in subsistence agriculture.[38] However, even when the food shortages were widespread, such protests remained essentially local in character.

The food shortages and price increases precipitated by the first appearance of the potato blight resulted in widespread food riots. Although Peel was generally praised for the speed and effectiveness of his response, especially in relation to food import and distribution, the early months of 1846 were a period of anxiety for relief officials in Ireland. The head of the relief operations, Sir Randolph Routh, suggested that increased supplies were necessary if food depots were to be effective, but the Treasury was determined that government intervention should be kept to a minimum. Similar anxieties were also expressed at the local level, particularly in the west where fewer administrative structures existed for the provision and distribution of relief. The parish priest in Kilmovee asked 'When are we to expect relief ? . . . I fear that as hunger breaks their will, so will their peaceable habits be very shortly turned to procure the means of subsistence in violation of the laws that hitherto regulated their conduct.'[39] The most portentous riots took place in the relatively prosperous south-east of the country. In structure and organization they resembled pre-famine popular demonstrations, with moral force and threats being bolstered by physical attacks on food stores rather than on property or individuals.

The outbreak of food riots in April 1846, especially in the relatively prosperous towns of Clonmel and Carrick-on-Suir, was widely covered in the Irish and British press. These disturbances demonstrated the potential danger of the food shortages in relation to the maintenance of order.[40] In the nearby ports of Cork and Waterford also, stocks of potatoes were 'seized by the mob'.[41] These areas were all economically important as centres of grain production and export. Clonmel, in particular, was an important trading and export centre, mostly via Waterford. Routh immediately ordered an inquiry into the riots in Clonmel, which reported that able-bodied vagrants from outside the towns had caused them. For the new Viceroy, Lord Lincoln, the riots throughout the south-east of the country were a salutary reminder of the potential for a breakdown in public safety and he responded to them by ordering more supplies of corn to the area, thus flouting the Treasury's directives.[42] Moreover, to avoid further disturbances, the relief officials in Dublin Castle notified all local committees to be prepared to respond to sudden distress. At the same time, the military were alerted to potentially dangerous situations and they were to be ready to rush to areas experiencing disturbances.[43] The determination of the authorities to safeguard the export trade in the commercially important south-east was apparent from the extensive use of the military; a number of barges leaving Clonmel being escorted by '2 guns, 50 cavalry and 80 infantry'.[44]

Attacks on food supplies increased following the second appearance of blight. These disturbances occurred immediately following the harvest period, reflecting not only a greater deficiency than in 1845, but also the fact that no new relief measures had been put in place. As early as August 1846, Daniel O'Connell warned the Prime Minister that 'there is the greatest danger of outbreaks in various parts of the County of Cork, the population driven to despair by want of food'.[45] The inadequacy and tardiness of the new relief measures also led to a sharp increase in food prices and inflamed an increasingly precarious situation. But even when government relief did become available, the situation continued to deteriorate. Following the harvest of 1846, public works were made the main source of relief; although the government imposed a ceiling on wages paid on the relief works, a corresponding ceiling on food prices was not introduced. As a consequence, wages on the public works fell in real terms in the second year of shortages. Moreover, as food prices rose steeply in the final months of 1846, a starvation gap emerged whereby poor people were not able to afford to purchase food. After 1846, many of the protests were concerned with either increasing the wages on the public works or with lowering the price of staple foods. Although the language used by the rioters was often threatening, the majority of protests were peaceful, attempting to exert moral rather than physical pressure. From the outset, however, the *Times* newspaper depicted the protests as a proof of the ingratitude of the Irish poor.[46]

The response of the authorities to attacks on food supplies was swift and increasingly severe, even though there was an acknowledgment that food prices had become exorbitant.[47] One of the first attacks took place in September 1846 in Youghal, a small town through which large amounts of corn were being exported. People from the surrounding countryside attempted to prevent a boat laden with oats from leaving the port. Dublin Castle responded immediately by sending additional troops to the town. The incident worried the British government and the Under Secretary, Redington, was ordered to travel to London to explain the situation.[48] Two days later, the government arranged for 2000 troops to be equipped to travel to any disturbed area at very short notice. Charles Trevelyan, who oversaw the arrangements, estimated that the troops would be required in this capacity for only six weeks on the grounds that 'food riots are quite different from organized rebellion and are not likely to be of long duration'.[49] As an extra precaution, however, naval escorts were provided for vessels carrying grain on a number of key waterways.[50] Military and police presence did not deter further attacks. Following a raid on flour carts in Parsonstown in October 1846, the military were called and five of the ringleaders arrested.[51] This response became the model for dealing with similar incidents. Despite a heavy presence of troops in the early months of 1847, food riots continued, most numerously in counties Cork, Kilkenny, Tipperary and Waterford.[52]

There were also isolated instances elsewhere, although the pattern of the demonstrations was similar. In Cong in County Mayo, the local poor marched to the town carrying flags and demanding food or work. They threatened to attack the Commissariat's food stores if their demands were not met.[53] In the nearby town of Belmullet the local Catholic priest, apprising the Lord Lieutenant of similar demonstrations, questioned 'how long a peasantry goaded by hunger may continue peaceable?' He also enquired 'who can stand the cravings of any empty stomach or be content while his neighbour's cattle walk the fields?'[54] Nonetheless, the role of local Catholic priests in curbing the anger of the crowds proved more effective than stand-offs with the military or the constabulary. Many of the clergy, following O'Connell's lead, initially had faith in the relief measures of the Whig government and urged the people to stay calm and be patient. When 1000 protesters marched on Castlebar in County Mayo to protest at the scarcity of food, the local priest, Father James M'Manus implored them to disperse on the grounds that they were being looked after by 'a humane and good government', and professed that 'no better man lived' than Lord John Russell.[55] Similar instances of clerical intervention were repeated in other parts of the country.[56] Food protests peaked in the critical winter of 1846–7, although they continued to recur intermittently but on a smaller scale than before.[57]

The workhouses were often focal points for the anger of the protesters, although they rarely sought admission. Demonstrations outside the workhouses – institutions that were a visible and countrywide symbol of poverty – also became a common way of protesting at the inadequacy and inefficiency of the relief provision. In the spring of 1846, as the impact of the first potato failure began to be felt, demonstrations took place outside a number of workhouses. Protesters at the Kilkenny workhouse were offered relief inside the institution but refused it, warning that unless they received an alternative form of relief 'they must resort to violence'.[58] In November 1846, an estimated 5000–6000 people marched to the workhouse in Listowel in County Kerry shouting 'bread or blood'. They also threatened to help themselves to provisions within the institution. A Catholic priest who was visiting a nearby convent appealed to the mob to stop, but without success. When he fainted, the workhouse authorities warned the mob that they were in danger of killing him. The crowd then dispersed quietly. The local newspaper exhibited sympathy with the protesters, reporting 'The poor unhappy people presented all the appearance of want. Their bodies could be scarcely said to be clothed, and their pallid visages showed what ravages gaunt famine had already made on their health and manly vigour.'[59] In April 1847 a large crowd gathered in Tuam, a number of whom had a loaf of bread fixed to their poles, and they marched to the workhouse where they asked for food. They had recently lost their jobs on the public works. The protesters did no damage.[60] Again, as the Famine progressed, the aims of the protesters changed. Initially, the protesters were seeking other forms of non-workhouse relief but the demonstrations increasingly changed to appeals for admission.

Whilst food protests were most often associated with rural areas, they also occurred in towns. The pressure for relief in the towns was exacerbated by the movement of paupers from the surrounding districts in search of employment or relief. Frequently, the migrants were blamed for increases in crime. In Belfast, the failure of the potato crop coincided with an industrial recession. As was the case in other towns, additional pressure was placed on the local relief authorities by the influx of people from the surrounding countryside in search of work or relief.[61] One of the most serious food protests occurred in November 1846 when a mob of between 50 to 100 labourers demonstrated at various bread shops in the town, demanding free bread on the grounds that they were hungry. Many of the protesters had recently lost their jobs on the Belfast railway. The ringleaders, James M'Cullough, William Walker and Henry Mason, urged their followers not to conduct themselves badly. At the first baker's shop, owned by Bernard Hughes, a Catholic businessman, they were refused food. The situation was defused when two passing 'gentlemen' gave them money to purchase bread. The men cheered in thanks and then proceeded to a second baker's where they threatened to take the bread if they were not given it. They were given bread. They then moved to a third bakery, but it was locked against them. Some of the crowd wanted to disperse at this point but M'Cullough retorted that 'it would be better for them to die than to leave'.[62] The police then arrived and arrested the ringleaders. In court, the leaders justified their actions on the grounds that they had been dismissed from work due to the frost and they and their families were hungry. The magistrate was unsympathetic. He noted with some satisfaction that the men were not natives of Belfast, and advised them that they should have gone back to their homes or applied to the soup kitchens rather than alowing themselves to become embroiled in 'very serious outrages'. Because the rioters 'had nothing to justify their offence', he decided to 'impose a heavier fine than he otherwise might be led to do'. Walker, the principal ringleader, was to pay either a fine of 40 shillings or to be imprisoned for a month; the other two were to pay 20 shillings or be imprisoned for a fortnight. Mason paid his fine immediately, which led a Dublin newspaper to comment, 'The food rioters of the north are men of wealth, in comparison to their suffering fellow creatures of the south.'[63]

Food riots also occurred in Dublin. In January 1847, there was a series of attacks on shops and stores containing bread or meal.[64] In one incident, 200 people attacked a bread cart in Dorset Street. Only a small number had been caught and 13 people were charged. The convicted were mostly young men from the country but, because a number of them had money in their pockets, it was assumed that they were not genuinely in want. In a separate incident, eight people were charged with attacking a cart in Bridgefoot Street. Again, it was claimed that the attackers were all from distant parts of the country and were not natives of Dublin. A number of bread carts coming into the city were also attacked.[65] The town authorities responded to the increase in attacks with additional mounted police patrolling the streets, but sporadic outbreaks continued.[66] An estimated 1000 people, who called themselves 'the Hungry

Mob', paraded through the Liberties district of Dublin taking bread from the bakers' shops and were only dispersed through the intervention of troops. Twenty-two arrests were made.[67] In the wake of this incident, combined with the general growth in plundering, the authorities decided to provide police protection for bakers and provision shops.[68] Food riots, concerned with obtaining cheap or free bread, were also taking place in other towns in Ireland. In Drogheda there were a number of food riots and attacks on bread carts leaving the town.[69] In February 1847, the Master Bakers in Cork threatened to close their shops and sell no more bread unless they received the protection of the police and the military. The city magistrates agreed that a party of military should patrol the various bakers' shops throughout the day and evening until the threat abated.[70]

Food riots in the late 1840s were not unique to Ireland, but were also occurring in other parts of the United Kingdom. A few instances were reported in the south of England, but they were more common in Scotland which had also suffered from potato blight and poor corn harvests in 1845 and 1846.[71] The protesters in Scotland were particularly opposed to the shipment of grain from the country and succeeded in preventing a number of grain cargoes from being transported.[72] In Ross-shire the local magistrates experienced difficulties in recruiting special constables from amongst the local population to prevent attacks on food cargoes, as many people believed that grain should not be exported whilst there was a general shortage in the area. A number of granaries were also attacked in Scotland. The attacks were often underpinned by a threat of violence. The forcible entry of granaries resulted in additional troops being sent to other areas involved with grain exports. A number of the conflicts also became violent. One of the most serious riots took place in Invergordon. An additional 200 soldiers were sent by boat to the area, but an estimated 1000 men, armed with bludgeons, prevented them from landing. Although grain continued to leave the port, many of the carts carrying the cargo were smashed. In the conflict a number of the rioters were wounded by the soldiers.[73]

Within Europe also, a series of bad harvests since 1845 had resulted in an increase in food riots. There were many similarities with the riots in Ireland, most of them originating from sharp increases in the price of basic food. Reports of such occurrences were carried in both Irish and British newspapers. In Ostend, for example, following a rise in the price of bread, a mob broke the windows of several bakers' shops and were only stopped from further acts of violence by the authorities meeting

their demands.[74] Sometimes the violence became more extreme. In
Grossewardein in Hungary, the taking of grain by rioters led to a
number of cavalry charges in which 30 persons were killed and more
were wounded. Jews were viewed as the main hoarders of grain and
following the incident, five Jewish merchants were found assassinated in
their homes.[75] Bread riots and food protests were also commonplace in
France and Germany.[76] In one incident in Mulhausen in France, the
mob plundered both the local bread and wine shops. The incident was
deemed to be sufficiently lawless for troops to be dispatched, which
resulted in the deaths of three or four persons.[77] Food riots, therefore,
were a widely used response to food shortages after 1846. But whilst
good harvest returned to many parts of Europe after 1847, in Ireland
the food shortages and distress continued.

The Breakdown in Relief

As the Famine progressed, there was an increase in attacks on relief officials. The announcement in August 1846 of the reduction in wages and
the transfer to task work was greeted with hostility. The first protest
against task work took place at the end of August 1846 in Westport in
County Mayo, where a 'mob' of up to 4000 persons listened to 'inciting
addresses'. Calm was restored only by the intervention of the local
Catholic priest.[78] An increasing number of attacks took place because
relief was slow to be established in an area or, as was frequently the case,
there was a delay in the payment of wages. In Castleisland in County
Kerry, for example, in mid-October a notice was posted warning that
unless public works commenced immediately, the people would resort
to plunder. Their desperation arose from the fact that they could not
'bear the cries of hungry children any longer'.[79] Although the large
number of people involved in collective protests alarmed the authorities,
most of the anger of the protesters remained directed at local inefficien-
cies rather than national policy. The staff employed on the public works
were generally held to blame for the delays and, consequently, a number
of relief officials were assaulted, most notably overseers of public works
and pay clerks.[80] Nonetheless, the number of threats greatly exceeded
actual cases of violence.[81] From the end of August 1846 to the beginning
of February 1847, the Board of Works who managed the public works
recorded 140 separate incidents of violence or outrage.[82]

County Clare, where at the end of 1846 over 21 per cent of the population was employed on the relief works, became a centre of agitation.[83] One of the most worrying incidents for the authorities occurred in the county in August 1846, when labourers employed on the public works near Ennis stopped work in protest at the new conditions.[84] The stoppage of work spread to other parts of the country as the impact of the changes in regulations began to be felt.[85] The new stringent conditions governing the provision of relief also caused dissent amongst the poor. In October, 2000 unemployed men in Ballingarry in Limerick persuaded those employed on the public works to stop working. It was followed by a riot, which was only terminated by military intervention.[86] Confrontations also occurred in west Cork, Galway, Kilkenny, Limerick, Mayo, Tipperary and Waterford, all areas where food riots had taken place a few months earlier. Although troops or constabulary were sent to the troubled areas, the government recommended that, in the first instance, the local officials should ask the local Catholic priests to intervene and pacify the protesters.[87]

But the apparent calm was sometimes short-lived and disturbances reoccurred when the various relief measures proved to be inadequate. Anger at the shortcomings of the public works fused with a more general dissatisfaction with the government's relief policies. Dungarvan, a small market town in County Waterford, had been a centre of disturbances in the early months of 1846 and, by the end of the year, food riots were being augmented by protests at the change to public works. The main complaints related to the slowness in introducing relief works to the area, the low wages paid on them, and the export of food from the area despite the fact that the people were starving. At the end of September, an estimated 4000 people protested in the local town and plundered stores in an effort to discourage merchants from exporting grain. Because of the disturbances in the spring, additional constabulary and military were quickly transferred to the area, but their presence angered the crowd and resulted in stone throwing. Although some of the ringleaders were arrested, the people did not disperse until the troops fired on the crowds. A number of the protesters were wounded and two were killed. Additional troops were dispatched to the area in order to ensure the resumption of the export trade.[88] During the following few days, large crowds gathered and fires were lit on the surrounding hills. The Resident Magistrate was pessimistic that the tension would not disappear until public works were commenced or food prices were reduced. The situation was diffused temporarily by the intervention of the local Catholic priest, but agitation resumed within days. By the beginning of October, public works had still not commenced. Although bread was offered to mollify the crowds, they refused it on the grounds of wanting a longer-term solution, which would require employment, fair prices and food not to be exported.[89] The arrest of the ringleaders led to stone throwing and violence during which some of the rioters were shot by the military, one of whom subsequently died. The local press were generally sympathetic, believing the cause to be hunger which would not be assuaged even when the public works did commence due to the government's insistence that wages should be lowered and dependent on task work.[90]

The incidents in Dungarvan were reported in a number of London papers, and the *Illustrated London News*, which was generally sympathetic to the Irish poor, sent an artist to illustrate the riots.[91] In the trial at the end of October, 51 persons were charged with riotous and unlawful behaviour and 'interfering with trade by violence and intimidation'. All of the accused pleaded guilty, but the counsel argued that they should not be sentenced. The ringleader, however, received 12 months' hard labour.[92] A few months later, the poor in Dungarvan again resorted to direct action when the public works were closed. The workhouse had been full since the beginning of 1847, but the closure of the relief works resulted in an additional 2000 people seeking admission, of whom the local Medical Officer said, 'neither food nor medicine could save from death'.[93] Because the institution was full, under the terms of the Poor Law no alternative relief could be offered. Instead, the military were deployed to keep the people away from the workhouse. The local bakers intervened by giving the unemployed workers bread in an attempt to protect their shops from being ransacked.[94]

Not all protests were on such a large scale or as sustained as those in Dungarvan. Many of the crimes were furtive and petty and were concerned with the immediate needs of the poor, such as cutting the tails off cattle or bleeding their necks for nourishment.[95] Other crimes were more ambitious but were not always successful. In Kilkenny, a pay-clerk of the barony of Kells and his police guard were both shot dead by a gang of six or seven men. One of the attackers was also shot dead in the affray. Nevertheless, the men did not get the money, an estimated £240, because the horse carrying it galloped away.[96] Some crimes were successful, although it was the poor who suffered the consequences. For example, when £300 was stolen from a coach travelling from Dublin to Ballinasloe, which was money sent by the Board of Works for payment of the labourers, no wages could be paid.[97]

The threat of violence was most apparent when local relief was inoperative, inefficient, or during the transition from one system of relief to another. A period of particular hardship occurred during the changeover from public works to soup kitchens in the spring of 1847, when the Treasury insisted on rapid closure even though alternative relief was not available. Ironically, workers who only a few months earlier had protested about the terms of employment on the public works, now resisted their closure with equal ferocity. Again, the protests were most numerous in counties Clare, Cork, Galway, Limerick and Tipperary; areas which had a high dependence on the relief works. In Youghal, the dismissed labourers held a meeting at which they asked the government to either restore the public works or to provide the people with the means of subsistence.[98] A few weeks later, notices were posted around the town threatening that the dismissed labourers would sack it and burn it unless they were given alternative relief.[99] Military and police were sent immediately to Youghal from Midleton, with the promise of additional troops from Cork.[100] In Nenagh in County Tipperary, 5000 men dismissed from the public works marched into the town. The protest was peaceful and was carried out because the workers wanted 'to show themselves as a memento of destitution'.[101] In Limerick, the closure of the relief works resulted in the plundering of food stores and the holding of public meetings described as 'tumultuous'.[102] In Galway, the local Coast Guard attributed the increase in theft and plunder to the closure of the public works and the slowness in opening soup kitchens. The final soup kitchen to be opened was in Ballinasloe on 16 June 1847. In the intervening period the dismissed labourers, who were described as a 'rueful and famine-worn band', had protested by marching daily through the local towns[103] Here, as elsewhere, the delay was fatal. The guardians of the local workhouses blamed the sharp rise in mortality on the slowness in opening the local soup kitchens.[104]

Food riots and other forms of direct action and crime decreased during the summer of 1847 when the Temporary Relief Act was operative. But even following the opening of soup kitchens there was still some unrest. The closure of the relief works and the change to gratuitous relief marked a decline in the status of the poor who became dependent on handouts rather than on employment. The poor also resented the inferior quality of some of the food served, preferring to receive meal rather than cooked food. The inferior quality of some of the soup led a juror to tell the Mayor of Clonmel that the food rations were 'totally unfit for human food'.[105] A similar incident occurred in Kells in County Meath, where people disliked the soup provided and asked for meal instead.[106] Nevertheless, for the majority of the poor there was no alternative to the government soup. Again, there were problems in the provision of relief. When the Corrofin soup kitchen ran out of stirabout, it was attacked, despite a number of police being on duty. The perpetrators tore down the brickwork and started to smash the soup boilers. They stopped only when the relief committee agreed to give out meal.[107] The soup boilers were also destroyed in Meelick and Cloonara in County Clare, and only the intervention of the police prevented others from being damaged.[108] In Middletown, an assault on the soup kitchen resulted in the ringleaders being put into jail.[109]

The destruction of the equipment at the soup kitchens was relatively short-lived, although dissatisfaction remained with the quantity and quality of the soup. A number of proprietors also disliked the soup kitchens, but on the grounds that giving free food was ideologically unsound and left the people with time for 'idleness and acts of crime'. They suggested that able-bodied people should be compelled to undertake employment in order to receive soup.[110] Protests and crime again increased following the poor harvest of 1847, although food riots had largely disappeared. Instead, collective action generally took the form of crowds gathered around the workhouses seeking relief. Although auxiliary buildings had been rented in every union, many of these were full. A number of Guardians responded by providing out-door relief to paupers who could not be accommodated in the workhouses, but they were reprimanded by the Poor Law Commissioners for not receiving prior sanction.[111] The pressure on workhouse resources also contributed to a breakdown in discipline and order in a number of institutions. In October 1847, the Dungarvan Guardians had to be escorted on to the premises by police to protect them from people seeking relief. Following a disturbance in the workhouse at the beginning of 1848, the clerk suggested that guns were needed for their protection.

Again, this form of protest was short-lived and by the end of the year, the Dungarvan workhouse was described by the local Commissioner as being well administered.[112] In general, the closure of the soup kitchens and the transfer to Poor Law relief in the autumn of 1847 resulted in little collective agitation and it marked the end of almost 18 months of popular protest and demonstrations. Individual crimes of theft did, however, rise in the autumn. Although Poor Law relief was also harsh and inadequate, and it marked a further decline in the status of the poor as they were officially classified as paupers, collective protests, either inside or outside the workhouse, had largely disappeared by 1848. Yet, the recurrent and widespread appearance of the protests during the early years of the Famine attested to an on-going dissatisfaction and frustration with the various relief schemes at the local level, which the recipients attempted to change. The authorities, in turn, even if they had sympathy for the rioters, made use of the machinery of law and order and increasingly the hungry people were treated as ordinary lawbreakers.

Crime and Punishment

During the Famine there was a dramatic increase in the number of committals, which peaked in 1848 when it was almost 100 per cent higher than its pre-Famine levels. Recorded crimes then started to fall but still remained above the pre-1845 levels into the 1850s.[113] The actual number of crimes was probably higher than the recorded numbers as the general dislocation meant that a large number of crimes went undetected or unrecorded. The nature of crimes changed also, with those classed as 'agrarian crimes' declining dramatically, whilst cases of theft increased substantially. Attempts to regulate food prices and distribution through popular protests were classified under 'plundering provisions'.[114] The greatest rise was in non-violent offences against property or goods, with only a smaller increase in crimes against persons. Yet, the later category received more publicity, especially following the murder of Major Mahon, a landlord in County Roscommon at the end of 1847.[115] Despite the harsh and well-publicized response of the authorities to Mahon's assassination, the number of committals for murder increased in 1848 by 67 per cent, from 117 committals in 1847 to 195 in the following year.[116]

Although it was hard to distinguish ordinary crime from famine-induced offences, many instances of petty theft were attributed to abject poverty. This was reflected by the fact that 'plundering provisions' became a separate category in crime statistics. Groups rather than individuals often perpetrated plundering, and in organization and aims it had a number of features in common with food protests. The most common crime was theft, which often reflected an immediate need rather than more long-term aims. The category of crimes classified as 'theft' showed the largest increase. Many of the offences in 1847 were committed in the early months of the year but declined over summer – usually the hungry months – when the Temporary Relief Act was operative, demonstrating

Table 5.1   Gross Committals in Ireland

1841	1842	1843	1844	1845	1846	1847	1848
20 796	21 186	20 126	19 448	16 696	18 492	31 209	38 522

Source: Criminal Tables for the Year 1848, PP 1849, xliv, p. 131.

the correlation between inadequate relief and high crime rates. In May, the number of crimes had been 2647 but it fell to 1672 in June. Lord Clarendon, who had arrived in the country a few weeks earlier, reported to the Prime Minister that his impression of the country was that it was 'tranquil', adding that 'if it were not for the harassing job of escorting provisions, the troops would have little to do'.[117] His optimism was short-lived. The increase in offences following the closure of soup kitchens led the Lord Lieutenant covertly to empower the magistrates to give a reward for the discovery of crime.[118] The number of committals peaked in 1848, when they increased by 24 per cent over the previous year (see Table 5.1) and then started to decline. The connection between distress and crime was acknowledged by the prison authorities who attributed the increase in committals to 'the general dearth which prevailed and the pressure of the severest privations . . . scarcity (and it is to be feared also its consequences) having extended to a class of person in the previous year exempted from such physical and moral calamities'.[119]

At the end of 1847 the introduction of a Vagrancy Law in 1847 – as part of the amended Poor Law – added to already swollen crime figures and to the prison population, although vagrants were not included in the official crime statistics.[120] The new vagrancy law also coincided with widespread evictions and a consequent increase in homelessness. An increase in other famine-related offences, such as larceny and bankruptcy, which were not crimes associated with the poor, put a further strain on the legal system. After 1849, when the country began a slow recovery from famine, the crime rate dropped dramatically. However, the reduction may also have been due to the fact that death, disease or emigration had removed a large number of the poorest groups who were most likely to perpetrate crimes. Jail or transportation did not seem to be a deterrent, but was regarded by some of the poor as an alternative strategy for obtaining food and shelter. In fact, pleas of guilty by the perpetrators increased in an attempt to be put in jail, with those who were not convicted quickly re-offending for the same purpose. Although the workhouse diet had originally been based on prison diet, during the Famine prison diets were more generous than in the workhouses, adding to the attractiveness of the former institution.[121] As late as spring 1849, at the assizes in County Kerry, two men who were discharged due to insufficient evidence against them refused to leave custody. In the July assizes they were formally acquitted so that they could be turned out of the gaol. The judge observed that 'to them their acquittal was a punishment'.[122] But the sudden and sharp rise in crime placed an inordinate burden on existing facilities which had been overstretched even before 1845. The increase in crimes meant that jails and courthouses not only became overcrowded, but were also incubators of disease. Fever, dysentery and diarrhoea quickly spread in these institutions. As a consequence, mortality in prisons and prison hospitals rose substantially: in 1845, there were 43 deaths, 103 in 1846, 1140 in 1847, 1051 in 1848, 1293 in 1849 and 597 in 1850.[123] Prison deaths, therefore, followed the general trend of famine mortality.

The increase in prison intake in 1847 worried the Inspector General of Prisons. The pressure was made worse by a temporary suspension of transportation. The poverty of those so incarcerated and the inability of the system to cope was illustrated by the rapid rise in prison deaths. The main causes were the dysentery, diarrhoea and fever already mentioned.[124] The number of first-time offenders also increased, indicating the existence of extraordinary circumstances. The evangelist Asenath Nicholson was secretly smuggled into the prison on Spike Island in Cork in 1848, because of a ban on visitors. There were 300 young boys in the prison schools and for the most part their crimes were petty theft, ranging from stealing a turnip to stealing a sheep. Their teacher commented that 'these people are docile, and I believe honest; their only crime being taking food when starving'.[125]

In towns crime levels also rose, partly as a result of poor people migrating to urban areas.[126] Crime levels in the towns were also inflated by the increase in begging. Begging had been common before 1845 and had generally swelled during periods of food shortages. During the Famine, beggars became more numerous and more visible. Moreover, after 1847 begging and vagrancy were made criminal acts as part of the amended Poor Law. As a consequence of the criminalisation of begging, the number of people convicted of vagrancy climbed from 25 810 in 1847 to 49 717 in 1848 – an increase of 93 per cent.[127] The new legislation stipulated that:

Every person wandering abroad or begging – or placing himself in any Public Place, Street, Highway, Court or Passage, to beg or gather Alms – or causing or procuring or encouraging any child or person to do so . . . shall, on Conviction thereof before any Justice of the Peace, if such justice shall think fit, be committed to the Common Gaol or House of Correction, there to be kept to Hard Labour for any time not exceeding One Calendar Month.[128]

Yet, not even the threat of hard labour was a deterrent. The Inspector of the Galway Union reported that 92 paupers had been caught begging, which they had done in the hope of being sent to prison.[129] The arrest of beggars in the later years of the Famine not only placed a burden on the gaols, but it proved to be an additional financial burden in the areas where they were situated. One taxpayer in Cork suggested that beggars should be sent to the workhouses rather than to gaols, as the cost of maintaining them in the former establishments was cheaper.[130]

Although the category of theft was wide and varied, in the majority of instances it had the objective of securing food. At the beginning of 1847, within the space of one month, 200 sheep were stolen on the Slievena-man mountain in County Tipperary in a number of small raids.[131] Those people who owned edible resources went to considerable lengths to protect them, employing people to guard fields, cattle and stretches of sea-shore, or setting 'mantraps', which were deep trenches, covered with bracken or grass and filled with water.[132] Cattle stealing reached such high levels that authorities in Dublin warned the government, 'it is committed with such apparent impunity, as to become a question of vital importance, threatening almost the very existence of that branch of the agricultural interest'. But although an average of 1200 cattle were being stolen each month by the beginning of 1848, few people were being committed.[133] Many of the perpetrators exhibited imagination and desperation, as even poaching or stealing cattle proved increasingly difficult. In Doneraile near Cork, a man was arrested for stealing and killing a horse for his family to eat, as he had been unable to find a cow or sheep to steal. The man was a small farmer who was not eligible for government relief. The owner of the horse was also a small farmer, the horse having provided him with a livelihood when the harvest failed.[134] One man convicted for stealing food in County Galway confessed that 'before he was driven to the theft, he and his family had actually consumed part of a human body lying dead in the cabin with them'.[135] The reporting of cases of cannibalism was rare. The impact of food shortages was also evident in parts of the country where the economy was more diversified. In Portadown in County Armagh, for example, which lay at the heart of the prosperous 'linen triangle', regular attacks on barges and boats carrying food resulted in troops being sent to guard the Newry canal. In each of the raids, only edible provisions were stolen, indicating that food shortages rather than dishonesty was the cause of the crimes.[136]

Not all attacks took place on dry land, as piracy also increased. Destitute fishermen were often blamed for these crimes. In May 1847 a vessel laden with provisions off the Mayo coast was boarded and her cargo plundered. The vessel was the fourth to be attacked in this way. The authorities suspected that the poor residents of Kildownet and Currane were involved, and the local coastguard was able to retrieve most of the meal.[137] A similar incident occurred near to Belmullet when 150 men in curraghs stole Indian corn off a ship. The local coastguard pursued the attackers and 34 of them were captured.[138] The imprisoned men appealed to the Lord Lieutenant to show clemency, claiming that they had acted in such a way because their families were starving and, since their imprisonment, members of eight of their families had died due to lack of food.[139] Again, the actions of the poor were sometimes desperate and, in some cases, the outcome was fatal. On an island off the coast of Connemara, a group of men in boats stole oysters from the beds of the local MP, Mr Martin, despite the presence of a number of guards. One of the attackers was killed in the raid and a number of others were injured.[140] Clarendon was unsympathetic to the plundering of vessels, especially as many of the raids were successful. He accused the perpetrators of preferring such 'piratical pursuits' to cultivating their land. Furthermore, he asserted that 'It is hard to tax the industrious paupers of England for the support of such ruffians.'[141]

Notwithstanding the fact that the majority of crimes were minor offences, some of the British press drew a picture of a lawless society in which the sale of guns had proliferated despite cries of famine. The pressure for more stringent legislation was also demanded by some sections of the British and Irish press. At the beginning of 1847, the *Times* warned that 'the very poorest of the peasantry have, in certain districts notorious for their lawless condition, availed themselves of the facilities which now offer for the possession of firearms without the risk of penal consequences'. It also asserted that, in parts of Tipperary, firearms were being carried in daylight. The *Times* verified its report by including articles from two Irish papers, the *Cork Constitution* and the *Tipperary Constitution*. The latter paper claimed:

While the victims of famine and destitution are dying in hundreds, numberless others scarcely removed from a similar fate, arm themselves... The country is in a fearful state. The law has become paralyzed... shots are to be heard at all hours of day and night, and the turbulent and evil-disposed of the peasantry have full license to follow their evil inclination – men of all shades of politics cry out against the policy of the government in allowing an indiscriminate arming of the people.[142]

By the beginning of 1847 there was widespread disaffection in the country. County Tipperary was particularly restless with three land-lords' agents being killed during the first three weeks of the year.[143] The carrying of firearms was also a source of concern to people in Ireland. In March, the Grand Jury of the North Riding of Tipperary sent petitions to both the House of Commons and the House of Lords regarding what was being referred to as 'the popular armament', asking the legislature to restrict the possession of firearms. The Grand Jury believed that the increase in firearms amongst the peasantry was 'greatly aggravated by the prevailing destitution, as the evilly dispossessed always avail them-selves of such a state of things as a pretext for crime and outrage'. More-over, they were apprehensive that outrages would increase following the stoppage of public works.[144] In May, one Irish paper, referring to the 'alarming state of Limerick and Clare', warned that the population were attacking not only the soup kitchens, but also the local police stations. Numerous firearms were believed to be in the district and so additional infantry was sent to the area.[145] In October, the Borrisoleigh Relief Com-mittee in Tipperary memorialized the Lord Lieutenant and warned that, whilst destitution continued to be unmitigated, it was useless to expect 'that the peace of the country could be preserved, or the rights of property respected'.[146] Police presence also increased in a number of areas at the request of the local magistrates.[147] A number of magistrates felt personally vulnerable and asked for an armed escort for when they left home.[148] One magistrate in Limerick received an armed guard of three policeman but, after they went off duty, his wife and son were murdered.[149] In Nenagh in Tipperary, following the murder of a magis-trate, his colleagues informed the Lord Lieutenant that 'a widespread, determined and well-organized combination exists to overturn all laws both human and divine, aimed principally at the rights of property'.[150]

Within parliament, also, alarm was expressed at the number of firearms in private possession and there were demands for Russell to introduce some coercive measures. The alarmist nature of such reports was made clear by Colonel McGregor, the commander of the constabulary, who informed parliament that the rumours had greatly exaggerated the increase of firearms in the country and that 'a very large portion' of the recent sales had been by 'respectable farmers and their dependents against the apprehended attacks of men driven to despair by want'.[151] His remarks, however, did not assuage the critics of government policy. Instead, the fact that the Whigs had introduced no additional coercion laws was blamed for the breakdown in law and order. Yet, the government had increased the number of troops in Ireland, particularly in the southern and western counties. By the end of 1847, Russell conceded that an arms bill would have to be introduced, regardless of the opposition of his Irish supporters.[152]

Landlords

The agricultural crisis precipitated by the Famine contributed to a deterioration in social relations between landlords and tenants, especially in the later years of the Famine. The indiscriminate evictions that intensified after 1847 were a recurrent grievance by tenants, although proprietors blamed evictions on the high level of poor rates. Many of the murders of landlords and their agents were frequently tied in with ejectments.[153] A number of wealthier farmers, despite having made large profits from grain sales, also claimed that poor rates were an oppressive burden; for poorer farmers, the poor rates and mounting rent arrears made eviction more likely. For some landlords, social dislocation proved an opportunity to evict unwanted or unprofitable tenants with little resistance. A number of landlords, including Lucius O'Brien in County Clare and Lord Sligo in Mayo, argued that land clearances had become a financial necessity. In addition to the sharp rise in poor rates, a clause which made the proprietor responsible for paying all rates on smallholdings of land valued at less than £4 was also seen as a major burden.[154] This clause put small tenants at the greatest risk of eviction. After 1847 evictions rose sharply, peaking in 1850 at over 100 000 persons.[155] The number was far larger when voluntary surrenders were included.

An early incident of a clearance, which received publicity in both Ireland and Britain for its callousness, occurred in County Galway in March 1846, when 270 people were removed in order that the area could be converted to pasture. The 'Gerrard evictions' (after the landlady, Mrs Gerrard) were discussed in parliament and in the press, and the general consensus was that the landlady had behaved irresponsibly.[156] Occurring as they did when the impact of the previous year's blight was beginning to be felt, there was an added concern that such actions would inflame agrarian unrest. A further source of anger was that landlords were carrying out such policies at a time when Britain was financing relief policies in Ireland. The *Illustrated London News* warned: 'English-men cannot see such barbarities practiced at the very moment they are paying enormous sums out of the taxes to support those whom the land-lords thus plunge into destitution.'[157] The idea that British taxes were subsidizing Irish evictions was a recurring theme in the later years of the Famine.

A further fear was that anger at evictions would lead to more agrarian agitation and that landlords would became the target of this hostility. Inevitably, the callous way in which a number of evictions were carried out, in the midst of an economic catastrophe, became a major grievance for tenants. Links between evictions and attacks on landlords were quickly evident from early on in the Famine. In Tipperary in October 1846, a 23-year-old agent was shot dead and his murder was attributed to the fact that he was about to evict three or four families in Galbooly for non-payment of rent.[158] Reform of landholding was thought to be necessary but, as had been the case with politicians before 1845, there was no easy answer to the land question. Consequently, coercion became an alternative to reform. Clarendon, within a few months of being appointed Viceroy, was convinced that extra policing was necessary to deal with the escalating problem. Russell was less sure, believing that 'this universal war between unfeeling landlords and barbarous tenants is not to be put down by an Act of Parliament'. He also doubted that the level of violence against landlords had increased to the levels being claimed.[159]

The British press had become a major forum for the debate about lawlessness in Ireland and, despite being largely anti-landlord, was sympathetic to them in relation to matters of law and order. The *Times*, which carried frequent reports of murders in Ireland, usually preceded them with an adjective such as 'frightful' or 'barbarous', thus reinforcing the opinion that not only was Ireland more lawless than other parts of the United Kingdom, but that crime there was particularly bloodthirsty.[160] Even the usually sympathetic *Illustrated London News* carried an article in October 1847 censuring the dishonesty and indolence of the Irish poor, and they included an image entitled, 'Three armed Irish peasants wait-ing for the approach of a meal cart'.[161] The lack of remorse of a number of the lawbreakers added to this viewpoint. In Westmeath, a man convicted of murdering a local landlord proclaimed that 'the jury might look out for their coffins, for that dead or alive he would be well revenged of them'. He also blamed the local landlord, Lord Castlemaine, for having brought him to this death. A minority of British newspapers, however, including the *Morning Chronicle*, argued that many coercion measures would be unnecessary if Irish landlords behaved more responsibly towards their tenants.[162]

British press anger climaxed following the much-publicized murder of Major Mahon in Roscommon in November 1847. He had assisted hundreds of his tenants to emigrate to Canada, but had punished those who had refused his offer with eviction – in the latter case amounting to over 3000 people. In the wake of this action, it was alleged that the local priest had denounced Mahon from the pulpit, thus precipitating the assassination. The nationalist *Freeman's Journal* regarded Mahon's murder as further proof of the need for an end to the system of 'barbarous clearances' in order to 'put an end to such criminal mutual extermination'.[163] For the *Times*, his murder represented a morality tale of good landlord against unlawful people, aided by their manipulative parish priest.[164] Some of the more dogged members of the Cabinet, including Lord Palmerston (himself a landlord in Ireland) recommended that the priest or priests responsible should be hanged or at least transported.[165] More liberal Whigs, including Russell and Somerville, believed that the murder of Mahon and other landlords had arisen due to long-seated grievances, which had been inflamed by more recent cruelty to their tenants.[166] They viewed the recent famine ejectments as being the latest round in a long continuum of evictions. Russell stated his case unequivocally when he said:

> It is quite true that landlords in England would not bear to be shot at like hares or partridges by miscreants banded for murderous purposes. But neither does any person in England turn out 50 persons at once, and burn their homes over their heads, giving them no provision for the future. The murders are atrocious but so are the ejectments. The truth is that a civil war between landlords and tenants has been raging for 80 years, marked by barbarity on both sides.[167]

Nevertheless, the majority opinion in parliament was for coercion measures to be introduced. Consequently, a Crime and Outrages bill was introduced in an emergency session in November 1847 – even though moderates within the Cabinet disliked it. Russell particularly resented having recourse to such a measure, especially as he had come to power as a consequence of his rejection of Peel's Coercion bill. Nonetheless, Clarendon persuaded him that the government had no alternative, especially in view of the activities of the Young Irelanders.[168] The bill was passed in both houses with large majorities. The main effect of the new act was that, after 29 December, people in the districts which were 'proclaimed' could not carry guns or have them in their homes without a license.[169] The new act also created a Special Commission that could convict people suspected of wanting to commit outrages. The act only had limited success and agrarian outrages continued to be perpetrated. More seriously, seven months after it was introduced a small, armed rebellion was attempted by Young Ireland in County Tipperary. Although the Young Ireland uprising was easily put down, the unstable political situation led to fresh proposals for an additional coercion bill or the continued suspension of Habeas Corpus. At the end of 1849 Clarendon admitted that he was disappointed that agrarian conflict appeared to be as bad as ever, with recorded crimes having increased over the previous year.[170] Russell was personally embarrassed that his administration had been forced to depend so much on coercion, and that it had proved impractical to balance coercive measures with remedial measures.[171] As a consequence of his coercion measures, Russell also lost the support of moderates within his party and of liberal members of the Irish Party.

The Police and the Army

In the decades before the Famine, Ireland maintained a larger police and military presence than other parts of Britain. In 1842, whilst in Britain the ratio of police to population was one to 1161, in Ireland it was one to 791, and by 1851 had risen to one to 480. The ratio of soldiers to Irish people was similarly high, being one to 747 in Britain and one to 491 in Ireland.[172] The most heavily policed counties were Tipperary, Kildare, King's and Kilkenny, areas traditionally associated with agrarian outrages and political agitation.[173] In 1843, to deal with the Repeal threat, extra troops had been sent to Ireland and barracks had been fortified. On the eve of the Famine, approximately 26 000 troops were maintained as a garrison force in Ireland. The size and duties of both the police and the army in Ireland following the appearance of blight increased. Not only were they increasingly used to deal with mounting crime and to control the crowds during periods of collective action, they were also involved in a range of civil functions associated with famine relief. To carry out their increased duties after 1845, additional troops were deployed in 1846 and 1847, despite the Whig administration's overt commitment to reform rather than repression. In the summer of 1847, 2000 mounted police and military were made available secretly to Clarendon, and a few months later, following the much-publicized murder of Major Mahon, a further 15 000 troops were rushed to Ireland.[174] During the revolutionary threat in 1848 the number was again increased, and Lord Clarendon secretly provided arms to the Orange Order to act as a native garrison.[175] In 1849 large-scale reductions were made in the British army, including those stationed in Ireland. Of the 10 000 rank and file ordered for reduction, 4000 were disbanded in Ireland.[176] These measures were largely for economic reasons, but they also reflected a return to more tranquil conditions in the country, despite continuing high levels of crime.

In addition to the large military presence, Ireland had been heavily policed before 1845, and a national network of resident magistrates supported them. The police force at the start of the Famine was approximately 9000 strong. The constabulary was a quasi-military force that was armed with bayonets and carbines. They were frequently unmarried, lived in barracks, and no member of the force was based in either his native county or a county with which he was attached by marriage.[177] There were approximately 1600 barracks in Ireland, which meant that the constabulary was a visible presence on the Irish landscape. During the most severe years of famine, the number in the constabulary increased substantially. By 1847, there were 10 639 constables and 67 stipendiary magistrates in the country, and in 1849, when the number peaked, it had risen to 12 828 police and 70 stipendiary magistrates. A mobile reserve force of constabulary based in Dublin also increased from 200 in 1844 to 400 in 1848.[178]

The use of the military to deal with famine-related disorder was evident during the food riots which occurred in the spring of 1846 and following the second appearance of blight. At the end of 1846, the government created a mobile force of 2000 troops to prevent attacks on food supplies.[179] As many of the raids took place when the food was in transit, a further job of the military was to oversee the safe import and export of corn.[180] Speranza, the pseudonym of the nationalist poet Jane

Elgee, who wrote for the *Nation* paper, chronicled the role being played
by soldiers in her poem, *The Famine Year (The Stricken Land)*

> Fainting forms, hunger-stricken, what see you in
> the offing?
> Stately ships to bear our food away, amid the
> stranger's scoffing.
> There's a proud array of soldiers – what do they
> round your door?
> They guard our masters' granaries from the thin
> hands of the poor.[181]

The deployment of troops to areas of distress was also resented, one
starving man in Mayo commenting: 'Would to God the government
would send us food instead of soldiers.'[182]

   The constabulary and army were employed also to protect and assist
rate collectors, which added to their unpopularity.[183] This was especially
necessary when the Poor Law became the main organ of relief following
the harvest of 1847. These duties also placed an additional burden on
the courts, a burden that increased in the later years of the Famine. For
the parties so convicted, it often proved to a be final straw financially. In
May 1847, out of 450 civil bills served at the Ballina Quarter Sessions for
non-payment of poor rates in Killala, over half of the people fled the
country before they could be brought to court, one died and was
declared insolvent, and a number of others were pronounced to be
destitute. In total, rates were recovered from only five people.[184] The
increase in crime rates in the large towns, especially Dublin, meant that
additional troops also had to be stationed in them. In October 1846, the
first division of the 6th Dragoons (known as the 'Caribineers') were
moved to Dublin, making them the third regiment of cavalry in the city.
In total, the Royal Barracks in Dublin consisted of the 3rd and 4th Light
Dragoons, the Caribineers, the 3rd Buffs, the 26th, 68th and 83rd
regiments of infantry, the 48th, a troop of horse artillery and three companies of foot artillery.[185]

   In addition to their conspicuous role in enforcing law and order, an
important part of the duties of both the constabulary and army was the
civil and administrative side of relief provision. The army had prior
experience of assisting in civil duties as they had been involved in carrying out an ordnance survey of Ireland between 1825 and 1841. During
the Famine, they were able to use their knowledge of local conditions to

good effect. The pivotal role of army officers in overseeing relief provision was evident from the first appearance of the blight. The Relief Commission, established in November 1846, included Colonel Harry Jones, an English Officer in the Royal Engineers; Colonel McGregor, Inspector General of the Constabulary; and Sir Randolph Routh of the Commissariat Department. The chairman Routh, aided by the Commissariat, was in charge of the supply and distribution of Indian corn in the government's relief depots. The Relief Commission, however, was ultimately under the control of the Treasury and Routh's ability to provide relief was stringently restrained by Charles Trevelyan.[186] Ironically, many of the food riots that the army had been called on to quell in 1846 and 1847 would have been ameliorated if the Commissariat department had been allowed more autonomy in food distribution. After 1845 the constabulary were important in collecting reliable data about crop loss, arranging burials and attempting to ensure that evictions were carried out legally. The constabulary were particularly useful in this capacity because they provided a national network of well-disciplined men. Also, as a result of their involvement in earlier government surveys, including the 1841 census report, they were acquainted with even the remotest parts of Ireland. However, their additional duties proved to be onerous. Following the outbreak of food riots in Drogheda, the local constabulary forces were described as 'almost fatigued to death with extra duty as escorts to bread, flour and other provisions leaving town'.[187] Not surprisingly, also, given their close contact with the poor, the infirm and the deceased, mortality and illness levels increased substantially amongst both the constabulary and military between 1847 and 1849, largely as a result of disease.[188]

Despite the oppressive role played by the army, especially in the latter stages of the Famine, a number of them did appear to have sympathy with the poor. In Dungarvan, where riots and protests were endemic throughout 1846, the commander of the troops deployed in the area was described by the *Cork Examiner* as being 'loved and esteemed by all classes, particularly by the poor peasantry for whose condition he and his men manifest such compassion'.[189] Large contributions were also made by individual regiments in the army for famine relief throughout the Empire, the first recorded private donation being sent by British and Irish soldiers serving in Calcutta at the end of 1845.[190] Troops in Ireland also raised money in a number of imaginative ways. Major Bushe and the officers of the 7th Hussars in Galway decided to hold a subscription ball in order to raise funds for local distress. In Killarney, the officers and men of the 55th and 47th gave one day's pay for the relief of the poor. Officers in the garrisons in Limerick and in Dublin held amateur theatricals in order to raise money on behalf of the poor.[191] Soldiers in the Regent's Park Barracks in London raised £3000 for famine relief.[192] As the Famine progressed, the police and military were increasingly used in a repressive capacity against the victims of the hunger rather than to facilitate the provision of relief. Although, in folk memory, stories endured of soldiers deliberately firing over the heads of people who were attacking food supplies, such recollections were rare. Overall, the use of the police and the military to guard the movement of food and to assist with evictions and rent and rate collection meant that they were despised for their role both during the Famine and in the post-Famine decades.[193]

Throughout the Famine, the nature of both popular protest and crime changed, as did the response of the authorities. Not only did the sympathy with the poor which had been evident in the early stages of the Famine dissipate, so too did the official attitudes change as the status of the poor declined. As the early food protests demonstrated, the very poorest classes were relatively passive, with the more militant protests being concentrated in areas where there was a developed commercial sector and a tradition of protest. Moreover, many of the protests were intra-communal – being directed against local merchants, shopkeepers, farmers and landlords, or against local relief agencies – rather than against the government. Yet, many of the decisions which were being objected to, such as the export of food and the low wages on the public works, were the result of policy formulation at the highest government level. Inevitably, it was against the groups who were responsible for implementing these policies, notably the local relief officials and the military, that the anger and frustrations of the people were directed. The popular protests were generally short-lived; by the end of 1847 they had largely disappeared and collective agitation had been replaced by the individual and immediate needs of survival. Increasingly, the responses to popular agitation demonstrated that law and order were being used to protect people with property or commercial interests rather than to provide for the rudimentary needs of the poor and destitute.

6

RELIGION AND THE CHURCHES

The role of the various churches in Ireland throughout the Famine, especially Protestant churches, has been largely untold.[1] An exception is the work of the Society of Friends who not only left a record of their part in providing relief, but who were almost universally praised for their commitment and non-partisan approach to relief.[2] The role of religious organizations has also been tainted by the attempts of some evangelical groups to proselytize, popularly referred to as 'souperism'. Despite their relatively small success rate, the folk memory of using the hunger of the people as an instrument to win converts has been long and bitter.[3] The controversy attached to proselytism also tended to overshadow the wider contribution of the various churches in providing relief. Moreover, in the post-Famine period, it was seen as being a particularly Catholic grievance against the Protestant Church and the larger Protestant establishment, with little distinction being drawn between the various denominations within Protestantism.[4]

The Famine also brought to the surface a number of tensions; some members of the Protestant churches believing that their position had been repeatedly undermined; by the granting of Catholic Emancipation in 1829 and in 1845 – the same year that blight appeared in Ireland – over the increased grant to Maynooth seminary and the attempt to establish non-denominational universities, which were mockingly referred to as 'Godless Colleges'. The hierarchy of the Catholic Church, whilst enjoying more authority and influence than it had for centuries, was increasingly caught between the needs of its distressed followers and the task of not offending the British authorities. Internal theological squabbles also contributed to the impression that the hierarchy of the Catholic Church did too little too late to help its congregation. Yet, the Catholic Church in the second half of the nineteenth century emerged as even stronger and more influential than it had been prior to 1845.[5]

The Churches and Relief

Prior to the Famine religious ministers played a vital role in community life. Catholic priests were especially important as over 80 per cent of the population belonged to this Church. Contemporary commentators agreed that the Catholic Church played a pivotal role in society and this role was increasingly acknowledged by British politicians, most notably Lord John Russell, who regarded the winning over of the leaders of the Church as essential to successful government.[6] Clergy also exerted a considerable influence on the political and social life of the communities which they served. Like the constabulary, they possessed an unrivalled knowledge of their neighbourhood and its people. However, in matters of law and order they were probably more influential than the constabulary. During the Famine ministers of all religions played a crucial role in the provision of relief; clergymen of all denominations were active members of relief committees in 1845–6 and 1846–7, and they played a central part in both raising and distributing private charity which was particularly important after 1846. The role of clergy in private relief organizations was especially important as many charities worked through existing local networks. Many of the main charitable bodies established in 1847 used the local ministers as a conduit for distributing their funds. In each of these endeavours the majority of religious bodies were praised for working together. The nationalist *Freeman's Journal* paid tribute to the fact that 'The Catholic and Protestant clergymen vie with one another in acts of benevolence. They are the most active members of relief committees – they confer together, remonstrate together, evoke together the aid of a dilatory government, and condemn together its vicious and dilatory refusals.'[7]

From the outset both Catholic priests and Protestant ministers were involved in the administration and distribution of government relief. In 1846, the new rules governing the formation of relief committees stipulated that the lieutenant of each county was to ensure that a clergyman of each denomination was represented on the committees. But, there were a number of complaints that Catholic priests were being deliberately excluded from the committees, including protests from John MacHale, Catholic Archbishop of Tuam. Although the Lord Lieutenant published additional instructions concerning the religious composition of committees, these were sometimes ignored.[8] One of the most publicized instances of religious discrimination being shown on relief committees occurred in County Mayo. It resulted in a court case which was tried on the Queen's Bench between the Earl of Lucan and the owner of the local newspaper, the *Mayo Telegraph*. The latter had accused Lucan, in his capacity as Lord Lieutenant of the County, of excluding Roman Catholic priests from local relief committees under the Labour Rate Act of 1846, even excluding those who had served on similar committees in the previous year. Although Lucan admitted that he had excluded Catholic priests, he argued that he believed it was his right to do so. He was found not guilty on the grounds that no malice could be proved.[9]

In addition to their work on relief committees, local clergymen continued to carry out their usual church duties, which became more onerous as the Famine progressed, especially in relation to looking after the sick and ministering to the needs of the dead or dying. Consequently, the local clergymen of all denominations witnessed and coped with the impact of the food shortages and evictions on a daily basis. A number of them also died as a result of coming into contact with the famine sick.[10] The Famine also affected religious issues in a number of less obvious ways. For example, in January 1847 the Catholic Primate pronounced that Catholics had permission to work on the relief works on holy days, which were generally considered days of rest in the church's calendar.[11] In 1849, when the Poor Law Commissioners ruled that Catholic inmates of workhouses should be allowed to observe their nine holy days of the year by not working, Protestant Guardians in Belfast led a protest on the grounds that treating Catholics in such a way would increase religious discord in the workhouses.[12]

In many instances, it was the local clergy who brought local suffering to the attention of relief officials. One of the most significant examples was the intervention of Mr Caulfield and Mr Townsend, two Anglican clergy from Skibbereen in West Cork, who travelled to London in December 1846 to meet with Charles Trevelyan at the Treasury. People had been dying of hunger since September and the public works were failing to keep the people alive. The Relief Commissioner, Sir Randolph Routh, had already informed the Treasury of the dreadfulness of the local situation. The people needed food and Caulfield and Townsend urged that it be sent to the area.[13] Intervention in the form of food was refused, but Trevelyan supplied the ministers with a list outlining the wealth of local landlords whom he considered responsible for the suffering rather than the government. The ministers kept up their pressure on the government. A local JP wrote an open letter to the Duke of Wellington which was published in the London *Times*, and at the beginning of January a delegation from the area again travelled to London to meet the Home Secretary.[14] They also lobbied Members of Parliament whilst they were there. Although none of these actions resulted in increased aid for Skibbereen, it brought the suffering of the area to a wider, international audience which increased charitable donations to the area, whilst making the name of Skibbereen a benchmark of suffering during the Famine. Moreover, those who visited Skibbereen in 1847 were struck by the dedication of the local ministers in the town.[15] Yet, in the neighbouring and equally poor parish of Schull, accusations of 'souperism' or proselytism based on relief not only divided the local ministers, but resulted in additional Catholic clergy being sent to the area to counteract the impact of the proselytizers and bring back the converts to the Catholic faith. Ultimately, for many Catholics the actions of the proselytizers eclipsed the memory of the collaboration and exertions of men such as Townsend.[16]

Ministers of all denominations were involved in distributing relief on behalf of the main relief agencies. The Society of Friends was particularly impressed with the support that they received from Anglican clergymen who generally were assisted by their wives and children. The conferring of the sacraments and the last rights by Catholic priests possibly left them less time to become involved in providing relief, the needs of the dead increasingly vying with those of the living. Anglican ministers also had more financial resources than Catholic priests did, as they were not dependent upon their congregation for an income. As the Catholic poor became further impoverished they were less able to contribute to the upkeep of the church. Catholic nuns also played an important, although less public, role in the provision of relief and, in particular, medical support. The Sisters of Mercy in Limerick, for example, were active not only in providing charity, but in tending to victims of fever and cholera.[17]

The various churches were influential in raising money. In this regard the Catholic Church was particularly successful due to the vast international network of Catholic churches. The Presbyterian Church was particularly strong in Belfast and money was raised in the town both for the local poor and also for the destitute in other parts of the country. The

Presbyterian Church in Scotland also contributed significant amounts but much of the money was used by proselytizers, which tainted the involvement of the church in general. The Anglican Church, although less able to draw on funds from overseas sources, was particularly successful in raising funds in England. Its success was helped by the involvement of Queen Victoria, who was head of the Anglican Church throughout the Empire. In January 1847 she issued a 'Queen's Letter' appealing for aid for both Ireland and Scotland which was to be read in all Anglican Churches. The full text of the letter was also published in the *Times*.[18] A day of 'General Fast and Humiliation before Almighty God' was also announced for 24 March 1847 which linked the Famine with providentialist interpretations of the catastrophe and emphasized the need for atonement and redemption. The House of Commons was adjourned for the day although members could attend divine worship in the House. The Anglican Churches were also to hold religious services throughout the country, but, as the MP John Bright pointed out, by linking the day with the Established Church, the majority of the population in Scotland and Ireland who were not members of the Anglican church were excluded from participation. Bright also disliked the fact that the government – a civil power – was visibly coupling the food shortages with divine intervention. He predicted the outcome would be to engender 'on the one hand, gross superstition, and gross infidelity on the other'.[19] Within Ireland, however, both the Anglican and the Presbyterian churches adopted the day as a day of prayer and humiliation, with additional services being held and collections made.[20] The first Queen's Letter was successful, raising almost £172 000.[21] A second Queen's Letter in October 1847 indicated that much of the initial sympathy for the Irish poor had dissipated when it raised only £30 167 14s. 4d. Its failure was not helped by the fact that the *Times* led a campaign against contributing to the second appeal, comparing the lazy Irish peasants with the hard-working industrial classes of Britain. They also published a series of letters in a similar vein.[22]

Regardless of the involvement of Protestant ministers in relief provision at all levels, a feeling existed that the Anglican Church in particular, which received income from the state, was not doing enough. In January 1848, John O'Connell opined that the property of the Protestant churches should be used for the poor.[23] In 1849, as the government contribution was reduced further and dependence on private charity increased, there was wide-ranging anger that people with money were not doing more. A donor to Archbishop MacHale asked angrily: 'What are the bishops of the Established Church doing with their several thousands a year, or where are those very reverend gentlemen; do they think it beneath them to attend to the affairs of charity?'[24]

One of the first Catholic bishops to get involved in fund raising was Bishop Murray of Dublin. Despite being 80 years old, he personally supervised the distribution of monies that he received and passed on in small amounts directly to local parish priests. Two other Catholic clerics who were particularly active in raising funds were John MacHale, Archbishop of Tuam and James Browne, Bishop of Kilmore.[25] Each of these bishops worked without a formal structure or organization. A Carmelite Father, John Spratt, organized a relief committee based in Dublin which was avowedly non-sectarian. In 1849 when most official and private relief had dried up, a deputation from Spratt's committee visited the Prime Minister to plead for more support. One of the unique features of the relief channelled through the various Catholic clergymen was that it continued long after other forms of charity had dried up. The most overtly political of the relief providers was Archbishop MacHale of Tuam, who described the money being sent to him as an attempt to 'make some reparation towards our neglected people for the shortcomings of ministers and legislation'. He also blamed centuries of colonization and anti-Catholic legislation which had forced so many people to depend on potatoes.[26]

Because many Roman Catholic priests supported the Whig ministry, for the most part they were relatively uncritical of the new relief policies following the disastrous harvest of 1846. An exception was John MacHale, who regularly used the columns of the newspapers to mount his attacks on the government. In August 1846, as it was becoming clear that the potato crop had failed totally, the government decided to close all of the food depots which had been established a few months earlier, even though they still contained supplies of meal. The decision alarmed a number of relief officials as it was evident that no alternative food supply was available, whilst MacHale informed Russell that 'You might as well issue an edict of general starvation as stop the supplies.'[27] He was also critical of the small amount of £50 000 made available by the government to support the new system of public works. MacHale compared the miserly amount being provided to save the Irish poor from death with the £20 000 000 of public money which had been provided as compensation to slave owners in the West Indies in the previous decade.[28] In March 1847 MacHale held a meeting in Ballinrobe in which he blamed the famine deaths on the government. He described the decision to bring the public works arbitrarily to an end as 'a melancholy proof of the hatred of Ireland'.[29] The *Northern Whig* described MacHale's comments as 'stupid invectives' which brought 'every death to the Englishman's door'.[30] A less public, but equally uncompromising, critic of government policies, especially the personal capability of Russell, was Edward Maginn, Bishop of Derry. In November 1846 he started to compile a list of deaths, distinct from normal entries in the parish register, which he believed were attributable to starvation. On 1 May 1847, the special list was wrapped in black crepe and placed in an archive. Its inscription read: 'The records of the Murders of the Irish Peasantry, perpetrated in A.D. 1846–47, in the 9 and 10 Vic., [public works act] under the name of economy during the administration of a professedly liberal, Whig government of which Lord John Russell was the Premier.'[31]

Other aspects of the new government's relief programme were also criticized by ministers and members of other denominations. One of the most scathing religious critics of Russell's decision to depend on the public works was a Presbyterian minister, W. Crotty, who was providing relief on the west coast of Connemara. In a letter to Russell which was also published in a number of Irish newspapers, he accused them of allowing hundreds of people to die of want while telling them that 'it is not the duty of government to intervene in providing cheap food for the people, lest the usual operations of trade be interrupted', averring that it was 'Miserable philosophy that would sacrifice one portion of the community to enrich and exalt the other.' He asserted that 'If Ireland continues a portion of the British Empire, is it not the solemn duty of government to come to the assistance of its inhabitants.'[32]

Some of the most relentless criticisms of both government and inactive landlords came from the Quakers, who were renowned for their philanthropy, lack of proselytizing and liberal views on a number of social issues. The Quakers had become involved in famine relief in November 1846 when Friends in Dublin decided to establish a Relief Committee of the Society of Friends that would operate distinctly from other relief groups. A committee concurrently established in London was responsible for raising funds in Britain, whilst both committees worked closely with Quaker organizations in America. Members of the Society of Friends travelled throughout the poorest areas of the west of the country in the early months of 1847, providing widely published reports of what they had witnessed. At the same time they provided immediate relief, usually in the form of soup or meal, bedding or clothing. As far as possible they preferred to work through local committees. In districts where the distress was most severe, they blamed the absence of a suitable local network for distributing food to the people. This deficiency they, in turn, attributed to an absentee or indifferent gentry class and the inappropriate administrative machinery provided by the government. Joseph Bewley, a leading Dublin Quaker, pointed out that the consequence of the government's policies was that the heaviest financial burden fell on the poorest areas. Moreover, the relief measures were a waste of resources in that they were bringing no long-term benefits to the country.[33] James Tuke, who visited Donegal in December 1846, repeatedly described the inadequacy of the government's system of relief to support the poor. He reserved his praise for the people who displayed 'good feeling, patience and cheerfulness under privation'.[34] In the autumn of 1847, when the Poor Law became responsible for relief, the Quakers decided to stop their relief work and instead to concentrate on measures which could help in the longer-term economic development of the country. Within a few months, however, the government asked them if they would consider providing relief as they had done 12 months earlier, but they declined to do so. They also refused an offer made by Trevelyan in 1848 of a subvention of £100 if they provided direct relief on the grounds that due to the severity of the crisis the level of intervention necessary was 'far beyond the reach of private exertion, the government alone could raise the funds and carry out the measures necessary in many districts to save the lives of the people'.[35]

Proselytism

Despite the co-operation of clergymen from various denominations on the relief committees, the theological differences between the three main denominations remained rigid, especially in regard to their views of salvation. Protestant evangelicals, in particular, believed that salvation could only be achieved through suffering and redemption. Each church also accepted that missionary activity was an integral part of their teaching. By 1845, for example, the Presbyterian Church in Fisherwick Place in Belfast supported collections for a Jewish Mission, a Foreign Mission, a Colonial Mission, a Mission to Old Calabar and, most importantly, a Home Mission, which distributed tracts amongst the local poor of all denominations within Belfast.[36] Nor was proselytism confined to Protestant Churches. In England Catholic proselytizing was particularly associated with Nicholas Wiseman, the vicar-general of the London district. In a number of sermons he and his followers declared their objective was 'the conversion of England to the Catholic faith'.[37] Even before 1845, therefore, proselytism – and the antagonisms which attended it – were present in Ireland and in other parts of the United Kingdom. However, what made proselytism particularly abhorrent during the Famine was that widespread hunger was used as a lever for persuading the poor to convert to Protestantism. Proselytism in Ireland was mainly associated with the two Protestant Churches, especially the evangelical wings. In the 1820s, a missionary campaign to convert Catholics, which was referred to as 'The Second Reformation', had been reactivated. Its prominence was largely due to the zeal of William Magee, the Anglican Archbishop of Dublin. The most common way of winning converts was through the distribution of religious tracts and Bibles and providing schooling.[38] The granting of Catholic Emancipation in 1829 added a new urgency to the desire to spread the Protestant religion. In 1830 the Protestant Colonization Society was founded, which signalled the onset of a new evangelical crusade. However, a consequence of the proselytizing campaign was that 'a religious war of words and missionary endeavour broke out between Catholics and Protestants'.[39]

Even before the appearance of blight, religious tension existed, especially between the more conservative or evangelical members of the Protestant and Catholic Churches. Since the granting of Catholic Emancipation in 1829 a number of Protestants had felt increasingly threatened by the growing political power of middle-class Catholics. In 1838 they complained that Catholics were being given preferential treatment by Dublin Castle, especially in appointments to the Irish Bench, and stated it was due to 'Popish artifice'.[40] Liberal Protestants and government ministers were also blamed for allowing this to happen. There was a number of calls for the Grand Orange Lodge, which had voluntarily dissolved itself in 1836, to be revived and reorganized.[41] Increasingly, Belfast, where the Presbyterian and the Anglican Churches were particularly strong, became the centre of proselytizing with the local Protestant press, notably the *Belfast Protestant Journal*, the *Warder* and the *Ulster Times*, declaring their major aim to be to weaken the hold of 'Romanism' in the country.[42] Although the west of the country was regarded as the main target for proselytizers, they were anxious that the evangelicals were not winning sufficient fresh recruits amongst the workers in the newly industrializing towns of the north. Even the poor in Belfast, who were predominantly Protestant, were described as manifesting 'spiritual destitution'.[43] In 1847 a number of Presbyterian churches in Belfast, largely influenced by the Rev. Edgar, intensified their local proselytizing activities in both Protestant and Catholic districts. They believed that an extra effort was necessary as a thanksgiving to God 'for the mercies of the last eventful year'.[44]

There was a belief that further proselytizing missionaries were needed throughout Ireland and that the Anglican and Presbyterian Churches should work together jointly to promote Protestantism.[45] The success of both Protestant Churches in the west of the country was attributed to the use of Scripture teachers who could speak the Irish language, which was spoken by about three million people in the country. Copies of the Scriptures had also been translated into Irish. One Presbyterian minister attributed the love of the poor people for the Irish language to the fact that 'they believe that it was the language used by Adam and Eve in Paradise, and that it is the language spoken by the saints in heaven'.[46]

The role of individual landlords in promoting proselytizing activities could be crucial; for example, Lord Farnham in County Cavan and the Earl of Roden in County Down were renowned for their work as evangelical lay preachers. Farnham, who was founder of the Association for Promoting the Second Reformation, combined spiritual persuasion with more practical inducements by evicting large numbers of Catholics from his estates and replaced them with Protestant tenants.[47] Lord Clancarty, a large proprietor in County Roscommon, combined introducing some of the most advanced farming techniques to his tenantry with proselytism. A journalist, Alexander Somerville, who visited the estate in 1847 noted that 'He mixes the produce of the farm-yard and the Thirty-nine articles together, the stall feeding of cattle and attendance at the Protestant church, the instruction on thorough drainage and the instruction on the church catechism ... The use of a bull of improved breed is associated with a renunciation of the bulls of Rome.'[48] The west of Ireland, however, which was overwhelmingly Catholic, was usually the target of proselytizers. In 1836 a group of landlords, together with local Anglican ministers, established the Connemara Christian Committee to promote Protestantism, with the expectation of eventually establishing a colony.

One of the most successful attempts to establish a Protestant mission took place on Achill Island off County Mayo. In 1831 Edward Nangle, a Dublin-born Anglican minister, decided to found a Protestant colony on the island. His arrival coincided with a subsistence crisis that had followed a poor harvest in the west of the country. Nangle, with his family and a small group of like-minded evangelicals, established a church, a number of schools and a printing press on the island. The latter was particularly important as it allowed the missions to disseminate their propaganda to a wider audience through the publication of a monthly paper. The mission also provided employment and medical support for the local population. The missionaries also learnt Irish to facilitate communication with the people. Within a few years the colony was firmly established in the community, but had made few conversions. Relationships between the mission and the Achill islanders deteriorated following a visit by Archbishop MacHale in 1837, when he spoke out forcefully against the missionaries and appointed a new parish priest whose task was to counter their work. In a sermon to the islanders he told them to:

> Have nothing to do with these heretics – curse them, hoot at them, spit in their faces – cut the sign of the cross in the air when you meet them, as you would against devils – throw stones at them – pitch them, when you have the opportunity, into the bog holes – nay more than that, do injury to yourselves in order to injure them – don't work for them though they pay in ready money – nay, don't take any medicine from their heretic doctor, rather die first.[49]

Nevertheless, when the potato blight appeared in the country, a Protestant crusade was well established. Although its success rate was low, some members of the Catholic hierarchy were engaged in a counter crusade that served to increase the divide between the main Churches.

The Protestant crusade gained momentum during the Famine throughout Ireland, both in existing missions and in the establishment of new ones. Evangelical Protestants viewed the Famine in providentialist terms and believed that it provided a God-given opportunity to convert Catholics. Consequently, proselytism became more widespread as starving Catholics were tempted with food, medicine, clothing or bedding in an effort to convert them. The offering of food, often soup, in exchange for conversion resulted in the nickname 'souperism', whilst those who converted were sometimes referred to as 'jumpers'. A number of different societies were involved, including the Exeter Society, the Orphan Association and the Belfast Society for the Relief of Distress in Connaught. Each of these societies received funding from the Society of Friends, although the Quakers themselves were renowned for their own aversion to proselytism.[50] England was also a major source of funding. The Reverend Alexander Dallas, an English clergyman (and supporter of pre-millenarianism) who had established the Society for Irish Church Missions even before the blight, used £3000 he received from English supporters to distribute 90 000 tracts in Connemara, entitled *A Voice from Heaven to Ireland*, in January 1846. Other tracts followed.[51] The primacy of proselytism over benevolence was clear in the way in which funds were used by this and other groups.

A number of Anglican and Presbyterian churches and landlords also mounted their own proselytizing campaigns. In January 1847 the Duke of Manchester, a landlord in County Armagh, and a number of other wealthy Ulster Protestants published a letter in the *Northern Whig*, stating that the purpose of 'the present favourable crisis' was to allow them an opportunity 'for conveying the light of the Gospels to the darkened mind of the Roman Catholic peasantry'. The mission society set up by Manchester, the Irish Relief Association, also received considerable funds from England and, significantly, Alexander Dallas was an honorary secretary.[52] One evangelical group, in a personal appeal to Lord John Russell, likened Irish Catholics to the people of Israel who underwent a famine because 'They lacked the knowledge of God – they were superstitious and idolatrous: they were in consequence wicked, and in consequence of all this God held a controversy with them ... the ignorance of God, the superstition and idolatry, and consequent wickedness of Ireland, are the cause of its misfortunes.' They told Russell not to give any form of relief which would support the existence of Popery as to do so would make the people 'more degraded, miserable and vicious'. Instead, they suggested that he must 'endeavour to bring the word of God to every cabin in Ireland'.[53] What made conversion particularly objectionable during the Famine were the methods employed to win converts – food, clothing, bedding being used to attract people who were bereft of any of these basic commodities. Children were also particularly targeted, as schools were opened in which the study of the Scriptures was the main activity. In contrast to the destitution of the people, the missionaries appeared to have limitless financial resources.

On Achill Island Nangle, like many other evangelical Protestants, believed that the potato blight was a judgement partly caused by 'idolatry in the professing people of God, especially when sanctioned by the rulers of the country'. In particular, he believed that the British government had precipitated the Famine through its grant to Maynooth College in 1845, pointing out that 'It is done, and in that very year, that very month, the land is smitten, the earth is blighted, famine begins, and is followed by plague, pestilence and blood.'[54] The total failure of the potato crop on the island in 1846 caused an upsurge in demand for the services of the mission and by spring of 1847 it was employing over 2000 labourers and feeding 600 schoolchildren each day. In this capacity it provided an invaluable supplement to official relief, but Nangle believed that the main purpose of providing such relief was to convert the population to Protestantism. But, as the distress intensified and the resources of the people disappeared, the mission distributed aid to all who were deemed to need it in return for employment.[55] By 1848, the number of schoolchildren attending the mission school had increased to over 2000 and 3000 adults were employed carrying out relief works, out of a total population of 7000. In the absence of other provision, the mission was the main agency for providing relief on the island. But hopes that the success of the mission during the Famine years would result in Ireland becoming Protestant disappeared after 1850. As conditions on the island slowly began to improve, the souls of the islanders were bitterly fought over by the mission on one side and John MacHale and his supporters on the other. The Catholic Church, which was reinvigorated in the post-Famine decades won, as by 1880 the mission was virtually defunct.[56] Some Catholic priests were aware that only biting poverty made the poor appear to be receptive to the teachings of the missionaries. One parish priest in Mayo maintaining that 'it cannot be wondered at if a starving people be perverted in shoals, especially as they go from cabin to cabin, and when they find the inmates naked and starved to death, they proffer food, money and raiment, on the express condition of becoming members of their conventicle'.[57] The battle for the souls of the people left a legacy of bitterness and mistrust between the main religions, which outlasted the failure of the potato crop. The activities of the proselytizers also cast a shadow on the work done by relief committees, on which all denominations had worked peaceably together. Consequently, in folk memory all private philanthropy – with the exception of the Quakers – became tinged with accusations of sectarianism.[58] Yet, in attempting to 'save' the Catholic poor, the proselytizers undoubtedly saved lives, if not souls, during the Famine.

The spread of proselytism intensified in 1847 with the stoppage of government relief and the tightening up of provisions governing entitlement. In September 1847 the nationalist *Freeman's Journal* warned that 'the stoppage of all government relief was the signal for a general attack on the consciences of the poor'. It also reported that some of the mission societies were being financed by the Society of Friends, 'but it is hoped without the consent of the Society'. It appealed for public funds in order to save other orphans or destitute people from falling into the hands of the proselytizers. The *Freeman's Journal* condemned the practice, describing it as 'nefarious un-christian wickedness'.[59] A letter published in the *Cork Examiner* described the extensive practice of proselytizing through the establishment of Bible schools as 'a new accompaniment to famine'. In these schools food was only distributed after five or six hours of lecturing by a 'Bible master or mistress'. The writer also pointed out that money used to purchase Bibles and to pay the salaries of the teachers meant that less money was available to relieve the poor. He blamed much of the suffering on the role played by both proselytizers and corn merchants and asked, 'what will be done with these two traffickers? ... Their very names should be set forth on the wings of the press as individuals base and degraded, to an extent unmatched in any other country calling itself civilized.'[60]

The proselytizing groups regarded the power of the Catholic Church over the peasantry as potent. In 1847 the Moderator of the Presbyterian Assembly warned that 'These people are the blinded and bigoted children of a fallen church. They hold their errors and cleave to their superstitions with tenacity almost remarkable.' The fact that large numbers of Catholics were emigrating was also viewed as potentially dangerous for the reason that 'Wherever they go, they carry their principles and habits with them. They are filled with the spirit of Proselytism. In Ulster, Scotland, England and America they are the same as in Munster and Connaught. Whoever may change, Irish Roman Catholics never change, and wherever they have the power, they exercise it.'[61] Theological objections to Roman Catholicism also became merged with political concerns. A number of Protestant groups suggested that the aim of the Catholic Church was to purge Ireland of all Protestants. The zealous *Belfast Protestant Journal*, in an article on 'Popish Bloodthirstiness', explained that 'We have often expressed it as our decided conviction that Popery possesses at the present moment an equal desire for extermination and persecution ... All the hypocritical cunning of the Agitator [Daniel O'Connell] and the Jesuitical policy of the priesthood, will not restrain the sons of Belial from the perpetration of their frightful and nocturnal orgies.'[62]

Similar fears were expressed by the National Club, which had been formed in 1840 and attempted to unite the Protestant people throughout the Empire. In their address in 1846 they warned that Protestantism was in danger in Ireland, where 'No people in Europe are so governed by their priests', whose power was based on 'popular superstition, popular ignorance – this is the power of the Church of Rome'.[63] On the eve of the General Election in 1847, the paper cautioned that the main enemy was Popery, 'whereby all that is left to us of our once Protestant constitution is threatened with immediate extinction' and being replaced 'upon the ruins of that Protestant state with an empire based on Popery'.[64] The Dublin Protestant Association and Reformation Society warned John Russell in 1847 against establishing diplomatic relations with the Pope, saying that they regarded him as 'the very Antichrist foretold in Scripture'.[65] But, even within the Established Church, there was some separation between Protestants in England and in Ireland. An incident which received much attention occurred in 1847 when the Bishop of London refused to appoint an Irishman from the Established Church as minister of the Belgrave Chapel. The matter was raised in parliament by Lord Monteagle, who argued that the decision not to appoint him was not 'on account of insufficient doctrine, morals, or learning, but his disqualification was because he was an Irish clergymen'. Moreover, Monteagle believed, this action was contrary to the principles of the Act of Union.[66]

Many of the proselytizing organizations had bases in Belfast, which was a predominantly Protestant town. An Evangelical Alliance was active in the town and it was supported by ministers from the two main Protestant Churches. The Earl of Roden who was a prominent Orangeman and Member of Parliament was also an active member.[67] Many Belfast evangelicals viewed the food shortages as an opportunity to extend their work. One of the main bodies, the Ladies' Relief Association for Connaught, had been founded by John Edgar, Professor of Divinity in the Royal College of Belfast. By 1849 it had collected £15 000 which was used to set up industrial schools in Connaught, which Edgar referred to as 'wild Connaught'. The funds which they raised were largely matched by donations from the Society of Friends. Thirty young women were sent to open the schools and they, in turn, were supervised by 'ladies of high rank and influence there'. As the girls worked, the Bible was read to them and each day there was some religious teaching or devotional exercises. At the beginning of 1849 Edgar made an appeal through the *Banner of Ulster* for additional funds. He explained that whilst his schools were proof that Irish people could be improved if well directed, they had encountered many difficulties with the people of Connaught: 'utter ignorance of order, punctuality, manufacture or manufacturing implements . . . lying, thievish habits, dark houses unfit for work, irregularity of means of conveyance, ignorance of the English language – but over and above all, the opposition, with a few exceptions, of the Romish priests, of which I could tell strange tales'.[68] Another Belfast association in which women played a principal role was the Irish Society. It had been founded in 1847 for the purpose of communicating through the medium of the Irish language the saving truths of the Gospel to the Irish-speaking population of the country'. It also held educational meetings in Belfast for its supporters, their main objective being to explain 'the blasphemous and anti-scriptural doctrines of the Church of Rome'.[69]

Women and children were regarded as fertile targets for proselytizers especially through the establishment of Bible schools. One of the main successes of the Presbyterian missionaries was the conversion of Michael Brannigan, a Catholic who was also an Irish speaker. In 1847 he established 12 schools in counties Mayo and Sligo, and by the end of the following year this had grown to 28, despite 'priestly opposition'. He claimed that the people were no longer afraid of 'priestly denunciation', but that the attendance numbers in each school had fallen because 'the famine, alas, has driven many of the scholars of our schools into the workhouse, where they are deprived of a Scriptural education'. The drop in attendance was due to the fact the British Relief Association had been supporting the schools by providing each child with a half-pound of meal every day, but they had closed their operations on 15 August 1848 as their funds were exhausted. Brannigan, in a letter to the *Banner of Ulster* appealing for financial support, disclosed that 'Many were so uncharitable as to conclude that it was the food, and not the Bible, that the children loved, and that so soon as they were deprived of the one, they would reject the other', but he rebutted such claims, saying that the children forced into the workhouses 'are not happy in that place of confinement – they have no Bibles there – no catechism except the one belonging to the Church of Rome'. He concluded by claiming that one cwt of corn weekly would be sufficient to keep 32 children in attendance at a school and thus prevent them from going into a workhouse, where 'They will then be registered as children of Roman Catholics – be entirely deprived of all Scriptural education, be trained up in degrading subjugation to the priest, and habituated to the soul-destroying service of the mass.'[70]

Even a number of Protestant philanthropic organizations which claimed to distribute funds to all denominations appeared to favour Protestants in the distribution of their charity, although this may have reflected a reluctance by Catholics to be associated with charities of another denomination. One example was the Dublin Parochial Association, which was founded by clergymen from the Established Church in March 1847 with the aim of giving relief equally throughout the city. However, less than 25 per cent was expended on the relief of 'Romanists', despite the fact that Catholics formed approximately 80 per cent of the city's population.[71] Occasionally, the bias of charitable donors was more obvious, as was evinced by a clergyman in Exeter in England who announced that he intended to preach on behalf of 'the Protestant portion of the starving Irish'.[72] In Belfast, also, in the impoverished but largely Protestant district of Ballymacarrett, the unemployed weavers were described as preferring 'a cheap loaf, only if it came to them through a Protestant channel'.[73] Nevertheless, some leading Protestants disliked accusations of proselytism. The Anglican Archbishop of Dublin, Archbishop Whately, denounced the existence of proselytism but believed that few of his ministers were involved.[74]

The government also appeared not to give support to any overtly sectarian organizations. This attitude was most evident when Queen Victoria visited Ireland in 1849. The Providence Home in Dublin asked the Queen for a gift to mark her visit, but this was refused on the grounds that she would not support any charitable institution which was exclusively Protestant.[75] Asenath Nicholson, an eccentric but warmhearted American evangelical Protestant, arrived in Ireland in 1844 with the object of bringing the Bible to the Irish poor. She returned again and in January 1847 established a one-woman relief operation in Dublin. Nicholson disapproved of religious groups which used the hunger of the Irish poor as an instrument for conversion. She believed that such conversions would not be permanent, but would terminate when good potato crops returned.[76] Some of Nicholson's sharpest criticisms were reserved for Nangle's mission on Achill Island, which she had visited before the Famine. When she returned at the end of 1847, she also criticized the efficacy of the relief provided by the mission, noting that 'the scanty allowance given to children once a day, and much of this bad food, kept them in lingering want, and many died at last'. She felt that the men employed by Nangle fared little better, as their average wages were only three or three-and-a-half pence per day. Moreover, these men had families to support, yet 'must work till Saturday, then go nine miles into the colony to procure the Indian meal for the five days' work'.[77] Yet, in spite of her criticism of various proselytizing activities during the Famine, Nicholson made a clear distinction between the proselytizers and the many Protestant clergy who worked tirelessly to help the poor without any attempt to win converts.[78]

The threat of proselytism was taken seriously by the Catholic Church, especially in the targeted areas. At the beginning of July 1847 an address was read in each of the Catholic chapels in the city of Limerick, warning the poor against 'an extreme section of fanatics', who were attempting 'by largesse of old clothes, to convert the benighted people, as they term those who do not come under the sphere of their enlightenment'.[79] In September 1847 a meeting was held in Ballina in County Mayo, convened by clergy in the surrounding diocese to protest against the intensive system of proselytism in the district.[80] The parish priest in Rooskey in County Roscommon castigated 'Exeter Hall Christianity' for making 'famine and fever the agents of proselytism'. He also suggested that much of the money raised in England for the relief of destitution had been given to Irish parsons, and thus had been 'perverted by vile fanatics into a powerful engine to convert to Protestant the Catholics of this country'.[81]

Fellow Catholics occasionally imposed their own form of justice by ostracizing converts or those who 'took the soup'. In a number of cases, the military was deployed to protect the converts as they attended Protestant religious services.[82] In Newmarket in County Cork, a number of the Catholic inhabitants set fire to a tar barrel and then proceeded to a cross where they burnt Protestant Bibles and threw them at some of the houses in the town.[83] Bitter disputes took place also in County Kerry, where the Anglican Church had established a Protestant mission in the small town of Dingle. The mission proved particularly successful in winning converts within the workhouse where, during 1848, 50 Catholics converted. But when they left the workhouse, they were ostracized by the local community and sometimes physically attacked, apparently at the instigation of the local parish priest. The *Banner of Ulster*, which reported this story, described the incident as painting 'as repulsive a picture of Popish cruelty as ever yet revolted and disgraced the instincts of human nature'. In a separate article, the paper described the activities of 'the skull-cracking practices of the Irish priests' who, it was contended, used whips or skull crackers in order to keep their flock faithful.[84] Attempts to proselytize in Kenmare, at the other side of County Kerry, also resulted in bitter divisions within the community and an acrimonious correspondence between the local Catholic priests, Father Sullivan and Father Ahern, and the Rev. James Rogers of the Established Church. The altercation resulted in a public meeting which was attended by over 1500 people, most of whom were Catholic. The mood of the meeting was fractious; Sullivan describing it as a *park a churine* (battlefield). Rogers, who was accused of trying to convert a man on his death-bed who had already received the last rights from the Catholic priest, left the meeting on the grounds that the discussion would be 'all one side'.[85]

The Catholic bishops were also concerned about the spread of proselytism among a defenceless people. When the bishops presented a memorial to Clarendon in 1847, they protested about 'the unchristian abuse of public and private charities evinced by the wicked attempts at Proselytism'. Clarendon, however, refused to comment on the issue.[86] Even the Pope felt sufficiently worried to urge, on a number of occasions, the Catholic hierarchy in Ireland to resist the works of the proselytizers. On one occasion he reprimanded the bishops for not protecting their flocks sufficiently.[87] As the Famine progressed, the attempts at proselytism intensified and became more organized. In 1848, the bishops made a further protest against proselytism, but again the government took no action. At the Synod of Thurles in 1850, proselytizers were condemned, although a distinction was drawn between Protestants who supported the missionaries and those who objected to them.[88] But a number of Catholic bishops, including Daniel Murray in Dublin and Cornelius Denvir in Belfast, were criticized for not having opposed proselytism more strenuously.[89] During the national synod of the Catholic Church in 1850 one of the main topics was the preservation of the Catholic faith. Inevitably, in view of the experiences of the previous few years, Protestant proselytizers were depicted as the main enemy of the Catholic Church and the synod encouraged Jesuits and Vincentian fathers to establish their own Catholic missions.[90]

Even after good harvests returned to Ireland, the work of the proselytizers continued. At the beginning of 1849 the Presbyterian Church in Belfast began to advertise for people who possessed a 'missionary spirit' and 'popular and acceptable talents as a preacher'. Those who agreed to work in a mission for one year would receive £50, but those who agreed to stay for three years would be paid £100 per annum.[91] One of the most active societies was the Irish Church Missions to Roman Catholics founded by the Reverend Alexander Dallas, which operated throughout the whole of the United Kingdom but had targeted Connaught in the west of Ireland even before the Famine. By 1854 the Society had established 125 mission stations in Ireland. Its base was in Exeter Hall in London and most of its funding came from England. The Society provided proselytizers with a network and organizational structure based in England. Their missionaries not only targeted the west of the country, but also made a concerted effort to win converts in Dublin.[92]

A number of proselytizers also believed that one of the effects of the Famine had been to extend the influence of Catholicism outside Ireland. In 1853, when speaking to the Sixth Annual Conference of the British Organization, which had been founded in 1847, John Edgar of Belfast delivered a paper entitled 'Ireland's Mission Field', in which he warned that the 'great New World of the West, Glasgow, Edinburgh, Dundee and the other towns of Scotland are oppressed and defiled by increasing swarms of illiterate, profligate, Irish Romanists'. He stated that crime had increased in the major cities of Britain as a result of their arrival and in London the City Mission had formed a special organization

> to bring reforming influences to bear on the increased masses of Roman heathens... We have no serpents in our land but our Romish population, like fiery flying serpents, are spreading over the face of our lands. Here are the headquarters of infection from which goes forth disease more fatal than cholera or plague. Here the reckless spirits are trained who destroy the peace of England, Scotland and America; our Maynooth produces more priests than Ireland needs and thus the public funds of Britain are employed in training agents for ill, ringleaders in rebellion and riot in lands across the sea.[93]

By 1851 the main proselytizing groups claimed that they had won 35 000 converts and they were anxious to secure even more. Shortly afterwards, 100 additional preachers were sent to Ireland by the Protestant Alliance.[94] This claim of the proselytizers, made after six years of shortages which had decimated the Catholic peasantry, inevitably angered the Catholic hierarchy. The continuation of the Protestant campaign also made them feel vulnerable, especially as the Protestant churches appeared to be forging an alliance against them. In the post-Famine decades the struggle became even more bitter as various institutions intended to look after the poor, such as workhouses and orphanages, became battlegrounds. One consequence was that religious divisions deepened concurrently with deepening political divides. For members of the Catholic Church hierarchy the struggle against proselytism – real or imagined – became a priority. The fear was also reflected in the attitudes of bishops in regard to issues such as education. The 1861 census demonstrated that proselytism had made few inroads, but the mistrust created during the Famine years and immediately after was hard to counteract.

Politics and Religion

The suspicion and antipathy between the churches was also exploited for political reasons. Even before the Famine, Protestants were concerned that Catholics were being given too many rights by a misguided and overly liberal government. In 1838 some Protestants complained that, as a consequence of the Whig/O'Connell alliance, a disproportionate number of Catholics was being appointed to the judiciary, in an attempt to 'fill the Irish bench with Papists'.[95] The government was accused of being 'partisan and anti-Protestant' and having performed 'a breach of faith with the Orange party'. In order to defend the interests of Protestants within Ireland, it was suggested that Orange lodges should reorganize. The Orange Order needed to organize openly because 'In *secret* movements, Protestants are no match for Roman Catholic priests.'[96]

In 1845 the Grand Orange Lodge was re-established in Ireland and in the same year Peel's government decided not to renew legislation which had banned political parades in 1824. The Lodge believed it was necessary to reform because:

> the present disorganised and deplorable state of Ireland can only be attributed to the base policy of statesmen who have treacherously betrayed the trust confided to them by Protestants, in granting unjustifiable concessions to popery, and that no attempt to remedy existing evils will be successful until the Romish Emancipation Bill, the Maynooth Endowment Bill, and all such measures are entirely repealed, and the constitution restored to its original integrity.[97]

The immediate outcome was a growth in membership of Orange lodges and the revival of marches on the twelfth of July. The parades became occasions for voicing fears against Catholic encroachments and disloyal Protestants. On the eve of the twelfth of July anniversary in 1846, the *Belfast Protestant Journal* cautioned that because not all Protestants supported the march, the twelfth would be 'a day of deep humiliation', adding that 'The Protestants of Ireland have lost much by their own supineness. They have folded their arms in cold indifference whilst the enemy has been invading their vantage ground.'[98] The Belfast Orange lodges were also warned not only against cunning Catholics, but also against 'liberal' Protestants.[99] The early years of the Famine, therefore, coincided with a period of increasing religious and political tension between Catholics and Protestants.

The Orange Order, in particular, viewed Catholicism as being inextricably connected with disloyalty. The rising of 1848 seemed to vindicate this belief. The Order claimed that the Protestant religion had been betrayed by successive governments since the 1820s and, on the annual twelfth of July commemorations, there were regular calls for the Catholic Emancipation Act of 1829 to be overturned and the grants to Maynooth College to be withdrawn. During the twelfth of July meeting of the Belfast lodges in 1848, the Reverend Campbell complained that the government had systematically trampled on the rights of Protestants. At the same time, he suggested that Catholic priests had become so powerful 'because they agitated and looked for what they called their rights'. He recalled a time when a priest could not look him straight in the face, 'but now he appears as independent as a Protestant clergyman does'. The Rev. Campbell concluded by saying that he would never be content until he obtained a repeal of the Emancipation Act of 1829.[100]

The relationship between the British government and the Catholic Church in Ireland was ambivalent. The Catholic hierarchy generally welcomed the return to power of a Whig government. Many Catholic priests, following O'Connell's lead, believed that with Russell as the new Prime Minister more concessions would be gained for their church. The main Protestant Churches also welcomed the fact that Peel had fallen from power because they believed that he was 'especial friends' with Roman Catholic priests, referring to his role in the granting of Catholic Emancipation in 1829 and the increased grant to Maynooth seminary in 1845.[101] Russell was also anxious to conciliate the Catholic priests and one of his schemes to bring justice to Ireland involved the payment of Catholic priests. By this measure, he would have removed a considerable burden from the poor, but the proposal was disliked by many of his party, and also by the Catholic hierarchy and the two main Protestant Churches in Britain and Ireland. The opposition of the latter hardened during the Famine. In 1848 when he raised the issue of payment again, Russell abandoned it because 'the repugnance of Episcopal, Presbyterian, Baptist, Independent and Roman Catholic was such as to defeat any measure for the present'.[102]

By the beginning of 1847 even Catholic priests had grown disillusioned with the government's policies. When Clarendon arrived in Dublin in the summer of that year, he described the Catholic priests as being 'bitterly hostile to the government whom they accuse of starving the people'. For Clarendon, a solution to the alienation of the priests was for them to be paid by the state, but he contended this was not possible because 'the bigotry of England and Scotland puts a veto'.[103] As disillusionment with the relief spread, criticism of the government by parish priests became more vocal. The involvement of priests in Irish politics was an on-going source of concern to the British government. The majority of priests supported O'Connell's moral force movement with a smaller portion approving of the physical force tactics advocated by a number of Young Irelanders. Clarendon was concerned that priests should not get involved in the general election in 1847.[104] He hoped that the election would weaken both the Repeal Party and the influence wielded by the priests, although he believed that it would take a long time for Catholics to acquire 'better ways or even to diminish the burning hatred of England'.[105] Clarendon attempted to influence the local priests through the bishops. He particularly wanted to meet the outspoken Archbishop MacHale, but believed that it was unlikely on the grounds that MacHale 'would be as soon thinking of calling upon Beelzebub or the Bishop of Exeter as upon me'.[106] One of his first official duties after arriving in Dublin was to visit the seminary at Maynooth, where he was pleased to find that the young students were not allowed to discuss politics.[107]

Throughout the Famine the Catholic bishops appeared divided on a number of issues, such as national education and the setting up of universities, and this lack of unity meant that the poor suffered. When Clarendon arrived in Ireland in July 1847, he regarded it as a priority to win the support of the Catholic hierarchy and he believed that this would have been attainable were it not for the distress. On 25 October Clarendon met a deputation of the Roman Catholic bishops and archbishops, describing the encounter to the Prime Minister as 'rather an important day'. To Clarendon's surprise, MacHale was present and the viceroy described him as 'a vain, turbulent, ambitious man but not a bad one I believe'. The memorial presented by the bishops had been drawn up by MacHale, and Clarendon referred to it as 'about as mischievous a document as could have been devised at the present moment'. The memorial had already been modified by the other bishops in a special meeting or synod, leaving Clarendon to speculate privately that 'the original production must have been a charming production'.[108] Clarendon's public response to the memorial was conciliatory, but he queried if it was right that 'men, who will make neither sacrifice nor exertion themselves' could accept help from the government when 'hundreds of thousands' in England faced the prospect of unemployment and becoming as poor as the most destitute class in Ireland? He concluded by saying how pleased he was to have met the bishops who exerted such great influence over the people of Ireland.[109] Clarendon invited the bishops to stay for dinner, which only MacHale refused to do. Overall, Clarendon was pleased with his meeting, especially as the bishops agreed that 'the clergy should inculcate habits of industry and order upon the people'. He described them as being 'in high good humour' and they had parted company 'with all the appearance of good friends'.[110]

The memorial of the bishops and archbishops, which was published in a number of Irish and British newspapers, stated that the Famine had filled them with 'grief and alarm', the impact of which was 'but too visible in the numbers of the most pitiable objects imploring relief'. They attributed the suffering to a lack of food in some southern and western districts and a want of employment elsewhere. They also criticized the suggestion that the catastrophe was due to 'the innate indolence of the people'. Whilst the blight had triggered the food shortages, the main causes of distress were historical – that is, rooted in the penal restrictions of earlier centuries which had prevented the great bulk of the people from possessing property – and although these restrictions had been removed, their legacy remained. The synod deprecated outbreaks of violence, but stated that no other people on earth displayed such a respect for law and order despite deprivation. The bishops believed that the Poor Law was inadequate for the mass of destitution that existed, suggesting that relief needed to be commensurate with the magnitude of the problem.[111]

The writing of the memorial was significant in that it showed that the bishops had become recognized by British officials as a power in Ireland. Yet the actions of the bishops met with objections from sections of the English press, the conservative *St James Chronicle* accusing them of having usurped the titles they used and Lord Clarendon of having encouraged them. The paper also posed the question: 'When the Romanist bishops insolently address the Queen's representative with an illegally signed address and, instead of prosecution, receive favour and blandishment, how can we wonder at the contempt of law manifested by the Romanist peasantry of Tipperary?' It warned that Clarendon's actions had served to 'pamper a disloyal ambition in a class already too well prepared to indulge it beyond all ambitions'.[112] The appointment of a new pope, Pius IX, in 1846 initially heralded a more liberal phase in Catholic Church politics. But the attempt by Italian nationalists in 1847 and 1848 to bring about a united Italy not only resulted in the Pope fleeing from the Vatican, but was followed by a more conservative period of church government.[113] The Pope's escape was achieved with British naval assistance. In return, Clarendon suggested that they should ask the Pope to intervene with the priests in Ireland and tell them to concentrate on spiritual matters.[114] As the political tensions in Ireland intensified in 1848 in the wake of the Revolution in France, the involvement of the priests in radical movements was regarded with concern. Following O'Connell's death in May 1847, many Catholic priests remained faithful to the repeal movement. Within a year, though, events in France and inept leadership by John O'Connell had resulted in a number of younger priests expressing support for the Confederation, which had been formed by members of Young Ireland, especially following the arrest and conviction of John Mitchel.[115] Nevertheless, the formation of the Irish League in the summer of 1848, which attempted to reunite Old and Young Ireland, was opposed by the majority of older priests on the grounds that members of the Confederation had not renounced violence.[116]

In the early months of 1848 Ireland appeared to be on the verge of an uprising. Support for it split both nationalists and the Catholic community. In parliament there was a fear that there would be intimidation against Roman Catholic farmers and gentry who opposed a rebellion, and who consequently would be branded as 'Orange Catholics'. They were regarded as more treacherous than Protestants.[117] The political tension also increased mistrust between Catholics and Protestants. On St Patrick's Day in 1848, which had been designated as the occasion for signing a national repeal petition, Protestants in Clonmellan in County Westmeath were notified that if they did not show support for the day's activities, 'it was intended to burn their houses and massacre the inhabitants'.[118] Although such threats were rarely carried out, they added to suspicion and misgivings within local communities. The role of the Catholic priests in the anticipated rising was regarded as crucial. In July, only a few days before the rising was attempted, Lansdowne publicly praised the great number of priests who had acted as a 'remedy' against sedition and had been 'the most effectual means of preventing the formation of clubs'. He believed that if an uprising were attempted, 'the Government of Ireland will be sustained by the support of one part at least of that highly respectable and religious body'.[119] A few days later the Earl of Glengall reported to the House of Lords that the role being played by priests in Ireland was favourable, the great bulk of them being opposed to the insurrection. Nevertheless, he noted that there were 'several young Roman Catholic priests who were urging the people on to join the clubs', and he cited the example of a Dublin priest who, a few days earlier, had said that 'the British government ought to be laid low in Ireland'. Glengall recommended that those priests who urged rebellion should read history 'and they would find that every revolution had been fatal to the Roman Catholic religion', pointing out that 'In the very last revolution in France, had not the Roman Catholic Archbishop been murdered and was not the Pope himself at this moment critically situated in consequence of revolutions?' If the Irish priests stirred up rebellion, he believed it would ultimately damage their own religion.[120]

The British press also praised the support of the priests for the government. The *Illustrated London News* referred to 'the wise and humane exertions of the Catholic priesthood in dissuading their flocks from embarking on this mad enterprise with the would-be patriot O'Brien'.[121] Gratitude was quickly replaced by hostility at the fact that an uprising had taken place at all. At the beginning of 1849, when anger was expressed by both landlords and the Catholic bishops at the smallness of the grant assigned to the most distressed Poor Law Unions, Clarendon pointed out that large amounts had previously been given in a 'spirit of brotherly love and true kindness'. He believed that this 'love had turned to bitterness' because of the ingratitude with which it had been received 'and the attempts to shake off English rule . . . The great body of the Catholic clergy promoting all of this.'[122]

The Catholic Church was also visibly disillusioned with the British government. The death of so many poor Catholics and the toleration of Protestant proselytism during the Famine were only components of the deteriorating relationship. The cordial relations which had initially existed between the Whigs and the Catholic Church had largely dissipated as it became clear that Russell's promise of church reform – especially ending the privileges of the Established Church – would not be fulfilled. In 1849 the *Freeman's Journal* complained that, despite years of Whig government and promises of justice for Ireland, the Irish Catholic Church was still in a condition of 'subjugation to a Protestant Queen – to a Protestant Prime Minister, and to an almost entirely Protestant parliament'.[123]

In the midst of this dispute, it was announced that Queen Victoria was to make her first visit to Ireland. The visit of Queen Victoria in August 1849 was generally regarded as a success, but her stay awakened existing religious and political tensions. Clarendon was particularly concerned about the reaction of the Catholic archbishops.[124] John MacHale and Michael Slattery felt that the occasion should be used to inform the

Queen of the suffering caused by the Famine. MacHale refused to put his name to the text of the address, which was drawn up by the more moderate Daniel Murray, because it contained 'no allusion whatever to the sufferings of the people, or the control of legislative enactment by which their sufferings are still aggravated'. Although Murray modified the document to include a reference to 'the many woes of our suffering poor', it still did not satisfy the other two archbishops. Slattery also refused to attend a levee to meet the Queen and considered presenting his own alternative address. In the end, however, he decided that he would treat the visit with silence. A number of bishops and other clergy also objected to the visit, especially the lavish celebrations being planned while people in some areas of the country were still dying of want.[125] The Catholic hierarchy had again failed to act together in defence of the people who had suffered during the Famine, even individuals who had strong feelings preferring silence to confrontation.

In Belfast the visit of Victoria caused little dissent amongst the local Catholic clergy, who used the address to reaffirm their loyalty and devotion to the crown. The Catholic bishop and clergy of Belfast praised Victoria for so ably ruling over 'many lands and procuring for many millions of people, of varying hues, of different dispositions, and divided sentiments, the greatest amount of happiness'. Only oblique reference was made to the Famine as they alluded to the fact that her reign coincided with 'commotions abroad and unparalleled distress in some portions of our afflicted country'.[126] The visit to Belfast was not without religious controversy. The address of the Lord Bishop of Down and Connor on behalf of the Established Church had intentionally avoided political or ecclesiastical issues.[127] Nevertheless, Dr Drew, one of the leading members of the Anglican Church in Belfast, warned that if Victoria visited the new university college in the town – which was at the centre of the debate about non-denominational education – he would withdraw his loyalty from the Queen. His action had little support even amongst the Protestant press of the town.[128] During Victoria's brief drive around the town she demonstrated her government's disapproval of religious partisanship by refusing to visit the Protestant Deaf and Dumb Institute which had gained a reputation for its sectarian policies.[129] Earlier, she had refused to make a gift to the Providence Home in Dublin on the grounds that she would not 'subscribe to the funds of any charitable institution which is exclusively Protestant'.[130] The determination of the government to disassociate the monarchy from religious partisanship was reinforced in the wake of Victoria's visit when, on her behalf,

Clarendon sent £300 to the bishop of Down and Connor for the use of the General Hospital in Belfast. Clarendon's accompanying letter added that 'I am anxious that Her Majesty's name should not, even in the remotest manner, be mixed up with political or sectarian discussions.'[131]

The Presbyterian Church used the Queen's visit to affirm its allegiance to both the monarchy and the Union. The address of the Elders of the General Assembly of the Presbyterian Church, who met Victoria in Dublin, stated that, to guarantee the 'best preservation of national prosperity and peace, we and our people will continue to support the legislative union of your Majesty's empire'.[132] The address by the Presbytery of Belfast, led by the notorious extremist, Dr Henry Cooke, recalled the last visit of a sovereign to Belfast, William of Orange, who had 'come to assert the public liberties in a time of war'.[133] The Queen's visit to Belfast was regarded as a triumph by the local press, especially as it reaffirmed the strength of the Union whilst demonstrating that 'The intoxicating idea, cherished by so many, that there was strength in the Roman Catholic portion of Ireland to resist successfully the British power, was proved to be a delusion.'[134]

Despite the professions of loyalty or the silence of the Catholic clergy during Victoria's visit, there was dissatisfaction that more had not been done to create religious equality. Since the Act of Union, a continuing source of discontent for Irish Catholics was the privileged position of the Anglican Church that had been confirmed by the Act of Union. In August 1849 an appeal signed by 36 Irish MPs was made to the people of Great Britain, making a plea for disestablishment. It averred that, as long as the Established Church continued in its special position, it was 'a symbol of conquest, a perpetuation of religious inequality, and a most potent cause of the social depression of the great body of the people of that kingdom'. It added that no permanent tranquillity could be expected 'so long as sectarian ascendancy is maintained in Ireland'.[135]

A more serious challenge to the authority of the British government was made in August and September 1850 when a synod was held in Thurles in County Tipperary. The bishops agreed the need to strengthen the influence of the Catholic Church in Ireland, particularly with a view to countering the impact of a period of intensive proselytizing. They also decided to oppose non-denominational education at all levels, although the issue of the new university colleges continued to divide the church. The synod also marked the rise to power of Paul Cullen, the archbishop of Armagh, who had firm links with Rome and was strongly anti-Protestant in his outlook. He dominated the Irish Catholic Church until his death in 1878, leaving it a far more powerful and conservative organization than it had been in 1850.[136] In 1850 an upheaval triggered by Russell's support for the Ecclesiastical Titles Bill, which restricted the use of titles by the Catholic Church hierarchy in England, had repercussions in Ireland which alienated the Irish Catholic Church further from the British government. By this stage, also, many members of the Protestant Churches had lost faith with Russell's government, believing that their privileged position had been further weakened under his premiership. Two occurrences in 1849 increased this disillusionment: a conflict in Dolly's Brae in County Down in July 1849 – which resulted in the dismissal of the Earl of Roden from the judiciary and the banning of party processions in 1850; and the introduction of a new tax known as the Rate-in-Aid. In the north, the new tax was represented as being a simple transfer of funds from Ulster 'for the purpose of supporting the lazy and blood-thirsty ruffians of the south and west of Ireland'.[137] A number of protests also viewed the matter in religious terms, viewing it as the Protestants of Ulster being forced to support the destitute Catholics of Connaught.[138] The dispute linked religion and economics in a way that was divisive, suggesting a dichotomy between the experience of Catholics and Protestants, and a divide between the north (usually Ulster) and the south (everywhere else) during the previous five years. A myth also started to take root that the Famine had little impact on the Protestant community of the north-east of the country.[139] Nevertheless, the impact on the Protestant community was considerable and excess mortality amongst Protestants did increase, although on a smaller scale than that of Catholics.[140]

Priestly Jealousy and Popular Bigotry

As parts of the country were beginning to recover from the effects of the failures, a crisis arose in the Catholic Church which was to exacerbate existing tensions between Catholics and Protestants, and alienate the church hierarchy from the British government even more than the Famine of the previous few years. The crisis arose out of a change in the English Catholic Church which, since the time of the Protestant Reformation, had not possessed a church hierarchy. Although a minority church, in the late 1840s its membership had grown dramatically due to the influx of Irish poor, whilst the Oxford Movement had brought into it an educated group of followers. To reflect its new status and need for internal structures, in September 1850, Pope Pius IX issued a papal brief which allowed for the restoration of a hierarchy in the Catholic Church in England. The Anglican Church saw this declaration as a challenge to their supremacy and many other Protestants were offended by the insolence of the Pope in interfering in English affairs. The *Times* also inflamed public opinion by publishing a series of articles decrying 'papal aggression'.[141] The issue took on a major political significance when Russell wrote a public memo, known as the Durham Letter, in which he condemned the action of the Pope and, in what appeared to be an insult to the Catholic Church, referred to 'the mummeries of superstition'. He also implied that he was considering introducing legislation banning ecclesiastical titles in the Catholic Church, although it was unclear whether the legislation would also apply to Ireland. Russell's letter angered Catholic communities in both Britain and Ireland, who had generally regarded the premier as being religiously tolerant. It also paved the way for more public onslaughts on the Pope with the *Times* construing the Pope's actions as representing an attack on the Reformation itself.[142] The controversy also became tied in with general attacks on Catholicism in Ireland, one editorial stating that Ireland was 'the spoilt child of the empire' and that the Union, instead of raising standards in the country, had served 'to sink England to the level of Ireland'.[143]

Although the controversy did not directly involve Ireland, the attacks on the Pope and the Catholic Church generally were noted and condemned – by the hierarchy led by Dr Paul Cullen and by both Catholic and Protestant politicians. The anger increased at the beginning of 1851 when Russell introduced the Ecclesiastical Titles bill, which was to extend to Ireland also. Apart from restricting the use of ecclesiastical titles, the bill made it difficult for the Catholic Church to receive donations or bequests. Even moderate bishops were outraged at this inclusion. Archbishop Murray of Dublin, who had previously been a supporter of both Clarendon and Russell, issued a pastoral letter to his local clergymen warning that 'The hand of persecution is about to be once more extended over us.' On a practical level, he was concerned about the implications of the bill on his ability to raise and distribute funds to famine victims. He also saw the bill as an act of betrayal in the light of the loyalty of the clergy in 1848, declaring, 'this is the return which the Catholic clergy are to receive for their efforts in the hour of trial for the preservation of public order'.[144] Furthermore, in a rare display of unity, the 27 Catholic bishops signed a protest petition which was sent to parliament, with a separate address being sent to the Queen.[145]

Meetings of the local Catholic clergy were also held throughout Ireland to express support for their sister church in England. At one such meeting in County Cork a speaker alleged that the Pope's action had caused such a commotion because the growing stature of the Catholic Church in the country has aroused 'priestly jealousy and popular bigotry'. It was also suggested that the outcome of the papal brief would only have been to place the English Catholic Church on the same administrative basis as the Catholic Church in other countries. The remains of the repeal movement led by John O'Connell also took up the issue. O'Connell argued that if the bill were passed, it would mark a return to penal legislation in Ireland.[146] The belief that the bill marked a return to penal discrimination against Catholics was regularly repeated and the belief that the Catholic Church was again under attack served to reunite Catholics who had been deeply divided over a number of issues in the previous years, most especially over support for O'Connell or the Young Irelanders, the government's relief policies and the issue of non-denominational university education.[147] Clarendon warned Russell that 'the priests are making political capital of the Bill and are recovering much of the influence which I hoped they had lost for ever'. His only solace was that 'Luckily, there is no O'Connell to move the masses.'[148]

The debate over ecclesiastical titles occurred at a time when there was considerable resentment in England at the Irish Catholic Church, which was felt to have exceeded its role at the Synod in Thurles when it had advised on many non-church matters. Moreover, the attitude of many bishops in rejecting the establishment of university colleges was regarded as ungrateful.[149] The manner of addressing Catholic bishops in Ireland had also proved difficult and Clarendon had caused offence in Britain in 1847 when he established a precedent at his first meeting with them by addressing them as 'My Lord' and 'Your Grace'.[150] A number of Irish Protestants also believed that Clarendon's conciliation of the Catholic Church had gone too far and that he was unfit to be viceroy.[151] The bill was therefore approved of by many in England, the *Nation* describing it as 'a mere placebo for English Protestants' who wanted to humiliate the Catholic Church.[152] In Ireland the bill was supported by some conservative Protestants and by supporters of the Orange Order who were still smarting from their public rebuke following the conflict at Dolly's Brae. Even within parliament, some of the debate was expressed in offensive, divisive terms. Henry Drummond, the MP for Surrey, described Irish convents as 'prisons or brothels' and accused Irish Catholic immigrants of having brought with them 'a cargo of blinking statues, of bleeding pictures, of liquefying blood, and the Virgin Mary's milk'.[153] However, many Protestants in Ireland regarded the bill as divisive and supported the protests against it, thus winning the praise of the bishops and the nationalist press.[154]

Apart from the opposition of the Catholic Church, the bill also offended Irish politicians. One of the most outspoken critics was Thomas Redington, a Catholic landowner and member of the Dublin Castle Executive, who regarded Russell's intrusion into the matter as ill-judged and divisive and who threatened to resign in protest.[155] In parliament the Irish members, like the bishops, produced a display of unity which they had not managed to achieve during the height of the Famine. They decided not only to oppose the Ecclesiastical Titles bill, but also to vote against all measures introduced by the Whig government. Clarendon was more pessimistic than at any point since he had become viceroy in 1847, believing the impact of the bill had 'lowered Whig popularity 20 fathoms deep and we shall not live to see it dug up again'.[156] In February 1851 Russell tendered his resignation, ostensibly due to a lack of support for a franchise bill, but in reality due to the controversy arising from the Ecclesiastical Titles bill. A still divided Conservative Party was unable to take power and Russell continued in office until the general election in the following summer. The new ministry was a coalition of Whigs and Peelites led by Lord Aberdeen. Before the election, the bill was introduced and was passed by a huge majority, but it was a much watered down version and its provisions were never enforced. It was repealed by Gladstone in 1871.[157]

The bill, therefore, ultimately achieved little, but it had served to arouse religious animosities and suspicions. This controversy was the most noteworthy achievement of a lack-lustre ministry in its final year in power. But by becoming so closely involved with such a sensitive issue, Russell had ignited anti-Catholic fervour in England as 'all the old suspicion of Rome welled up in fervent Protestant imaginations'.[158] In Ireland, he had stirred up mistrust of both the Protestant Churches and also of the Protestant state. In order to defend Catholic interests, the Catholic Defence Association was established in August 1851. The first meeting, held in Dublin, was attended by Catholics from England and Scotland. Within a short time, also, donations were being sent from Catholics in other parts of Europe to fight against 'Protestant fanaticism' and 'to combat Protestant propaganda' in Ireland.[159] Although the fight against proselytism was made a priority, from the outset the Association combined a religious with a political agenda.[160] Overall, the mishandling of the Catholic Church did more to damage the standing of the Whig government in Ireland than their handling of the food shortages. It also increased mistrust between Catholics and Protestants in both Ireland and Britain. Russell, whose premiership had been marked by a massive human catastrophe in Ireland, ended his period in office by creating a religious division which was to cast a long shadow over the Catholic and Protestant Churches in both Ireland and Britain.

The majority of those who had died were poor peasants who had been members of the Catholic Church. Their allegiance to Catholicism had changed even before the Famine, the campaign for Catholic Emancipation giving them a strong political identity. The Famine strengthened rather than weakened the influence of the Catholic Church over the people, although tenant farmers rather than peasants were the main supporters of the post-Famine Church. In the hands of Archbishop Paul Cullen, also, the Catholic Church became far more orthodox and conservative, moving closer to the unprogressive ultramontanism of some European churches.[161] During the Famine the relations between the main Churches had deteriorated due to the actions of the proselytizers, the divisions caused by the 1848 rebellion and the sectarian clash at Dolly's Brae. As a consequence, Irish Catholics became hostile not only towards Protestantism, but increasingly towards Britain and the British government. As the Catholic Church became more organized and politically powerful, it was resented and feared by some sections of Protestantism. One consequence was that political and religious affiliation became fused, increasing alienation between Catholics and Protestants. Political differences were also cemented by the devotional and evangelical fervour which was manifested during the Famine and flourished in the post-Famine decades, each of the main religions continuing to vie for the souls and allegiance of the people.

7

REPEAL, RELIEF AND REBELLION

On the eve of the Famine the Irish population was one of the most politicized in Europe, largely due to the activities of Daniel O'Connell, a Catholic barrister and MP who had dominated Irish politics since the 1820s.[1] Involvement in the parliamentary process, however, was recent and small scale. Catholics had only gained the right to vote in 1793, but continued to be barred from sitting in parliament. O'Connell's role in securing Catholic Emancipation in 1829, which gave Catholics throughout the United Kingdom the right to sit in Westminster, marked a significant victory against the British government. But the achievement of Emancipation was counterbalanced by a simultaneous reduction in the Irish franchise. As a consequence of the Emancipation Act, the county franchise in Ireland was raised from 40 shillings to ten pounds for freeholders, thereby disenfranchising many of O'Connell's supporters. The size of the electorate continued to decrease after the Reform Act of 1832, despite the rapid growth in population. This was partly due to the reluctance of landlords to grant long leases, hoping to maximize their income through shorter-term lettings. By the 1840s, less than one in every 116 county dwellers had the vote, compared with one in 24 in England.[2] After 1829, therefore, O'Connell was forced skilfully to balance popular mobilization with parliamentary presence. Due to the small size of the Irish electorate, also, many of O'Connell's activities were extra-parliamentary, although he made repeated demands for an extension of the franchise. During the Famine, the Irish electorate collapsed completely, falling from approximately 121 194 in 1845 to 45 000 in 1850.[3] In response, the government introduced the Irish Franchise Act of 1850 that permitted a lower franchise based on the occupation of property in

182

relation to Poor Law valuation. As a consequence, the electorate increased immeditely from 45 000 to 164 000.[4]

Politics and Famine

Throughout the course of the Famine political tensions both within Ireland, and between Ireland and Britain, increased. The successive crop failures increased dissatisfaction with both the system of landholding in Ireland and with the Union with Britain. Within parliament there was no united Irish parliamentary party to make demands on behalf of the country. The renewed alliance between the new Whig administration and O'Connell in 1846 also served to weaken the effectiveness of the Repeal Party in Westminster. Following the second appearance of blight, the moderate Lord Sligo attempted to form a coherent grouping for the purpose of watching over Irish interests in the British parliament, but was unsuccessful. The Marquis of Londonderry, renowned for both his unprogressive attitudes and his parsimony, objected on the grounds that 'Looking to the discordant materials of which such a party must be composed, and embracing, as it does, men of the most adverse political opinions, his lordship conceives that the experiment would prove to be a total failure.'[5] The political fragmentation evident in the latter years of the 1840s, however, was to have a significant impact on subsequent Irish political developments.

The early years of the 1840s had been dominated by repeal agitation under the leadership of Daniel O'Connell and the Repeal Association, with its headquarters in Conciliation Hall in Dublin. O'Connell had established the Loyal National Repeal Association in 1840, as a result of his disillusionment with the policies of the Whig administration towards Ireland.[6] The activities of the Repeal Association peaked in 1843, the 'repeal year', but they ended with a humiliating defeat for O'Connell. Sir Robert Peel's determined handling of the repeal agitation contributed to a decline in O'Connell's personal authority and in the movement generally. When the potato blight appeared in Ireland, therefore, the repeal movement was in decline. The second, almost complete failure of the potato crop coincided with the return to power of a Whig government in the summer of 1846. O'Connell welcomed their return to power, as it provided a means of bolstering his flagging political influence. However, O'Connell's response to the failure, more especially his alliance with the new Whig government, damaged constitutional nationalist politics. It also paved the way for the political vacuum to be filled by the radical Young Irelanders, a loose collection of intellectuals and writers who believed that Ireland had a distinct cultural identity from Britain. Their view of nationalism had much in common with the European style of romantic nationalism. Young Ireland found an outlet for their views when they established the *Nation* in 1842, which by 1845 claimed a readership of 250 000, making it the most popular journal in Ireland.[7]

Although they were initially loyal to O'Connell, a number of the Young Irelanders increasingly opposed his narrow, Catholic approach to politics. In July 1846, the Young Ireland group formally withdrew from the Repeal Association, ostensibly over the use of physical force, which they refused to renounce. In January 1847, the split between the two repeal bodies was formalized with the establishment of the Irish Confederation, whose leaders included William Smith O'Brien and John Mitchel. Increasingly, those Repealers who supported Daniel O'Connell, and, following his death in May 1847, his son John, were referred to as 'Old Ireland.' But even within the Confederation, there were splits over policy and strategy, which came to a head in early 1848, in the wake of revolution in France and other parts of Europe. Mitchel's radical brand of politics, which were both anti-British government and anti-Irish landlord, resulted in his official departure from the Confederation in April 1848. In the wake of his departure, Smith O'Brien attempted to reconcile his own genteel and inclusive view of Irish nationalism with the revolutionary fervour unleashed by events in France. At the same time, Mitchel's departure paved the way for a reconciliation between the Young and Old Irelanders. In July 1848, on the eve of the uprising, the Confederation reunited without the O'Connellites to form the short-lived Irish League.

The attitude of the Young Ireland group to the British government's relief policies after 1846 was more overtly critical than that voiced by O'Connell's supporters, many of whom continued to pay lip-service to the alliance with the Whig Party. From 1845, the *Nation*, the journal of the Young Irelanders, published articles, letters and poems describing the progress of the Famine. Smith O'Brien warned Peel's government following the first potato failure that the Irish poor 'will not lie down and die'.[8] The Young Ireland group was especially critical of Russell's relief policies, notably its decision not to intervene in food exports, and they repeatedly called for food to be retained within the country. As the Famine progressed, Smith O'Brien's criticisms of government policy became increasingly acerbic. Even following the second appearance of blight, he believed that Ireland still possessed sufficient resources to feed all of the people, suggesting that the prohibition of grain exports would prevent any starvation.[9] Instead, Smith O'Brien maintained that 'English horses are now consuming provisions that would have afforded sustenance to our starving population'.[10]

Smith O'Brien frequently spoke in the House of Commons concerning famine policies, accusing parliament of indifference and 'apathy towards Ireland'. During the opening session of parliament in January 1847 he asserted that the suffering in Ireland 'could not be exaggerated, and could not be described'. He admonished parliament for not having convened three months earlier with a view to introducing comprehensive relief measures, imputing that 'if the calamity existed in this country instead of Ireland, it was the course which would have been adopted'.[11] At a meeting of the Irish Confederation in Dublin in April 1847 Smith O'Brien announced that he would not return to parliament as he believed that he could do more good for the country in Dublin. At this stage, he unequivocally blamed the suffering on both the government and the Union, claiming that 'the present misery of Ireland was not occasioned by a visitation of Providence, it was all the doing of England and of the English Government, which had neglected to provide food for the people, and which had rejected Lord George Bentinck's comprehensive plan for the employment of the people'.[12] Smith O'Brien was particularly opposed to the Quarter Acre Clause, introduced in the autumn of 1847 by a fellow Irish MP and landlord, William Gregory. He regarded it as punitive to the poorest classes and predicted that a person who was forced to give up their land in order to obtain relief would become 'a beggar for ever'.[13] The escalating mortality rate gave conclusive proof to the Young Irelanders that the policies of the Whig administration in Ireland had failed. By May 1847, the *Nation* estimated that there had been '2 000 000 Murders', by which it meant unnecessary deaths from hunger and disease, which the paper blamed on the government's mishandling of the food shortages.[14] Overall, the official response to the potato blight hardened and embittered Smith O'Brien's relationship with the British government.[15]

Unlike earlier subsistence crises in Ireland, the potato blight coincided with a period of political agitation, which gave the food shortages a revolutionary potential that had not been present during previous food shortages. The repeal agitation, the emergence of Young Ireland, the Chartist agitation in Britain and the various insurrections throughout

Europe in 1848 – all of whom believed their causes to be linked – meant that the Famine coincided with a period of unparalleled revolutionary unrest within Europe. In Ireland, as a consequence of O'Connell's agitations, the revolutionary fervour apparent in 1848 impacted on a people who were already highly politicized. Anger at the handling of the Famine increased the dissatisfaction of many Irish people with the British government but demand for repeal within Ireland was not unanimous. Since its foundation in 1795 the Orange Order had regarded itself as a native garrison and in 1848, as in earlier crises, it offered to act as a counter-insurgency force in defence of the political connection with Britain.[16]

In 1848 the demand for the repeal of the Act of Union, fuelled by events in France, again became high on the political agenda. The revolution in France changed the character of the repeal debate by making a nationalist uprising appear a possibility. The continuing food shortages, combined with disillusionment over the government's mishandling of the situation, had also hardened the attitude of moderates such as Smith O'Brien. Nonetheless, essential ideological divisions within the movement remained unresolved, especially over the issue of physical force. The Young Ireland group, inspired by the recent revolution in France, argued for a republican revolution to end the political connection with Britain.[17] Notwithstanding their fiery rhetoric, a number of Young Irelanders (including Smith O'Brien) hoped that an armed rising would not prove to be necessary.[18] Moderate Repealers also continued to oppose an uprising. Furthermore, given the despondent situation of the poorest classes, it was unlikely that an uprising could attract mass support. Overall, both sections of the repeal movement appealed to social groups that were above any immediate danger of starvation such as small farmers, tradesmen and artisans. Many within the repeal movement also, including some of the Young Irelanders, hoped to win the support of landlords to their cause. More radical members, such as John Mitchel, deemed landlords to be an enemy who had to be opposed not wooed. When an uprising did take place in July 1848, it was small, lacked popular support and presented no threat to the authorities. Moreover, its occurrence had been precipitated by the actions of the government rather than by the insurgents.[19] But although the rebellion was short-lived, its repercussions were significant. The failure of the uprising in 1848 destroyed the repeal movement and considerably weakened the republican cause in Ireland. It also served to reawaken the Orange Order's clims to be loyal subjects and the true defenders of the British connection. Consequently, the uprising contributed to a polarization between those who wanted an independent Irish parliament and those who supported the continuation of the Act of Union.

Land Agitation

The recurring poor harvests in Ireland and concurrent collapse of some sectors of the Irish economy exposed the fragile nature of the system of landholding, especially of landlord and tenant relationships in Ireland. Even before the potato blight, the issue of land ownership was an ongoing source of grievance and by the 1840s it was also dominating parliamentary discourse. Sir Robert Peel viewed a resolution of the land issue as central to his policies of reconciliation in Ireland after 1841. He also regarded it as a means of undermining O'Connell's renewed agitation for repeal which, by 1843, appeared to be bringing Ireland to the brink of civil war.[20] To ensure that the political initiative on land reform did not pass to the Whig Party, in 1843 Peel appointed the Devon Commission to examine landlord and tenant relationships. The completed report was one of the most comprehensive investigations carried out on behalf of the British government in the nineteenth century, containing testimonies of over 1000 witnesses and over 100 appendices. Yet, its impact on government policy was negligible. When the report was submitted in February 1845, the Commissioners, whilst admitting that some reform was already under way, identified a number of areas of weakness; there were few landlords and a portion of them were either absentee or in debt; there were too few leases; and subdivision of land was extensive in a number of areas. They did praise the small number of 'improving' landlords who they believed could provide a model for future developments. Whilst defending landlords from many criticisms against them, the report recognized that the poor quality of landlord and tenant relationships was detrimental to progress being made. The consolidation of property that was highly sub-divided was viewed as a necessary prelude to reform, although its impact was to be softened by subsidized emigration. The Commissioners admitted that the Ulster Custom of tenant right had conferred some benefit, but overall regarded it as an infringement of the rights of property.[21]

Overall, the recommendations for reform made by the Devon Commission remained unfulfilled not merely because of the appearance of blight shortly after the report was completed, but also because of the opposition of vested interests within parliament. The first potato failure alarmed the government that Ribbonism and repeal agitation would unite together. Ribbon societies were agricultural, secret organizations that combined elements of both tenant protection and desire for an independent Ireland. By the 1830s, the Ribbon societies were generally blamed by the government for agrarian crime and disaffection. Ribbonmen were predominantly Catholic and in parts of Ulster they were involved in sectarian clashes with the local Orange lodges. O'Connell had traditionally been opposed to agrarian agitation, arguing that such societies hindered rather than helped the demand for repeal.[22] The leaders of Young Ireland, who regarded winning agrarian support as essential in their struggle for independence, also advised peasants against getting involved in Ribbonism, which they believed detracted from their political struggle.[23] Following the first appearance of blight, however, a number of Young Irelanders, who had previously been opposed to Ribbonism, began to argue for the benefit of united action.[24]

The failure of the potato crop at a time of political uncertainty worried successive administrations in Dublin Castle. In April 1846 the Lord Lieutenant, Heytesbury, warned of the potential threat if a union between Ribbonism and the repeal movement took place, saying: 'It is only in a crisis like the present that the evils arising from Repeal agitation are fully developed.'[25] O'Connell's revival of the Mansion House Committee in October 1845 – ostensibly for the purpose of providing relief – also appeared as a vehicle for tying in crop failure with political aims. O'Connell, however, was old, in poor health and, following the accession of the Whig government, was no longer viewed as an effective opposition. One American newspaper, commenting on the increase in lawlessness and disillusionment with British rule, remarked: 'If the part of O'Connell were not finished, or if some popular agitator were to take possession of the part which the Liberator has ceased to act, this social disease would soon be transformed into a rebellion.'[26] The death of O'Connell in May 1847, en route to Rome, coincided with the highest number of people being in receipt of government relief during the Famine.

The increase in crimes, especially organized, collective crimes was attributed to Ribbonism by the government. In counties Cavan and Fermanagh where Ribbonism was extensive, Ribbonmen were held responsible for sending assassination notices to local landlords and agents.[27] In November 1847 the Lord Lieutenant issued a proclamation in the most disturbed districts, asserting that although the crimes were being carried out:

under pleas of distress, yet it is notorious that the Ribbonmen are armed and night attacks in Limerick and Clare ... as well as atrocious assassinations which have disgraced Tipperary, King's County and Roscommon, are not induced by pressure of want but are acts of habit-ual disturbers of the public peace who, by seeking the perpetration of such crimes, desire to intimidate all other classes.[28]

The proclamation also warned that there would be 'the severest punish-ment on those who give them shelter or protection'.[29]

For the leaders of Young Ireland, the food shortages meant it was difficult to organize an uprising, hence in 1848 they advised peasants to 'fight for the harvest' and not allow their crops to be sold.[30] When a small uprising did take place in July 1848, it lacked popular support most notably amongst the poorest classes. A few weeks later it was clear that blight had reappeared, as virulently as in 1846. Moreover, hunger was exacerbated by homelessness, as the impact of a fourth year of food shortages was accompanied by an increase in evictions. In some areas, the continued deterioration of the condition of the poor was accompan-ied by a resurgence in Ribbonism.[31] The government regarded the rural disorder as arising from disaffection that had led to the 1848 rebellion combined with a general dissatisfaction at the agricultural collapse, espe-cially amongst small farmers. The government's anxiety was apparent by the fact that it organized a confidential survey of magistrates, requir-ing them to comment on the condition of the districts which had been involved in the 1848 uprising and the likelihood of further agitation. The responses were generally despondent, one from County Clare warning that 'some of the better class of farmers, endeavouring to hold their position, complain of the severity of the landlords, and some crimes may be anticipated'.[32] Although land reform continued to be viewed as a solution by some members of the government, the perennial problem continued to be that no agreement could be reached on what form it should take, taking into consideration the need to appease British public opinion, Irish landlords and prevailing ideological con-cerns about the rights of property.

Demands for tenant right also became tied in with the repeal move-ment, especially the O'Connellite section.[33] The tenant right movement was particularly strong in the north of the country where the existence of the Ulster Custom had traditionally provided some protection for tenants and compensation for improvements, but where it was felt to be under threat. The Devon Commission, however, had viewed the Ulster Custom as flawed, as it could work adversely against proprietors. The Commission recommended its abolition and replacement with a system that fostered a better relationship between landlords and tenants.[34] The suggestion that the Ulster Custom should be rescinded had made tenants in the north apprehensive that they would lose their traditional rights and, consequently, they became more sympathetic to the tenant right movement. The leading proponent of tenant right was William Sharman Crawford, a liberal landowner in County Down and a radical MP for Rochdale. John O'Connell and a large number of Catholic clergy also supported tenant right. Throughout 1847 and 1848 numerous tenant right meetings were held, especially in the north of the country. Large numbers of people were present at the meetings. But although the movement was committed to protect and respect the rights of properties of landlords, few landowners supported the movement.[35] In October 1847, 5000 farmers and labourers attended a meeting in Waterford. A large number of military and mounted and foot police were also in attendance. In 1848, the government was afraid that these demands would become fused with more general grievances and local magistrates and constabulary was alerted to keep a special watch on meetings for this purpose. For the most part, though, the various movements remained distinct and peaceful.[36]

For a small number of Young Irelanders, the demands of the tenant right movement were too moderate. One of the most radical advocates of land reform was James Fintan Lalor.[37] Both he and Mitchel advocated the total elimination of the landlord class and a social revolution as an integral part of the national revolution.[38] Through the columns of the *Nation*, Lalor advocated the necessity of a social revolution as part of political independence, as a constitutional change alone would not solve the problems of Ireland. Lalor believed that the devastation on society was so deep that 'it stands dissolved, and another requires to be constituted'. He also warned the landlords of Ireland that unless they declared their unanimity with the people they would be displaced by them. Lalor's analysis was significant because it placed the land question at the heart of any resolution of Ireland's situation. Lalor died in 1849 at the age of 42. Both John Mitchel and, later, Michael Davitt were greatly influenced by his writings and as a result Mitchel increasingly drew away from the more socially conservative members of Young Ireland. Lalor also, perhaps more than any other individual in Ireland or Britain, realized the momentousness of the Famine in the long-term development of Ireland averring that 'In the presence of famine men are blind to its effects.' He believed that:

The failure of the potato, and consequent famine, is one of those events which come now and then to do the work of ages in a day, and change the very nature of an entire nation at once. It has even produced a deeper social disorganization than did the French revolution – greater waste of life – wider loss of property – more than the horrors, with none of the hopes.[39]

Repeal and Relief

Daniel O'Connell dominated Irish politics from 1824 until his death in 1847. Throughout this time, although his rhetoric was often fiery and seditious, he remained committed to constitutional means to bring about a repeal of the Union with Britain. Two issues dominated the final two years of O'Connell's life: the ideological conflict with the Young Ireland group over the use of physical force and non-denominational education, and the response of the government to the Famine. His moderate stance on both issues served to weaken the repeal movement at a time of economic crisis in Ireland and revolutionary fervour within Europe. In the 1830s, O'Connell had formed an alliance with the Whig government and he welcomed the new Whig administration in 1846, believing that he could work with Russell and the new Lord Lieutenant, Bessborough, to bring about a number of concessions for Ireland. O'Connell had the support of other Repealers and of the nationalist press in renewing the alliance with the Whigs. Young Ireland opposed it, however. To demonstrate his commitment to constitutional politics and to the Whigs, O'Connell expelled the Young Ireland group from the repeal movement, ostensibly on the issue of physical force.[40] In 1846, in an attempt to strengthen links with O'Connell and his followers, Russell restored the pro-repeal magistrates who had been dismissed by Peel in 1843. A number of important administrative positions within the Irish Executive were given to supporters of O'Connell. But even within the Cabinet, these concessions proved to be unpopular.[41] They also angered the Orange Order, which had re-emerged as a powerful voice in Irish politics following the reformation of the Grand Orange Lodge in 1845. Moreover, the renewed political alliance between O'Connell and the Whigs was forged without any awareness that a second potato blight was about to strike Ireland which would be even more devastating than in the previous year.

Disillusionment with Whig measures was rapid, especially with the reliance on public works following the second potato failure. Demands for more relief, therefore, became tied in with demands for the repeal of the Union. Disappointment with Whig policies drew together a diverse grouping of Irish politicians and O'Connell, despite his failing health, attempted to maximize their influence on future relief policies by convening a meeting of 26 MPs in Dublin in January 1847. The outcome was negligible, with little consensus being reached, and the opportunity to form an effective Irish parliamentary party was lost.[42] Within Ireland, also, support for O'Connell had waned, with attendance at repeal meetings falling.[43] His death in 1847, therefore, occurred at a time that constitutional nationalism was in decline. By the end of 1847 the Repeal Association, discontented with the relief policies of the Whig administration, called for a number of measures which included a tax on Protestant churches and an absentee landlord tax. They also wanted the recently introduced amendments to the Poor Law to be repealed, especially what they described as 'the hideous and cruel quarter acre clause'.[44] The Young Irelanders were also disillusioned with the policies of the government. In March 1847 William Smith O'Brien calculated that 240 000 persons had already died of starvation, yet he believed that it was within the ability of the government to have prevented these deaths.[45] He was also critical of the Treasury's determination to close the public works and ruthlessly dismiss those who were employed on them.[46] By the end of the year, whilst both sections of the repeal movement were disappointed with the policies of the Whig government, the repeal movement was in disarray, damaged by the split between Young and Old Ireland, weakened by O'Connell's death and the withdrawal of Smith O'Brien from parliament, as the country faced a fourth year of shortages.

Repeal without O'Connell

O'Connell's death in May 1847 left a vacuum in Irish constitutional politics which his son John was unable to fill. It also left Repeal MPs in Westminster without leadership in parliament with which to resist the new relief policies, which were based on an amendment of the Poor Law. The activities of the Repeal Association were overshadowed by the more dynamic appeals of the Young Ireland group, leading John O'Connell to make desultory appeals for support and cash. The *Nation* was particularly scathing about John O'Connell's ability to lead the Repealers, especially a union between Old and Young Ireland, observing that 'A leader is one who leads . . . but a fat young gentleman of five and thirty, without eloquence to sway the multitude, or passion to stir them, or imagination to elevate them, or humour to please them, is he a leader?'[47] Feargus O'Connor, the Irish-born Chartist leader who supported repeal yet disliked the Catholic Church, warned that 'John O'Connell will be made the little mouthpiece of the Irish Catholic hierarchy, and those of his order who now pledge themselves to repeal, will advocate the equality of the Catholic priesthood. That is their prostitution.'[48]

Daniel O'Connell's death, however, created an upsurge of support for the Repeal Association that they were able to exploit in the General Election in July 1847. Yet, despite electoral success, popular support for the repeal movement under John O'Connell was declining and within Westminster it no longer had political respect.[49] Within Ireland, apathy towards their politics was shown by the substantial drop in income from 'repeal rent'.[50] The Whig Party, despite its earlier commitment to justice for Ireland, fought the election on a policy of non-intervention in Ireland and financial retrenchment. The Repeal Party, therefore, even without O'Connell, was able to maintain earlier electoral successes, winning 38 seats largely at the expense of the Whigs in Ireland. The only Confederate candidate, William Smith O'Brien, who had been an MP since 1828, retained his seat.[51] Thomas Anstey, an English lawyer, who was a supporter of Smith O'Brien also won a seat in Youghal, although he did not officially join the Confederation until August.[52] The success of Repealers in the election was interpreted in England as an example of Irish ingratitude, Lord Palmerston opining:

> I see that almost all of the Irish Elections have gone in favour of Repeal candidates; and this is after Two or Three millions of Irish have been saved from Famine and Pestilence by money which, if the Union had not existed, their own parliament would never have been able to raise. This is not natural.[53]

Although the Whig Party was returned to government in 1847, within England a number of moderates in the party lost their seats to candidates who combined their antagonism to Irish landlords with demands for financial retrenchment.[54] Russell's personal position was also weakened, which he largely attributed to disapproval of his measures in Ireland, leaving him to lament: 'We have in the opinion of Great Britain done too much for Ireland and have lost elections for doing so. In Ireland, the opposite is true.'[55]

St Patrick's Day in 1848 gained a new significance as a consequence of the recent events in France. John O'Connell asked Repealers to sign a monster petition to the Queen demanding a native parliament, while John Mitchel called for an uprising to take place on that day. The Catholic Church was to play a crucial part in the management of the signing of the mass petition. The vast majority of the clergy supported the repeal movement, but was opposed to physical force and therefore sided clearly with Old Ireland. In the wake of the revolution in France, the O'Connellites were particularly concerned that the political initiative should not pass to Young Ireland who increasingly were adopting republican rhetoric. Parish priests were made responsible by John O'Connell for preparing the local copies of the petition which were to be signed following the Sunday mass. During mass, many priests exhorted their congregations to behave well.[56] In addition to the repeal petition, the leadership in Conciliation Hall suggested that congratulations could be offered to the people of France. If possible, also, monster meetings were to be held, although few actually transpired. One of the largest occurred in Portumna in County Tipperary which was attended by an estimated 4000 people. The speaker counselled the people to be peaceful and to support constitutional means only.[57] The government was apprehensive that demands for repeal might become fused with more general dissatisfaction at the government's relief measures. Although the petition was widely adopted, few meetings took place and those that did were generally poorly attended. The economic crisis probably contributed to the widespread apathy. In Leitrim, one Resident Magistrate suggested that the lack of enthusiasm was because it coincided with the spring harvest and therefore 'the poor people seem to be much more intent on getting in their crop than anything else.'[58]

The Resident Magistrate in Limerick, an area where the distress continued to be extreme, warned that whilst the people might not be interested in political matters:

Yet there is reason for apprehension when such large masses of people are called together under exciting circumstances, and at a period when want of employment and want of food, presses so severely on a great portion of them lest, depending on the number, they be induced to proceed to plunder and outrage.[59]

Both Dublin Castle and the Home Office in London were kept fully informed of the outcome of the meetings through the drawing up of local reports by both the constabulary and the magistrates. Clarendon, in anticipation that an uprising might take place on St Patrick's Day, placed the armed forces and the students of Trinity College on full alert.[60]

Some of those who signed the petition seemed to be unaware of the ideological conflicts that separated the two bodies of Repealers. In Clogher in King's County, although no large meetings took place, copies of the petition had been signed at several chapels. The constabulary report describing the day also observed that 'the minds of the people are much excited. They expect a war and consider that it will be a religious war and that those who are killed in it will go to heaven.'[61] A number of Catholic clergy were anxious to separate the demand for repeal from events taking place in France. In Wicklow town, the Reverend Grant prepared a repeal petition but made it clear that he disapproved of offering congratulations to France.[62] A repeal meeting in Maryborough in Queen's County ended with three cheers for the Queen.[63] A few Catholic priests openly supported the possibility of an uprising. The Rev. Mr O'Sullivan in Newmarket, County Cork, informed his congregation that pikes were being sold as cheap as old iron and suggested that they should practice firing their guns. He added that they should read a new newspaper called the *United Irishman* in order to find out what was going on in other nations.[64] In Templederry in County Tipperary also, the Rev. Kenyon, a member of the Confederation Council, told his congregation to arm and prepare for a revolution that he predicted would take place within six months.[65] The devastation and suffering caused by the Famine generally played a minor part in the anti-government debates and demonstrations. An exception was in Drummcona in Meath where the Rev. Mr Fulton 'accused the government of having caused the death of 2 500 000 of the people and urged the people to study the glorious effort of France and get rid of this terrific [sic] government'.[66] Repeal rather than famine relief was the main business of the day's activities, however.

Green against Orange

The political tensions within Ireland in the late 1840s served to increase rather than diminish tensions between Catholics and Protestants. On the eve of the Famine, there were under one-and-a-half million Protestants in Ireland (representing approximately 12 per cent of the population) most of whom were concentrated in the eastern counties of Ulster. Politically and economically, they were a powerful group. Many were supporters of the Union, whilst the Orange Order combined pro-Unionism with anti-Catholicism. Leaders of the Repeal movement were aware of the necessity to win the support of Irish Protestants, especially as in the 1798 uprising members of the Orange Order had acted as a successful counter-revolutionary force.[67] Although O'Connell had visited the north in 1841, including Belfast, his reception had been generally antagonistic. In 1843, the designated 'Repeal Year', O'Connell decided not to hold monster meetings in the north so as not to provoke Protestant anger.[68]

Many of the Young Ireland leaders were Protestant or from the north of the country, yet its enemies associated the movement with Catholicism. Unlike O'Connell, they had little support amongst the Catholic clergy. The Young Irelanders recognized that militant Protestants were an obstacle to an independent Ireland and they repeatedly appealed to all Protestants to support their non-sectarian movement. The emergence of Young Ireland as a distinct group also coincided with the advent of a more militant form of Protestant pro-unionism, mostly centred around a revived Orange Order, that objected not only to the activities of the Repeal movement, but also to various concessions made by Peel's government to Catholics, in particular the increased grant to Maynooth seminary in 1845. Many Protestants also indelibly associated Peel with the granting of Catholic Emancipation in 1829. The Young Irelanders, through the columns of the *Nation*, tried to counter Protestant enmity by proclaiming that the Orange Order was again – as in 1798 – being manipulated by the British government in whose interests it was to keep settler and native apart.[69] Smith O'Brien, himself a Protestant, wrote an appeal to the Protestants in County Down in 1845 suggesting that, in the spirit of the 1798 uprising, they should forget their more recent hostility to Catholics and rally to the repeal movement. He attributed the long-running antagonisms between Catholics and Protestants to British manipulation.[70] This theme was also apparent in the optimistic ballad written by the Young Irelanders, Thomas Davis's, *Orange and Green will Carry the Day*.[71] Davis, a Protestant, desired to foster a form of nationalism that was based on uniting all religious traditions. His unexpected death in 1845 at the age of 30 deprived Young Ireland of one of its most talented and charismatic leaders and polemicists.

The Young Ireland group had the support of a number of prominent Protestants, including Isaac Butt and Samuel Ferguson who were associated with the conservative *Dublin University Magazine*, but who came to share a similar view of cultural nationalism.[72] Although neither Butt nor Ferguson desired a repeal of the Act of Union (Butt had been a member of the Orange Order), their disillusionment with the response of the British government to the food shortages led them to join Smith O'Brien in early 1847 to form an Irish Council, with the aim of establishing practical relief measures.[73] The Young Ireland leadership also hoped to win the support of ordinary Protestants rather than just middle-class intellectuals and so, in November 1847, a small number of meetings were arranged in Belfast for 'the friends of Irish nationality'.[74] Their main aims were to reassure Belfast Protestants that the country would not suffer under an independent legislature and that Protestants' rights would not be damaged. Although the Belfast meeting sold out in advance, many of the audience were members of Old Ireland who were determined to disrupt the proceedings. One of the key speakers, the young and charismatic Thomas Francis Meagher, tried to reassure the few Protestants present that a repeal of the Union would not result in the creation of a 'Catholic Ascendancy'.[75] The radical Mitchel, a northern Protestant, whose father was a Unitarian minister, repeated the same message. He asserted that he had 'joined with Catholics because I know they would cut off their right hands before they would hold them up to advocate any measure of intolerance'.[76] By the time the third meeting was held, the attendance had dwindled to a small number of enraged supporters of O'Connell who repeatedly interrupted the speakers until the meeting was abandoned. The Young Irelanders had to receive a police escort to their hotel to protect them from their former colleagues in the repeal movement.[77] Overall, the main aims of the mission had failed as too few Protestants had attended, whilst the meetings confirmed the ideological gulf which existed between Old and Young Ireland.

On St Patrick's Day in 1848, Repealers in Belfast, still hopeful of winning Protestants to the cause of repeal, placed posters around the town, proclaiming that 'Orange and Green will carry the Day'.[78] They also invited Protestants to attend a meeting and demand a repeal of the Union and to offer messages of congratulation to France, similar to those offered by Presbyterians in the town in 1789, following the first French Revolution. Angry Protestants responded by positioning their own placards around the town and calling for a meeting at which to reaffirm their allegiance to Queen and Constitution.[79] In a number of other areas in the north-east of the country, Protestants registered protests against the activities of the Repealers of all shades, with Orange lodges being in the vanguard of the desire to proclaim their loyalty to the Union.[80] In Tyrone, a party of Protestants held their own counter-demonstrations on 17 March and played Protestant music, including *The Boyne Water*, in order to show their opposition to repeal meetings.[81] On 7 April a further attempt was made by Young Ireland to hold a meeting at the Theatre Royal in Belfast and again Protestants were asked to attend. At the last minute, the Repealers were refused access to the theatre and instead a speech was made from the window of a confederate club room. The evening ended without incident, helped by the presence of the military.[82]

Despite the failure of the visit to Belfast, the various groups within the repeal movement continued to make overtures to northern Protestants. Following the French revolution, Mitchel declared that in the imminent rising in Ireland, he would prefer to have the support of 5000 northern Protestants than 50 000 French men.[83] However, Meagher's public showing of the tricolour flag to symbolize unity amongst Irishmen angered some nationalists, who felt that Protestants were being given too much representation on the new national emblem.[84] Notwithstanding opposition, a Protestant Repeal Society had been formed in Ireland.[85] In May 1848, Protestant Repeal Associations were formed in Dublin and in Belfast.[86] Support for repeal amongst Protestants tended to come from tradespeople with little support amongst working-class Protestants or those from the landlord class. Within Belfast a number of confederate clubs were formed, although local magistrates estimated no more than five.[87] Nonetheless, a John Mitchel club was alleged to have been formed in Sandy Row, the heartland of Protestant Belfast. Twenty-nine Protestants were also expelled from the Orange Order for declaring their support for repeal.[88]

The various nationalist activities in the spring and summer of 1848 and the threat of a revolution widened the divide between nationalists and Protestant supporters of the Union. In April 1848, a meeting chaired by the Mayor of Belfast sent a memorial to the Lord Lieutenant stating their opposition to a repeal of the Union and offering the services of the townspeople if needed.[89] The *Belfast News-Letter* reminded its readers that the Orangemen of the north had made known to the government their willingness to 'act as a native garrison of their country'.[90] A number of Orange lodges also began to prepare to resist an uprising and asked the government to supply them with arms and ammunition.[91] Although both Russell and Clarendon toyed with the idea of arming the Orangemen, they decided not to do so. Yet, Russell cautioned Clarendon, '*in extremis* not to rebuff offers of help from Orange associations, and to envisage arming the Protestants'.[92]

The growth of revolutionary fervour in the summer of 1848 coincided with the annual festivities of the Orange Order. The Belfast Protestant Repeal Association appealed to rank and file Orangemen to use the Boyne anniversary to ask for a repeal of the union and for a native parliament to be established in Ireland. They added that the leaders of the Orange Order had reduced them to 'the ridiculous and humiliating positions of mercenaries, garrisoning your own country for the benefit of strangers'.[93] The appeal had little positive impact but it made the Orange Order even more determined to resist repeal, one lodge informing the Queen of 'the determination of these men to die rather than submit to a repeal of the union'.[94] Inevitably, the twelfth of July commemoration became an opportunity for Protestants to affirm loyalty to the Union and the Crown and to denounce the repeal movement, especially Protestant Repealers.[95] The Rev. McIlwaine, who addressed the meeting of the Belfast Orange lodges, began by asking the assembled crowd if there was a Protestant Repealer amongst them. He answered that if there was, he should 'immediately take the train to the asylum'. In Newtownards the speaker wished that the repeal prisoners in Newgate could be present to see that 'the Protestant population of the county of Down are true to their Queen and their country, and will never join with the disturbers of law and order'. The number and size of the July marches were reported to be larger than in previous years, which led one northern newspaper to conclude that 'It is evident that Repeal agitation in the south has inclined the North more in the direction of Orangeism.'[96] The *Belfast News-Letter* suggested that repeal had infused the Orange Order with 'more ardour' whilst giving it a new respectability amongst the wider Protestant population.[97] Increasingly, also, the Orange Order and its supporters were portraying the repeal agitation as being closely allied with Catholicism and the south of Ireland, whilst opposition to repeal had united Protestants and afforded the Orange Order a leading political role in the maintenance of the Union.

To prepare for an uprising in Belfast in the summer of 1848, special constables were sworn in and the local police were supplied with staves.[98] The authorities also started to arrest people known to have associations with the confederate clubs.[99] When at the end of July an uprising took place in Tipperary, the *Nation* appealed to the 'Catholics of Ulster and repeal Protestants' to arm themselves.[100] The insurrection was short-lived and ended in failure. Rather than bringing Catholics and Protestants together as the Young Irelanders had hoped, it had helped to divide nationalists and unionists. Moreover, the events of 1848 had strengthened the position of the Orange Order who promoted themselves as defenders of the British connection in Ireland, which was juxtaposed against the disloyalty of Catholics. On the twelfth of July anniversary in 1849, the Belfast lodges were reminded that 'this time last year, the Orangemen were, under God, the means of rescuing this country from carnage and the dreadful effects of a bloody civil war'.[101] In the wake of the 1848 uprising, the gulf between Orange and Green seemed even wider than before, whilst the non-sectarian aspirations of Young Ireland appeared increasingly ethereal.

Green against Green: Young and Old Ireland

Although all sections of the Repeal movement attempted to enlist the support of Protestants with varying success, the nationalists themselves continued to be troubled by internal divisions and splits. In January 1847 the Young Irelanders created the Irish Confederation in an attempt to bring about a reunion of moderate and radical Repealers. However, its establishment reinforced existing differences. To provide the Confederation with a network of local support, throughout the summer confederate clubs were established not only in Ireland, but also in Britain. They were mostly located in the towns and had little support in the countryside, where the same organisational structures did not exist. From the outset, the clubs were regarded as the militant, military wing of the Confederation, a view that gained credibility following the French Revolution. Russell responded to the revolutionary threat by secretly offering the Irish government the support of an additional 2000 constabulary and military.[102] The Lord Lieutenant, Clarendon, remained unperturbed by the efforts of the Young Irelanders. He comforted Russell with his conviction that in the summer of 1847, 'Young Ireland has no money, some talent, very little influence, and is losing ground.'[103] A few months later, however, he was more pessimistic about the political situation in Ireland, informing Russell that he felt that he was 'at the head of a Provisional government of a half-conquered country'.[104]

By the end of 1847, the Confederation was split over divisions between the more conservative and radical members of Young Ireland. John Mitchel, who was the leader of the latter group, was calling for rent and rate strikes, but this was rejected. At the beginning of 1848, the *Nation* announced that Mitchel and his followers were no longer associated with the paper.[105] His departure reflected an ideological split within the Young Ireland movement. Following his departure, Mitchel established his own newspaper, the *United Irishman*, in which he openly advocated revolution. The government kept a close eye on both the circulation and impact made by the paper, but decided to act surreptitiously rather than overtly.[106] On 2 February Mitchel debated with his former associates in the Confederation about the use of physical force. The majority, led by Smith O'Brien, asserted their determination to achieve an Irish parliament by peaceable means, thus deepening the rift with Mitchel.[107] This division further fragmented the already divided repeal movement.

Following Mitchel's quarrel with the Confederation, events in France propelled the remaining members of Young Ireland to adopt a more radical stand, with a number openly declaring their support for a revolution. Moreover, the revolution in France meant that the debate regarding the use of physical force was no longer merely a theoretical one. On 2 March Charles Gavan Duffy informed a meeting of the Irish Confederation that the time to act had arrived, saying: 'Nation after nation is rising into the light of liberty, while Ireland seems sinking more hopelessly into ruin, whilst famine and death hold her more mercilessly in their grasp.' He asked for 'Old Ireland and Young Irelanders, Protestant and Catholic, the gentry and the labourers' to unite. If this happened, he predicted that 'Ireland will be free before the coming summer fades into winter.'[108] The revolutionary aspirations of the Confederate groups were made more explicit on 9 March when they proposed that the Irish people should proceed with 'organizing and arming themselves'. Even Duffy, one of the more moderate leaders of the Confederation, suggested a National Guard should be formed, demonstrating that France was both a model and an inspiration to the Young Irelanders.[109] An address of congratulation to the people of France was prepared and a delegation delivered it to the provisional government in Paris. Although Smith O'Brien and some of the Young Irelanders hoped to win the support of France for an uprising, no assistance was forthcoming. However, at a meeting in Dublin to welcome the delegation back to Ireland, Meagher produced a flag of orange, white and green presented by the French provisional government and explained: 'The white in the centre signifies the lasting truce between the 'Orange' and the 'Green' and I trust that beneath its folds the hands of the Irish Protestant and the Irish Catholic may be clasped in generous and heroic brotherhood.'[110]

But although there was a general consensus that an uprising was imminent, there was still internal division regarding the strategy to be pursued. Supporters of John O'Connell, although sending messages of congratulation to France, still hoped that constitutional pressure might force concessions from the British government and organized the signing of a mass petition demanding repeal on St Patrick's Day. At the same time, congratulatory messages were sent to the French provisional government.[111] But events in France and the Chartist activities in Britain in 1848 fuelled rumours in Ireland that a revolution was about to take place, possibly in April. During the early months of 1848, also, closer links were forged between the Chartists and the Confederation, Mitchel in particular urging each group to support the other.[112] Despite considerable Irish presence in the British radical movement, particularly within the leadership of Chartism, the relationship between Chartism and repeal remained ambivalent and an alliance was never formalized, to the relief of the British authorities.[113] Since 1842, however, repeal of the Act of Union had been included in the introduction to the Chartist petition.[114] The lack of unity was largely due to Daniel O'Connell's prolonged condemnation of Chartism and his refusal to allow Repealers to belong to both organizations. O'Connell's attitude made an effective alliance difficult to achieve in the early months of 1848. Following the public humiliation of the Chartists at the monster meeting in Kennington Common in April 1848, the political initiative moved more firmly back to Ireland. When the anticipated uprising did not take place in Ireland in April, neither the Irish Confederates nor the government appeared to know how to act to resolve the tense situation. Increasingly the initiative was able to pass to the latter.

The timing of the uprising continued to be a cause of speculation throughout the summer of 1848. In Waterford, the home town of Thomas Meagher, tricolour flags were being flown over the local confederate club, known as the 'Wolfe Tone Club', from early March. The local Corporation addressed a memorial to the Lord Lieutenant which warned of 'the prevalent attempts to procure revolutionary outbreaks in this country'. It also asked for the town to be provided with a Stipendiary Magistrate and for a war steamer to be positioned in the harbour. Further reports were made alerting the government to the fact that pikes were being openly made and sold, and firearms were being practised with.[115] The revolutionary tension reached a climax in Waterford in July when Meagher visited the city, and was arrested and taken to Dublin. Although the local people barricaded the streets and threatened to rescue Meagher, he persuaded them not to do so but to let his arrest take place.[116] The *Waterford Chronicle*, which was a supporter of repeal, advised against an immediate uprising but urged Meagher's supporters 'to wait until England is engaged in a major European war. The *Chronicle* will equip 200 000 men to fight against England.' However, in the wake of Meagher's arrest, the fact that there were few disturbances in Waterford was attributed to the presence of additional troops and constabulary.[117]

The radical press was becoming increasingly intemperate, the *Nation*, for example, published an article on how to break down doors and blow up bridges.[118] But plans for an insurrection were juxtaposed against stories of suffering and hunger in the weeks before the harvest in the revolutionary press. The on-going distress had increased the dependence of the poor on the British government at a time when the Young Irelanders wanted to end it. In the early days of July 1848, as the arrests of leaders of the Confederation escalated, those remaining wanted to wait until the harvest had been secured and urged the people to be prepared to 'fight for the harvest'.[119]

Regardless of the calls for unity amongst Repealers, a major weakness within the nationalist movement was the split between Old and Young Ireland and internally between the leaders of the Confederation, especially between Smith O'Brien and Mitchel. Although a number of Young Irelanders desired a reunion with their former colleagues, they believed this was not possible as long as the Repeal Association continued to have an alliance with the Whig Party.[120] Furthermore, the increasingly radical politics of John Mitchel offended both Old Ireland and the moderate members of Young Ireland. On 23 March, Mitchel openly declared his desire for a separate Irish republic, the majority of Confederates, regardless of their revolutionary rhetoric, still had as their objective the return of a domestic legislature under the crown.[121] Mitchel had also made frequent attacks on the constitutionalism of the Repeal Association, especially the dead O'Connell, in the columns of the *United Irishman* describing him as 'the mortal enemy of the Irish working man, tiller and artificer'.[122] These sentiments offended not only the O'Connellites but also the majority of Young Irelanders who despite their differences with O'Connell had remained loyal to his achievements.

The ideological split between Mitchel and other members of the Confederation came to a head following a meeting in Limerick at the end of

April 1848 when the former was unexpectedly asked to speak alongside
Smith O'Brien and Thomas Meagher. Smith O'Brien and Meagher
were reluctant to share a platform with Mitchel, but felt to refuse to do so
would inflame an already difficult situation and give their opponents a
propaganda coup. However, supporters of O'Connell turned the meeting into a public brawl: an effigy of Mitchel was burnt; the meeting place
was set on fire; and numerous people were injured, including Smith
O'Brien.[123] The reaction of the Old Irelanders in Limerick in many ways
was similar to the group's activities in Belfast a few months earlier, when
they had been attacked physically by Young Irelanders. Police intervention
was minimal throughout the riot, which appeared to be a deliberate
policy by Clarendon to allow the repeal movement to be seen to be
divided.[124] Clarendon was clearly pleased by such public displays of
dissension and he was optimistic that the Young Ireland cause had been
badly damaged by internal fighting.[125] Nevertheless, events in Limerick
facilitated a reunion between the Old and Young Ireland as, in its wake,
Mitchel resigned officially from the Confederation. His departure made
a reconciliation between the two sections of the repeal movement a possibility. At the beginning of May, the two repeal bodies met and a
reunion was achieved in July with the formation of the Irish League.[126]

The Catholic Church opposed the creation of the Irish League. Many
priests and bishops disliked the programmes of the Young Irelanders,
especially the latter's support for non-denominational education. The
Young Irelanders had supported Peel's proposal to introduce non-
denominational universities in 1845, whereas O'Connell and the
Catholic hierarchy wanted Catholic universities to be established. The
opposition of the Catholic Church proved to be a major limitation to
the Confederates ability to organize a national movement. At the end of
1846, Dr Browne, the Bishop of Elphin, denounced them as being 'the
enemies of religion'.[127] The Catholic Church's opposition to the Young
Irelanders heightened following the February Revolution in France,
fearing that similar events could take place in Ireland. Although the
majority of priests continued to support the Repeal Association, the
events in France – and the memory of the anti-clerical backlash in 1791 –
led a number of priests to adopt a more conservative attitude to the
whole repeal movement. In Dunleer in County Louth, the priest was
described as 'absolutely kicking the people out of the chapel yard' if they
showed any desire to sign the repeal petition.[128] In the nearby parishes
of Dunleer, Clogher and Termafeckan, however, the local priests encouraged the people to take part in the latest round of repeal agitation.

There were other exceptions. In Blacklion in Cavan when some local men wanted to join the Molly Maguires, a branch of Ribbonism, they were commanded not to do so by their priest.[129] A few months later in March 1848 the same priest, like many others in the country, urged his congregation to sign the petition for repeal sent from the Repeal Association. More unusually, he suggested that if it was not granted, they should 'imitate the French people and force their freedom'.[130] For the most part, however, the opposition of both individual priests and the church hierarchy to radical or republican activity was clear. Consequently, they were opposed to the re-alliance between Old and Young Ireland in 1848, particularly as the Confederate Repealers appeared to be the dominant force in the union. They were also concerned that the alliance would reawaken the debate on the use of physical force.[131]

The ostensible lack of response by the government to the growth in revolutionary activity worried various groups and individuals in Ireland. The conservative press repeatedly called for resolute government action, especially in outlawing the revolutionary newspapers. The *Erne Packet*, for example, described the *Felon*, the *Nation* and the *Tribune* as 'preachers of Republicanism', adding that 'their vigour and determination being the most severe reproach that could be cast on the hesitation and incapacity of government'.[132] The likelihood of an uprising also concerned Irish MPs and in July 1848, 68 Peers and Members of the House of Commons connected with Ireland petitioned the government calling for decisive action. The main target of the petition concerned the network of clubs – modelled on the French example – which were described as being 'of the most treasonable, revolutionary and dangerous character'. The clubs were accused of wanting to overthrow 'by violent means' the Union between Great Britain and Ireland. The petition warned that if they succeeded, it would also lead to the dismemberment of the Empire. Recent events in France were cited as a warning to the government of the danger of delay in acting.[133] The response of the government was sanguine but reserved; whilst they were aware of the potential danger of the situation, they were confident that the peace of the United Kingdom would be preserved 'by a firm exercise of the powers which the law affords, aided by the support and co-operation of the loyal subjects of Her Majesty in Ireland'.[134]

Despite being criticized for their apparent inactivity, since the French Revolution the government had been secretly prepared for the possibility of an uprising within the United Kingdom. Although alarmed by the Chartist threat in Britain, they realized that the greatest danger lay in

Ireland, especially with the Young Irelanders. The government had in place an extensive network of spies, which had even infiltrated the clubs. The leaders of the Confederation were closely watched and the government opened their mail.[135] Furthermore, Clarendon was engaged in a war of propaganda in an attempt to counter the growing support for Young Ireland. The Lord Lieutenant surreptitiously fed articles to the *Times* and he subsidized the journal, the *World*, to use the news from France in such a way that it would undermine any revolutionary aspirations.[136] The *Dublin Evening Post* also proclaimed its support for the government and published articles by Dr William Cooke Taylor which were anti-French and pro-government. Cooke Taylor had been secretly employed by Clarendon to do so, and for this task the Prime Minister agreed to pay him £500.[137] As the French revolution became more marked by in-fighting and violence, this task became easier. An important propaganda tool was provided by the murder of the popular Archbishop Affré of Paris on 25 June, as he was trying to mediate on the barricades. As a consequence of his murder, Clarendon and his adherents were able to portray the revolution as out of control and anti-clerical.[138] The articles by Cooke Taylor acquired a new authority, leading a satisfied Clarendon to observe: 'What is more use than anything is Dr Cooke Taylor's articles in the *Dublin Evening Post* connecting the clubs with infidelity and proving that every Irish priest must expect the fate of the Archbishop of Paris.'[139] Clarendon believed that his use of propaganda following Affré's murder not only confirmed the Irish Catholic Church in their opposition to the Confederates and to physical force in general, it also ensured their support as a counter-revolutionary force. The Lord Lieutenant regarded their support as essential in turning public opinion against the clubs.[140]

Apart from the clandestine propaganda campaign, the British government was adopting a more overtly interventionist position. The Duke of Wellington was given a key role in preparing to meet the threat militarily of both Chartism in Britain and repeal in Ireland.[141] Troop presence in Ireland was increased and by the summer of 1848, there were 100 000 troops in Dublin alone. A number of Young Ireland leaders were arrested in March, including Smith O'Brien, Meagher and Mitchel, but they were released on bail. In April a Crown and Government Security Bill was hurried through parliament. It imposed severe penalties for acts which were defined as treason-felony, including seditious writing, and speaking in such a way as would encourage rebellion. Both could be punished with transportation for life. The bill passed through parliament with ease, although Smith O'Brien made a vigorous denunciation of it.[142] Smith O'Brien and Meagher were brought to trial in May, accused of inciting the people to rebellion. Both of the cases were dismissed, the juries being unable to reach agreement.[143] The release of the two men was a significant victory for the Young Irelanders and a public defeat for the government. Significantly, in the wake of the trial the number of confederate clubs increased in Dublin.[144] At the trial of Mitchel a week later, under the recently introduced Treason-Felony Act, the government was determined to get a conviction, especially as Mitchel was regarded as the most extreme and probably well known of the Young Irelanders. He was also the most controversial activist, having offended many in the repeal movement with his attacks on O'Connell.[145] The Chartist movement in England watched Mitchel's trial with anxiety, and widespread demonstrations were held in his support. The outcome brought both the Chartists and the Confederates closer together, and provided a temporary unity within both movements. Following Mitchel's conviction, on 29 May a mass meeting of an estimated 60 000 people took place in London, with Irish Confederates based in England playing a key role. On the following day the metropolitan police banned all meetings and demonstrations.[146] Mitchel was easily convicted by what was widely regarded as a packed jury that included no Catholics, and he was sentenced to 14 years transportation to Bermuda. His transportation was carried out quickly, the convict ship departing on 1 June. By early July Irish newspapers were reporting Mitchel's arrival in Bermuda, describing him as physically healthy although depressed.[147]

Further arrests of Confederate leaders followed in the summer of 1848. The radical press was also suppressed systematically and its proprietors arrested. Mitchel's revolutionary *United Irishman* was the first to be outlawed, followed by the almost equally radical *Irish Tribune* and *Irish Felon*, each having been in print for a few weeks only. The property of the revolutionary press, including the *Nation*, was also seized. From 20 July, proclamations were issued under the earlier Coercion Act making it illegal to carry arms in Dublin, Cork, Drogheda or Waterford, and punishable with two years' hard labour. The term 'arms' included firearms but also swords, cutlasses, pikes or bayonets. A bill suspending Habeas Corpus was also rushed through parliament and became law on 25 July. On 26 July the government issued a proclamation declaring that membership of clubs was sufficient grounds for arrest. It was immediately followed by the detention of a number of secretaries of repeal clubs.[148]

Although there was much speculation about an uprising and rumours relating to the movement of guns and men, overall there was confusion and a lack of central co-ordination, whilst the Young Ireland leaders remained ambivalent towards precipitating an armed conflict. However, the actions of the Whig government, particularly the introduction of the draconian legislation and the transportation of Mitchel, were opposed by even moderate Repealers and by the liberal nationalist press. In July 1848, the O'Connellites united with the Confederation to form the Irish League, although the former only agreed to join the League on the understanding that the latter would be pledged to 'a peaceful, legal and constitutional means' and that 'the Club organization be entirely dissolved'.[149] However, the actions of the government resulted in the League adopting a more radical stand. The suspension of Habeas Corpus had taken the leadership of the Irish League by surprise and they responded by appointing a War Council the same evening, with the object of preparing for an immediate uprising. Yet, whilst many leading Young Irelanders believed that an uprising was now inevitable, Smith O'Brien still remained reluctant to advocate one and was only persuaded to do so as a result of the suspension of Habeas Corpus. To avoid arrest, the remaining leaders did not meet but scattered to the countryside in the hope of raising support there. Despite the existence of a large club network in Dublin, the high troop presence meant that there was little chance of a successful uprising in the capital.[150] However, as Charles Gavan Duffy recognized: 'The measures of the conspirators were taken three months too late.'[151]

At the end of July, approximately 200 Young Irelanders, led by Smith O'Brien, mounted a small uprising near Ballingarry in Tipperary. Throughout, Smith O'Brien was concerned that the affair should result in few casualties – he even suggested that no blood should be shed except his own – and be conducted with honour.[152] A force of armed police easily routed Smith O'Brien and his followers, with only a few casualties. The leaders were arrested and sentenced to be hanged, drawn and quartered, which was later commuted to transportation for life. This sentence had been decided by Clarendon even before the trials were over, he informing Russell that 'It is clear to my mind that he ought not to be hanged but that this ought not to be said until after he is found guilty.'[153] The *Times* took pleasure in the fact that the insurrection had been put down without the intervention of the military and that it was 'a victory of Irishmen over Irishmen, Papists over Papists'.[154]

Although there were a few isolated incidents to support the rebels, they were easily put down. John O'Mahony, who mounted a seven-week campaign in the Comeragh Mountains from whence he orchestrated attacks on police barracks, led the most significant one. In November 1848 he had also assisted in an attempt to release the Young Ireland leaders from jail. More importantly the men involved in this rescue prepared for a further uprising to take place at Cappoquin in September 1849. The local police were informed that their barracks were about to be attacked. Additional military were also sent to the area. One of the attackers was killed in the raid and 11 more were subsequently tried and sentenced to deportation.[155]

In the wake of the 1848 uprising, repeal politics of all shades retreated. Although John O'Connell attempted to maintain the Repeal Association, support no longer existed. Moreover radical politics disappeared also; the leadership of the Young Ireland movement was in jail and recent developments in France had tarnished the revolutionary fervour.[156] The 1848 potato harvest was as poor as that of 1846 in many parts of the country, but sympathy for the Irish poor had disappeared in both the press and in parliament. Even the formerly sympathetic *Illustrated London News* viewed the failed uprising in terms of Irish ingratitude.[157] Irish landlords, constrained both by lack of rents and increased fiscal burdens, responded harshly to their tenants. One consequence was that evictions also gained momentum, the consequence of which meant that homelessness caused as much distress as hunger. As the *Times* observed in an article deriding the attempted insurrection: 'The potato still rots'.[158] Distress and starvation raged in Ireland as virulently as in the two previous years.

The various policies introduced by the British government during the Famine had demonstrated that, even in the midst of a crisis, Ireland was to be treated differently from other parts of the United Kingdom.[159] For a short period, however, and worryingly for the British government, Irish nationalists and English radicals concurrently challenged the authority of the British state.[160] Yet, despite the revolutionary rhetoric and separatist aspirations evident in Ireland in 1848, the expectation of achieving a native parliament was short-lived. Although the Famine provided an added incentive to have an independent legislature, it also weakened the likelihood of a successful uprising. Instead, in the wake of the uprising, the Act of Union between Britain and Ireland appeared to be even more firmly entrenched, whilst within Ireland divisions between nationalists and loyalists had been reawakened. The 1848 uprising was a further defeat for nationalist aspirations and for the physical force tradition in Ireland. In contrast, the uprising contributed to the reinvigoration of Orangeism that increasingly looked to Belfast and London rather than Dublin for political leadership. In the long term, therefore, the 1848 uprising contributed to a polarisation within Irish politics in the late nineteenth century which was based on religious lines, and which was the antithesis of the vision of the Young Irelanders.

Overall, the leadership of the 1848 uprising lacked the co-ordination, ruthlessness and support to turn radical rhetoric into a genuine threat to the British State. Three years of famine had also left the poorest sections of the population without resources, stamina or interest in an ideological battle that was not rooted in their immediate need to survive. The rising occurred when many of the Irish poor were despondent, demoralized or dead. Furthermore, the reappearance of blight in 1848 proved that the crisis was far from over. Disillusionment with the policies of the British government could not be translated into support for ending the political union. The food shortages and destitution in Ireland also shaped the response of the Young Ireland leadership, most notably those of John Mitchel and Smith O'Brien. Smith O'Brien's prevarication was rooted in his desire that an uprising should not interfere with the period of harvest, whilst he feared that a defeat would lead to further oppression of the people.[161]

In contrast, propaganda and the resolute and well-timed intervention by the British authorities were too much against adversaries who were honourable, idealistic and – to a large extent – reluctant rebels. Moreover, clerical opposition proved to be coherent and vehement, with few exceptions.[162] Yet this fact did not prevent the Orange Order from immediately denouncing the Catholic clergy for providing widespread support to the rebels.[163] Whilst these claims were exaggerated, the actions of both Daniel O'Connell and his son John had reinforced the conviction amongst many Protestants that Catholicism and nationalism were intertwined, and that the outcome was rebellion. One of the few beneficiaries of the uprising was the Orange Order, who gained both in numbers and in prestige as a result of presenting themselves as defenders of the British interest in Ireland. The insurgents had not only to contend with both the military and economic power of the British government, which was underpinned by an efficacious propaganda machine. Also, from within Ireland, they had to counter the impact of the Catholic hierarchy, the Orange Order, a divided repeal movement, and a demoralised and decimated peasantry.

EPILOGUE

The prospects for a healthy and abundant harvest in 1849 created a spirit of confidence that had not been evident for a number of years. The *Times* asked:

> Can it be that there is a 'good time' coming? ... a feeling of hopefulness is beginning to spring up, while the sense of utter despondency which seemed to have overpowered all classes is gradually giving way to a more healthy course of action, in the (perhaps over-sanguine) belief that the 'crisis' has passed and there is still sufficient stamina in the country to recover from the shock of a three years' famine.[1]

The massive fall in population since 1846 was viewed also as a positive factor in Ireland's regeneration. This optimism was evident in the Census Report for 1851 (published in 1854) when the Commissioners concluded:

> We feel it will be gratifying to Your Excellency to find that although the population has been diminished in so remarkable a manner by famine, disease and emigration between 1841 and 1851, and has since been decreasing, the results of the Irish census of 1851 are, on the whole, satisfactory, demonstrating as they do, the general advancement of the country.[2]

Blight did appear in 1849 but it was confined to counties Clare, Kerry, Limerick and Tipperary. The fact that plenty of food and fuel was available in the country demonstrated that the contribution of simple crop shortages to famine was now in decline. The poorest groups, however, continued to lack entitlement to either food or shelter. After 1849 the regional dimension of the Famine became more marked. For some areas, the cumulative consequences of successive years of shortages were

211

overwhelming. In parts of counties Clare and Kerry the number of people receiving poor relief in 1849 and 1850 was higher than it had been in the previous year.[3] The Kilrush Union, in particular, suffered as a result of the longevity and devastation of the Famine. Despite a population fall of up to 50 per cent in some parts of the union, up to 50 per cent of those who remained continued to be in receipt of Poor Law relief.[4] The *Illustrated London News* predicted that:

> Kilrush, which gives its name to a Poor-law Union, will be celebrated in the history of pauperism. With Clifden, Westport, Skibbereen, and other places, it forms one of the battle-fields of Ireland, in which property, under the guidance of legislation, has fought with poverty... The Board yesterday agreed to petition the Poor-law Commissioners on the state of the Union, and said that the guardians would not be morally responsible for the deaths that may occur through starvation ... The present condition of the Irish, we have no hesitation in saying, has been mainly brought on by ignorant and vicious legislation.[5]

The optimism of some commentators could not disguise the shock and anguish that the preceding four years had wrought on Irish society. Ireland in 1850 was vastly different from what it had been only five years earlier. The loss of almost one-quarter of the population, through a combination of death and emigration, changed the structure of Irish society. Most of the lost population came from the lower ends of the social scale who had been potato growers. Those who died had been overwhelmingly Catholic and Irish-speakers, but whilst the Irish language continued to decline after 1850, the Catholic Church emerged from the Famine organizationally stronger than ever. Emigration from Ireland, always substantial, had become a torrent after 1846 and showed no signs of abating as a remittance system financed subsequent generations of emigrants. Those who emigrated were generally young adults and were amongst the healthiest and most enterprising in society, thus further depriving Ireland of generations of youthful energy.

From the first appearance of blight, legislation had served the dual purpose of both providing relief and facilitating long-desired changes within Ireland. At times, the former objective was sacrificed to the latter aim. The repeal of the Corn Laws, opportunistically forced through parliament following the first potato failure, had not helped in alleviating famine distress, but rather had contributed to a long-term social revolution in Ireland. In the post-Famine decades, pasture replaced tillage with increased regional specialization in both crop and livestock production. Evictions were viewed increasingly in terms of sheep replacing people, which sometimes resulted in a number of attacks on sheep.[6] One consequence was a dramatic decline in the number of people employed working on the land. The introduction of reaping and threshing machinery from the 1860s, however, contributed to a decline in the demand for agricultural labourers. The poorest groups remained dependent on potato cultivation. In 1855 one newspaper, reporting on the widespread planting of potatoes, remarked, 'it is evident that the previous failure of the crops has not diminished the favour or the confidence of the minds of the country people'.[7] Overall, living standards did rise slowly for all groups in the second half of the nineteenth century.[8] Although the potato and other crops failed intermittently, notably in 1861 and 1879, there were few deaths from starvation in Ireland after the Great Famine.[9] The use of the word 'famine', however, to describe periods of scarcity, even if no deaths occurred, indicated that a consciousness of famine had become embedded in the psyche of both the poor and the relief officials.[10]

The British economy, in contrast, had weathered the storm of the late 1840s and emerged economically stronger. The commercial crisis of 1847 and the accompanying increase in unemployment proved to be short term in their impact.[11] In 1851, the Great Exhibition was a powerful symbol of Britain's economic supremacy and, by making industrial power a tourist attraction, even the poor could feel pride in the country's achievements. Whilst celebrating such achievements, it was easy to forget that only three years earlier famine was devastating part of the United Kingdom and a revolutionary threat had existed in both England and Ireland.[12] An industrial exhibition organized in Cork in the following year led one Irish journal to observe: 'There is not, in the history of our country, a more melancholy reflection than that suggested by the manufactured objects in the Exhibition.'[13] The Great Exhibition in London was, unintentionally, a symbol that after 50 years of union, the British and Irish economies had become even more divergent. Dependence on Ireland as a cheap supplier of food and labour, however, remained strong.

Apart from the loss of the poorest groups, the economic situation between 1845 and 1850 forced changes at all levels of Irish society, which had long-term repercussions. The British government had helped to facilitate the removal of inert and indebted landlords through the Encumbered Estates legislation of 1849, which had made it easier to

sell estates. The Encumbered Estates Acts, by sweeping away the insolvent landlords, meant that those who remained were resilient. They were
a small group, numbering less than 10 000, with over half of the country
being owned by less than 1000 of the largest proprietors. For the most
part they were wealthy, being, in the words of W. E. Vaughan, 'one of the
best-paid vested interests in the British empire'.[14] Apart from economic
power, they possessed considerable parliamentary power, especially in
the House of Lords. Moreover, they wielded substantial local power,
through acting as magistrates, Poor Law Guardians, school managers
and so forth. Yet, although they emerged from the Famine as a formid-
able group, within 30 years their economic, political and social power
had been challenged. Social relations within Ireland were transformed
by the disappearance of the landless labourers and indebted landlords.
Instead, strong farmers and rich merchants, who had survived the
Famine and were economically stronger than before, occupied a new
economic middle ground.

Landlord and tenant relations did not improve after the Famine, even
where new landlords were in place. All landlords regarded evictions as
a necessary tool in the progress towards modernization. In 1855, the
Freeman's Journal reporting on the 'Progress of Extermination', outlined
the case of an improving landlord who, having bought an estate in
County Galway, had then evicted 3000 people and burnt their homes.
The paper appealed to the government to intervene, saying that whilst
such evictions were legal, they were immoral.[15] Evictions received widespread publicity in the press and in parliament, whilst the notorious
Derryveagh evictions in 1861 were the subject of two ballads and one
novel.[16] Whether instigated by new or established landlords, evictions
added depth to existing anti-landlord feeling, whilst becoming a key
concern of Irish nationalists. Following the Derryveagh evictions, the
Nation predicted that 'bad work has been done in Donegal; work full of
sorrow and sin; work that will bear bitter and bloody fruit'.[17]

During the latter years of the Famine, the issue of tenant right was
regarded by liberals as a solution to Ireland's system of landholding.
Despite being defeated repeatedly in parliament, by the time of the General Election in 1855 tenant right had emerged as a significant political
issue.[18] A decade later, the land question had become central to Irish
political discourse. The establishment of the Land League in 1879 was a
powerful reminder that solving the land issue had become a central part
of the nationalist project within Ireland. Significantly, it was founded
following a year of poor harvest and food shortages in the west. The

League provided a nation-wide organization for providing resistance to landlords and transforming tenant farmers into owners. Many of its objectives had been earlier articulated by James Lalor, writing during the late 1840s, but it took the threat of a further famine to provide a catalyst for allying the land question with the nationalist question. Under the leadership of Michael Davitt, whose family had been evicted from Mayo in 1850 when he was aged four, the land question was transformed into a mass movement.[19] Consequently, the General Election in 1880 was fought in Ireland on the land issue.[20]

Ultimately, the Land War exchanged one form of inequality for another, with wealthy farmers emerging as the clear winners whilst landless labourers gained little. The death of Daniel O'Connell in 1847, at the height of the Famine, marked the end of a phase in constitutional nationalist politics. Since 1829 O'Connell had been a principal figure within Westminster, but after 1843, both politically and physically, he had been in decline. His authority had also been challenged from within his own party by the progressive, Eurocentric and avowedly non-sectarian Young Irelander group. The spread of their radical brand of politics had been assisted by the revolutionary fervour that swept Europe in the wake of the revolution in France in February 1848. Following the defeat of the Young Ireland movement in 1848, however, republican nationalism had gone into decline also and, instead, the majority of Irish politicians followed the British Liberal and Tory divide. Extra-parliamentary activities, however, were beginning to revive by the end of the 1850s with the foundation of the Fenian movement, and they looked for inspiration to the physical force tactics used in 1798 and 1848.[21]

Religion, particularly the relationship between the main churches, was a casualty of the crisis. One of the most significant legacies of the Famine was the fear of proselytism, which had played a major part in creating mistrust between the Catholic and the two main Protestant churches. After 1846 the battle for the souls of the Irish poor coexisted with the struggle to save their lives. Furthermore, after 1850 there was a fear that proselytism was becoming institutionalized, with accusations of it being widespread in a number of workhouses.[22] Consequently, each watched the actions of the other jealously; in 1855, for example, complaints were made that proportionately more Protestant than Catholic priests were being sent to the Crimea to tend to the needs of the soldiers.[23] Moreover, divisions between the Catholic hierarchy and the British government had also intensified, largely as a consequence of the controversy over the Ecclesiastical Titles bill. In the 1850s, religious battles appeared to replace political battles. The religious tensions evident in the later years of the Famine 'sharpened the hostility of Irish Catholics not merely towards Protestantism, but towards the British connection'.[24]

In the post-Famine decades also, religious and political affiliations became more strongly allied, fueled by the events of the late 1840s. In the wake of Catholic Emancipation, British politicians of the two main parties introduced a variety of measures which were intended to conciliate Catholic opinion in Ireland. For a number of Protestants, especially evangelical Protestants, the concessions were both theologically and politically dangerous.[25] Robert Peel was closely associated with two of the most unpopular measures – the granting of Emancipation in 1829 and the increased grant to Maynooth Seminary in 1845. The latter measure contributed to the revival of the Grand Orange Lodge which provided the local lodges with a national network and organizational structure. In 1848 the Orange Order viewed itself as being in the vanguard of a counter-insurgency movement. They had opposed the Act of Union in 1800, but less than five decades later regarded themselves as a native garrison and as defenders of the British interest in Ireland. The re-emergence of the Orange Order contributed to Irish politics splintering along religious lines, which was far removed from the non-sectarian vision of the Young Irelanders. Increasingly, also, Belfast rather than Dublin became the centre of pro-Union activity.

Political developments during the Famine shaped patterns of protest and division which became more marked in subsequent decades. One divide that become increasingly evident within Ireland after 1850 was that between the north and the south – areas that were imagined rather than real, but which came to represent deep political divisions in the post-Famine decades. During the Rate-in-Aid dispute in 1849 ratepayers in the north-east, in an effort to avoid paying a new national tax, created a geographic and economic distance between themselves and the rest of the country. The debate was heated and mirrored many of the stereotypes which had been apparent in some of the discussions in the British press, one Ulster ratepayer demanding to be told why 'the industry and exertions of one part of the country [should] support the improvidence, the worthless and the dissipation of the others'.[26] In the post-Famine periods, as the economy of the north-east pulled even further away from the rest of the country – boosted by linen and shipbuilding – such attitudes appeared to be vindicated.

By 1854, however, divisions within Irish society appeared to have become secondary to a war being fought hundreds of miles away in the

Crimea. The large Irish presence within the Crimea gave the country a direct interest in the outcome of the conflict. Even the nationalist press was dominated by war reports, carrying extensive accounts of battles, letters from soldiers and appeals for contributions to numerous patriotic funds.[27] Within a few decades, however, the attitude of nationalists to Britain and to fighting British wars had become more ambivalent. At the end of the century, the Boer War elicited a very different response from nationalists than the Crimean War had.[28] When Queen Victoria, wheelchair ridden and enfeebled, visited Ireland in 1900 in the hope of raising troops, she was designated by a nationalist 'the Famine Queen'.[29] Attitudes to monarchy and empire had changed, and the Famine had become a tool of nationalist propaganda in creating anti-British feeling.

The Famine seemed to offer compelling evidence that Ireland was backward, poor and likely to be a dependent partner for many years in the United Kingdom. But was Ireland's reputation deserved? Within the context of the United Kingdom, Ireland was a principal producer of food – and her economy was sufficiently dynamic to be able to respond to changes in demand within Britain. Also, despite the association of Ireland with poverty and her reputation for dependency, on the eve of the Famine the total number of paupers relieved as a percentage of the population in England was 9.2 per cent, in Scotland it was 3.7 per cent, whilst in Ireland it was only 1.5 per cent.[30] After 1852 Poor Law expenditure dropped sharply, but it was not until 1859 that it reached its pre-Famine level. Many of the paupers were sick, with the workhouses accommodating few able-bodied inmates. The amount of relief being provided in Ireland was lower than in other parts of the United Kingdom, whilst the provision of outdoor relief was particularly small in Ireland, where one in 30 paupers received it, compared with 19 out of 20 paupers in Scotland and six out of seven paupers in England.[31] Despite the changes in legislation introduced in 1847, the Irish Poor Law continued to depend heavily on workhouse relief. Overall, poor relief in Ireland in the nineteenth century, apart from during years of poor harvest, was lower than in Scotland and in England.[32]

Was the Famine, as Tony Blair recently suggested, a failure by parliament in Westminster to respond with humanity to the crisis? Or was it a failure of the Act of Union, which had been imposed on a reluctant Irish parliament less than 50 years earlier? Moreover, the fact that plenty of food and fuel was available in the country throughout the Famine demonstrated that suffering and starvation was not simply caused by shortages of food. The recovery from such a tragedy was protracted and frequently painful, and the long silence which followed the Famine was a further manifestation of the cataclysmic nature of the event. The re-assessment of the Famine which commenced after 1994 – by academics, politicians, famine experts, descendants of famine survivors within Ireland and amongst the diaspora, local and international historians, psychiatrists and song-writers – has helped to break the long silence.

The failure of the British government is not only a judgement made with the benefit of hindsight. Various interpretations were expressed at the time of the Famine and they provided a foundation for subsequent debates and conflicting interpretations about the role of the British government. The view that the Famine demonstrated the failure of the Union was expounded by the *Times* as early as 1847, although the paper suggested that it was a failure not of Britain's making. As was so frequently the case, Ireland was portrayed as a burden on Britain (more usually England) and accused of ingratitude, asserting:

> We have been united to Ireland for 47 years by the ties of legislative association. During that time Ireland has enjoyed all the privileges that England enjoyed . . . The same advantages our people possessed, hers possessed also. The same commerce, the same seas, the same Indies, the same America, were for her to trade with as well as England . . . yet, notwithstanding these facts, she claims in alternate tones of supplication and menace that her poor shall be supported by our bounty, her improvidence corrected by our prudence, and her self-sought necessities alleviated by our mortgaged wealth.

It added: 'What have we – what has England – done to deserve this per-petual blister of thankless obligations and exacting obloquy?'[33]

An alternative view, that Ireland had been callously abandoned by Britain, was also expressed at the time. In July 1849 in the House of Commons, the MP Mr Horsman asked rhetorically, 'what have we done for Ireland?' His conclusions were gloomy, believing as he did that the people had been reduced to 'ruin, and misery, and death, and demoral-ization worse than death'. Moreover, as he pointed out, this suffering had taken place 'among our own people, within a few hours' distance of the richest metropolis in the world'. Horsman blamed the crisis in Ireland on the policies introduced by the British government. The transfer to Poor Law relief in 1847 was, he claimed, due to 'prejudice created on the English mind . . . the clamours of the press, as an easy solution to incompetent statesmen, who dared not go to the bottom of the subject – as a sop to the English public, at the cost of unpopular Irish landlords'.[34] Yet, parliament had also taken advantage of 'English prejudice and Irish helplessness'. Moreover, the relief measures chosen were 'stale devices, long ago tried and condemned in England, but exported, like damaged wares, to an inferior market, as not suited to fastidious England, but quite good enough for Ireland'.[35] He also denied that the potato failure had caused the suffering, but averred: 'Bad legislation, careless legislation, criminal legislation had been the cause of it all.' A further accusation made by Horsman was that such discussions had become 'wearisome and distasteful' to the British parliament. [36]

The government enquiry set up in 1849 to investigate the continued suffering in the Kilrush Union was also in no doubt that Ireland was treated differently stating :

> Whether as regards the plain principles of humanity, or the literal text and admitted principle of the Poor Law of 1847, a neglect of public duty has occurred and has occasioned a state of things disgraceful to a civilized age and country, for which some authority ought to be held responsible, and would have been long since held responsible had these things occurred in any union in England.[37]

In 1849, Edward Twistleton, the Poor Law Commissioner in Ireland resigned as he no longer felt able to implement Poor Law policy 'with honour'. Over the previous 12 months he had frequently clashed with Charles Trevelyan over the amount of relief provided, pointing out to the Treasury official that if people in England were made aware of the situation, 'they might say that we are slowly murdering the peasantry by the scantiness of the relief'.[38] Clarendon sympathized privately with Twistleton's decision to resign, informing Russell that Twistleton 'thinks that the destitution here is so horrible and the indifference of the House of Commons to it so manifest, that he is an unfit agent of a policy that must be one of extermination'.[39] Shortly afterwards he informed a government committee that the British government could have prevented much death and suffering, emphasizing 'the comparatively trifling sum with which it is possible for this country to spare itself the deep disgrace of permitting any of our miserable fellow subjects in the distressed unions to die of starvation'. Twistleton believed that the relief policies could have saved lives if the administrators had been given financial support with which to implement them. His concluding statement was a damning indictment of the policies that he had been responsible for managing, pronouncing:

> I wish to leave distinctly on record that, from want of sufficient food, many persons in these unions are at present dying or wasting away; and, at the same time, it is quite possible for this country to prevent the occurrence there of any death from starvation, by the advance of a few hundred pounds, say a small part of the expense of the Coffre War.[40]

A similar sentiment was expressed by the Marquis of Sligo, who condemned the parsimony of the Treasury, contending that:

> Money can be got if the Nation wills it, and would be forthcoming if the necessity of it were proved either for foreign war or for internal famine. It surely is equally the office of the Executive to protect from the latter as from the former and deliberately to allow a man innocent of all crime to perish for economy's sake would amount almost to an abdication of government.[41]

Such unequivocal criticisms of government policy, voiced publicly or privately by prominent officials, politicians and relief officials, were an admission that the treatment of Ireland was regarded by a number of commentators at the time as having been both inappropriate and distinctive.

The Famine occurred within the jurisdiction of not only the richest empire in the world, but one of the most advanced parliamentary democracies of the time. At each stage of the Famine, relief policies were discussed and debated both within parliament and within the press. The opposition to the various policies demonstrated an awareness of the limitations of relief provision and showed that other models of aid were possible. The various relief policies – with the partial exception of the soup kitchens – were inappropriate and inadequate. The defects of policy formulation were compounded by the government's refusal to intervene at certain key times – to restrict food exports, to curb evictions, to regulate emigration, or to prevent proselytism. As a consequence, a potato blight was transformed into one of the most lethal famines in modern history. Clearly, the Act of Union neither conferred economic advantages on Ireland nor safeguarded her population at a time of crisis. The Famine had demonstrated the existence of a less than united kingdom, provoking the Lord Lieutenant to suggest in 1849: 'I don't think there is another legislature in Europe that would disregard such suffering as now exists in the west of Ireland, or coldly persist in a policy of extermination.'[42] The needs of the Irish poor were made secondary to the demands of the British population, especially the commercial sector. Weak government, parsimonious administrators, entrenched financial interests, anti-Catholic, anti-poor and anti-Irish sentiments produced a particularly lethal combination of misguided intervention and injudicious non-intervention. The immediate consequence was the unnecessary deaths of over one million people. The long-term legacy of the Famine not only changed Ireland, but continued to influence British politics even after the passage of 150 years.

NOTES

1 Remembering the Famine

1. Speech by the Minister of State, Avril Doyle TD, Famine Commemoration Programme, 27 June 1995.
2. The text of a message from the British Prime Minister, Mr Tony Blair, delivered by Britain's Ambassador to the Republic of Ireland, Veronica Sutherland, on Saturday 31 May 1997 at the Great Irish Famine Event, in Cork (British Information Services, 212).
3. *Irish News*, 4 February 1997.
4. The designation of the event is contested; some nationalists find the use of the word 'famine' offensive and inappropriate given the large amounts of food exported from Ireland. For more on the debate, see Kinealy, *A Death-Dealing Famine: The Great Hunger in Ireland* (Pluto Press, 1997), Chapter 1.
5. The *Irish Times*, 3 June 1995.
6. The most influential work which laid the ground for much subsequent revisionist writing was R. D. Crotty, *Irish Agricultural Production* (Cork University Press, 1996).
7. The most polished and widely read exposition of the revisionist interpretation was provided in Roy Foster, *Modern Ireland, 1600–1972* (London, 1988).
8. Roy Foster, 'We are all Revisionists Now', in *Irish Review* (Cork, 1986), pp. 1–6.
9. Professor Seamus Metress, *The Irish People*, 10 January 1996. Similar arguments have also been expressed by Professor Brendan Bradshaw of Cambridge University, a consistent – but isolated – opponent of revisionist interpretation. See, for example, *Irish Historical Studies*, xxvi: 104 (November 1989), pp. 329–51.
10. Christine Kinealy, 'Beyond Revisionism', in *History Ireland: Reassessing the Irish Famine* (Winter 1995).
11. For more on this episode, see Cormac Ó Gráda, 'Making History in Ireland in the 1940s and 1950s: The Saga of the Great Famine', in *The Irish Review* (1992), pp. 87–107.
12. Edwards and Williams, *The Great Famine* (Dublin, 1956), p. xi.
13. For example, F. S. L. Lyons in *Irish Historical Studies* (1964–5), pp. 76–9.
14. Cited in Cormac Ó Gráda, *The Irish Famine* (Dublin, 1989), p. 11.
15. Foster, *We are all Revisionists*, pp. 3–5.
16. Mary Daly, *The Great Famine in Ireland* (Dundalk, 1986).
17. Lecture by Mary Daly in Linen Hall Library, October 1995, quoted in Gerard Mac Atasney, *This Dreadful Visitation: The Famine in Lurgan and Portadown* (Belfast, 1997), p. xv.

18. Speech by Doyle.
19. John Waters in the *Irish Times*, 22 August 1995; for an example of the kind of hysterical attack mentioned, an edition of the *Davis Show*, broadcast by RTE in February 1995, including in the invited audience, Eoghan Harris, a renowned spin doctor and media guru. He alleged that Famine commemorations were a ploy by the IRA to humiliate the British government.
20. Fintan O'Toole in 'Unsuitable from a Distance: The Politics of Riverdance', in *The Ex-Isle of Erin: Images of a Global Ireland* (Dublin, 1997), argues that *Riverdance* provides an authentic reworking of Irish dancing before it fell a victim of a conservative church and other influences. In the same year as Riverdance, Ireland's early successes in the World Cup, taking place in the United States, also won praise for both the footballers and their fans.
21. Lance Pettitt, *Screening Ireland: Film and Television Representation* (Manchester University Press, 2000), p. 177.
22. Deborah Peck, *Silent Hunger. The Psychological Impact of the Great Irish Hunger*, unpublished Ph.D. thesis, Massachusetts School of Professional Psychology, University of Massachusetts, 2000. She makes the point that psychological trauma is transgenerational and that recovery can only take place when people feel 'safe' and accepted. In the United States, Irish-Americans of the John F. Kennedy generation were the first to feel secure and so confront some of the more unpleasant aspects of their history. In the Republic of Ireland, it followed economic success and cultural recognition in the 1990s.
23. Jim Jackson, 'The Making of a Best Sellar' [sic], in *Irish Review* (Winter, 1991/2).
24. Tom Hayden (ed.), *Irish Hunger: Personal Reflections on the Legacy of the Famine* (Roberts Rinehart, Colorado, 1997).
25. Speech by Doyle.
26. *Irish Times*, 3 March 1995. The four historians were Cormac Ó Gráda and Mary Daly (both at University College, Dublin), David Fitzpatrick and David Dickson (both at Trinity College, Dublin).
27. The publication was Cormac Ó Gráda, *Famine 150* (Dublin, 1997), with the exception of chapters by Andrés Eiríksson and Joseph Lee it contained few original chapters. The research financed by the committee has still not been published.
28. Speech by Doyle.
29. Ibid.
30. Mary Robinson, *A Voice for Somalia* (Dublin, 1994), pp. 11–12.
31. *Church of Ireland Gazette*, 13 January 1995; *Irish Times*, 3 March 1995.
32. Speech by Doyle.
33. *Irish Independent*, 7 March 1995.
34. *Irish Times*, 30 December 1995.
35. Christine Kinealy and Trevor Parkhill (eds), *The Famine in Ulster* (Belfast, 1997).
36. For example, see Ó Gráda, *Black '47*, which provides a rare examination of the role of merchants.
37. Liam Swords, *In Their Own Words: The Famine in North Connaught, 1845–9* (Dublin, 1999).
38. This point has been made repeatedly by Dr Charles Orser, who has excavated a village in Gorttoose in County Roscommon which was occupied *c*.1790–1847

and provides many insights into daily life before the Famine, see Charles Orser, 'Why is there no Archaeology in Irish Studies?', in *Irish Studies Review* (vol. 8, no. 2, August 2000), pp. 157–65.

39. *Sunday Times*, 10 September 1995.
40. *Evening Press*, 26 April 1997.
41. AfrI, *Peacemaker* (Dublin, 1988), pp. 5–8; Cormac Ó Gráda, however, has argued that the practice of finding links and similarities between Ireland's Great Famine and modern famines is an invented tradition.
42. This point was made by Amartya Sen at the Ireland House Conference on Famine in New York in May 1995; Ó Gráda, *Famine 150*, pp. 132–3, has attempted to quantify mortality in the Third World in recent famines and confirms that more people died in Ireland in both absolute and relative terms, but in absolute numbers, the number who died during Stalin's Ukraine Famine in the 1930s and China's Great Leap Forward Famine of 1859–62 was higher. No hard, reliable data exists for population loss during the Irish Famine, although it is generally accepted that excess mortality was over a million people.
43. Benjamin Disraeli in *Hansard*, xci, 29 March 1847, p. 574; William Smith O'Brien had also asked parliament for a register to be kept of famine deaths, but his request was turned down by the Prime Minister, *Freeman's Journal*, 12 March 1847.
44. *Irish Independent*, 7 June 1997.
45. Sinéad O'Connor, 'Famine', on *Universal Mother* Album (1994).
46. *Evening Press* (Dublin), 26 September 1994.
47. Ibid.
48. Amartya Sen, *Poverty and Famine: An Essay in Entitlement and Deprivation* (Oxford, 1981). His theory probably has greater application to short-term famines rather than one as protracted as the Great Hunger.
49. *Evening Herald*, 26 January 1995.
50. John Waters, *Irish Times*, 11 October 1994.
51. *Liverpool Daily Post*, 20 November 1997.
52. The lawyer was Professor Charles Rice of Notre Dame University, who was an eminent and well-respected academic.
53. *New York Post*, 11 December 1996.
54. James Mullin, President of the Irish Famine Curriculum Committee and Education Fund in New Jersey, produced a Famine Curriculum which included a section on whether the Irish Famine could be classed as 'genocide'.
55. ABC World News Tonight, 16 March 1997.
56. *Sunday Telegraph*, 11 February 1996.
57. *Sunday Times* (Dublin), 16 October 1996.
58. *Wall Street Journal*, 10 November 1997.
59. *New York State*, 1 December 1996.
60. *New York Daily News*, 26 October 1996.
61. *The Times*, 13 October 1996.
62. *Sunday Tribune* (Ireland), 13 October 1996.
63. An Irish historian, Margaret MacCurtain, who had no particular expertise in the Famine, was chosen to head the review of the Famine committee.
64. For more on the New York Famine Curriculum Project, contact Maureen Murphy, www.geocities.com/hsse.geo or, CATMOM@Hofstra.edu.

65. This initiative was largely the work of John Lahey, President in Quinnipiac University and former Grand Marshall of the St Patrick's Day Parade in 1997. It was financed by a generous donation from the Lender family.

66. *Irish Times*, 21 January 1998.

67. Speech by Doyle.

68. *Irish Times*, 27 May 1997; *The Phoenix* (Dublin), 23 May 1997 wrote a disparaging article criticizing the Irish government for allowing the Famine event to descend into shabby commercialism.

69. *American Irish Newsletter* (21, no. 8, 1996), pp. 1–4.

70. Message from Tony Blair.

71. *Irish Times*, 5 May 1997.

72. For example, the Famine Genocide Committee based in New York, continued to threaten to take a 'class' action against the British government charging it retrospectively with genocide.

73. Kevin Whelan in the *Irish Times*, 21 January 1998.

74. Christine Kinealy, 'The Great Irish Famine. A Dangerous Memory?', in Arthur Gribben (ed.), *The Great Famine and the Irish Diaspora in America* (University of Massachusetts Press, 1999), pp. 239–55.

75. *Irish Times*, 21 January 1998.

76. For example, on 3 December 1998 a dedication service took place in Derry, which involved local schoolchildren throwing flowers into the quayside to mark the death of emigrants 150 years earlier from suffocation when they were forced below deck during a violent storm. Such horrific incidences, although rare, contributed to the folk tradition of 'coffin ships'. In August 2000, the same group who had organized the previous event opened a Great Hunger Education Centre in the City.

77. One of the murals is located on Crocus Avenue, near Springfield Road; see also Christine Kinealy and Gerard Mac Atasney, *The Forgotten Famine: Hunger, Poverty and Sectarianism in Belfast* (Pluto Press, 2000), Chapter 1.

78. Liam Kennedy, 'The Rural Economy', in Liam Kennedy and Philip Ollerenshaw (eds), *An Economic History of Ulster, 1820–1939* (Manchester University Press, 1985), p. 30.

79. Quoted in the *Irish Times*, 21 January 1998.

80. *Belfast Telegraph*, 4 February 1997.

81. *Belfast Newsletter*, 4 February 1997.

82. *Irish News*, 4 February 1997.

83. *Newry Telegraph*, 6 March 1849.

84. Gerard Mac Atasney, *The Famine in Lurgan and Portadown* (Beyond the Pale, 1997); Trevor McCavery, 'The Famine in County Down', in Kinealy and Parkhill, *Famine in Ulster* (Belfast, 1997), pp. 99–128; Kinealy and Mac Atasney, *The Forgotten Famine*.

85. For more on folk memory, see Cathal Póirtéir, *Famine Echoes* (Dublin, 1995).

86. Christine Kinealy, *A Disunited Kingdom? England, Ireland, Scotland and Wales, 1800–1948* (Cambridge University Press, 1999).

87. Dorothy Thompson, 'Ireland and the Irish in English Radicalism before 1850', in James Epstein and Dorothy Thompson (eds), The *Chartist Experience Studies in Working-Class Radicalism and Culture, 1830–60*, (Macmillan – now Palgrave, 1985), p. 145.

88. Thomas Bartlett, Kevin Dawson and Dáire Keogh, *Rebellion*, (Dublin 1998).

89. B. R. Mitchell and P. Deane, *Abstract of British Historical Statistics* (London, 1962).

90. There were a number of comprehensive government-initiated enquiries into social conditions in Ireland – the Poor Inquiry, chaired by Archbishop Whately, 1833–6 (PP, 1836, vols xxx–xxxiv); the Censuses of 1821,1831 and 1841; the Devon Commission into landlord-tenant relations, which reported in 1845 (PP 1845, vols xix–xxii).

91. *Third Report of the Commissioners for Inquiry into the Poorer Classes in Ireland*, PP 1837, vol. xxx.

92. Trevelyan to Routh, Public Record Office, London (hereafter PROL), T.64 368A, 10 January 1847.

93. Wood to Russell, cited in G. P. Gooch, *The Later Correspondence of Lord John Russell, 1840–1878* (London, 1925), p. 228.

94. For example, at the height of the Repeal crisis in 1843, Peel informed parliament that 'There is no influence, no power, no authority which the prerogatives of the crown and the existing law given to the government, which shall not be exercised for the purpose of maintaining the union; the dissolution of which would involve not merely the repeal of an act of parliament, but the dismemberment of this great empire', in Charles S. Parker (ed.), *Sir Robert Peel from his Private Papers*, vol. iii, (London, 1899), pp. 47–8.

95. Christine Kinealy, 'The Introduction of the Poor Law to Ireland, 1838–64' (unpublished Ph.D. thesis, Trinity College Dublin, 1984).

96. *Hansard*, xciii, Debate on Railways, 28 June 1847

97. Ibid.

98. T. M. Devine, *The Great Highland Famine: Hunger, Emigration and the Scottish Highlands in the Nineteenth Century* (John Donald, Edinburgh 1988).

99. Quoted in Donal Kerr, *The Catholic Church and the Famine* (Dublin, 1996), p. 11.

100. Peter Solar, 'The Potato Famine in Europe', in Ó Gráda, *Famine 150*, p. 113.

101. Ibid., p. 116.

102. Cormac Ó Gráda, *Ireland: A New Economic History* (Oxford, 1994), p. 120.

103. Mr and Mrs S. C. Hall, *Ireland, Its Scenery and Character etc*. (3 vols, first pub, London, 1841–3; reprinted London, 1984), p. 406.

104. Christine Kinealy, 'Peel, rotten potatoes and providence: the repeal of the Corn Laws and the Irish Famine', in Andrew Marrison (ed.), *Free Trade and its Reception* (vol. 1, London, 1998).

105. Eric J. Evans, *Sir Robert Peel: Statesmanship, Power and Party* (Routledge, 1991), pp. 4–19.

106. *Hansard*, cxi, 29 March 1847, pp. 570–4: Bentinck resigned leadership of the Protectionists in December 1847; he died in 1848 at the age of 46.

107. *Hansard*, lxxxix, 4 February 1847, pp. 703–802.

108. *Freeman's Journal*, 12 March 1847.

109. Clarendon to Russell, Clarendon Papers, Bodleian Library, 10 August 1847.

110. Frank Prochaska, *The Voluntary Impulse* (London, 1988), p. 39.

111. Ibid., pp. 34–5.

112. This bitterness was evident in the reception to the play *Souper Sullivan* by Eoghan Harris, which was produced by the Abbey Theatre in 1985 and portrayed the Protestant minister sympathetically but failed to understand that proselytism

was part of a wider and more long-term desire to make Ireland Protestant. The play was variously attacked and defended in the national press. See also Irene Whelan, 'The Stigma of Souperism', in Cathal Póirtéir, *The Great Irish Famine* (Dublin, 1997), pp. 135–6.

113. *Times*, 14 January 1880.
114. *United Irishman*, 7 April 1900.
115. *Cork Examiner*, 14 June 1995.
116. For example, Mary Daly quotes the figures unquestioningly: Daly, *Famine in Ireland*, p. 57; for original table, see Austin Bourke, *The Visitation of God? The Potato and the Great Irish Famine* (Dublin, 1993, first printed as an article), pp. 168–9.
117. Peter Gray, whose interpretation is generally post-revisionist, has claimed, 'Even if exports had been prohibited, Ireland lacked sufficient food resources to stave off famine in 1846–7', in Peter Gray, *The Irish Famine* (Thames and Hudson, 1997), p. 46.
118. Bessborough to Russell, Russell Papers, PROL 30.22.16.A, 23 January 1847.
119. *Hansard*, xciii, 30 June 1847, pp. 1057–9.
120. The Bills of Entry, which list the cargo of each vessel, are available for the ports of Liverpool, Bristol, Glasgow and London in the Maritime Museum in Liverpool.
121. Amartya Sen, *Poverty and Famines: An Essay on Welfare Economics* (Oxford, 1981).
122. See also Chapter 5 in this volume.
123. Hugh MacNeile, *The Famine a Rod of God: Its Provoking Cause, its Merciful Design* (Liverpool, 1847).
124. Trevelyan to Monteagle, Monteagle Papers, National Library of Ireland (hereafter NLI) Ms 13,397.11, 9 October 1846.
125. *Church of Ireland Gazette* (Belfast), 13 January 1995.
126. Kinealy and Mac Atasney, *Famine in Belfast*, Chapter 6.
127. *Freeman's Journal*, 10 July 1849.
128. Constabulary Reports, Galway, PROL HO45 2416, 2 March 1848.
129. *Times*, 8 June 1849.
130. A. K. Sen, 'Nobody need starve', in *Granta*, (no. 52, Winter, 1995).
131. Ó Gráda, *New Economic History*, p. 120.
132. Quoted in Ó Gráda, *Black '47*, p. 6.
133. *Belfast Vindicator*, 6 January 1847.
134. Blair Speech, 1997.

2   The Government's Response to the Crisis

1. *Gardener's Chronicle and Horticultural Gazette*, 16 September 1845.
2. For example, the Rev. Ivers of Tartaraghan stated of the local poor that 'Sometimes their breakfast, dinner and supper consist of potatoes', quoted in Mac Atasney, *Famine in Lurgan*, p. 17.
3. For more on potatoes, see Kinealy, *Death Dealing Famine*, pp. 41–53.
4. R. Floud, K. Wachter and A. Gregory, *Height, Health and History: Nutritional Status in the United Kingdom, 1750–1980* (Cambridge University Press, 1990).

5. Cormac Ó Gráda, *New Economic History*, p. 116; Ó Gráda also points out that many of the disparaging comments made by outsiders on mud cabins were 'culturally specific'.

6. A. Young, *Tour in Ireland* (Dublin, 1780); J. G. Kohl, *Travels in Ireland* (London, 1844).

7. Ó Gráda, *New Economic History*, p. 14.

8. David Dickson, *Arctic Ireland. The Extraordinary Story of the Great Frost and Forgotten Famine of 1740–41* (Belfast, 1997).

9. William Wilde's Table of Irish Famines, 900–1850, in E. M. Crawford (ed.), *Famine. The Irish Experience* (Edinburgh, 1989), pp. 3, 16; James Kelly, *Famine and Harvest Crisis in Ireland before the Great Famine* (paper delivered at the Parnell Summer School, 1995).

10. Timothy P. O'Neill, 'The state, poverty and distress in Ireland, 1815–45', unpub. Ph.D. thesis (University College, Dublin, 1971), Chapter 1.

11. J. H. Andrews, *A Paper Landscape: The Ordnance Survey in Nineteenth Century Ireland* (Belfast, 1975).

12. Eric Evans, *Sir Robert Peel: Statesmanship, Power and Party* (London, 1994), pp. 11–27.

13. Dr Lyon Playfair to Peel, 26 October 1845, Charles Stuart Parker (ed.), *Sir Robert Peel from his Private Papers*, vol. iii (London, 1899, 2nd edn) p. 225.

14. As late as 1849, accusations of exaggeration and corruption were still evident, For example the Board of Trade accused one MD of exaggerating the number of immigrants on one ship which contained 1700 passengers from Derry to Glasgow. The MD had to produce proof that this was, in fact, true, *Liverpool Mercury*, 7 August 1849.

15. For more on mechanics of relief, see Kinealy, *Great Calamity*, Chapter 2.

16. Sir Randolph Routh to Charles Trevelyan, 1 April 1846, *Correspondence Explanatory of the Measures adopted by Her Majesty's government for the relief of distress arising from the failure of the potato crop in Ireland* (hereafter, *Correspondence Explanatory*) PP, 1846, xxxvii, p. 139.

17. *Belfast News-Letter*, 17 February 1846.

18. *Freeman's Journal* (hereafter, *Freeman's*) quoted in Mary Daly, *Famine in Ireland*, p. 69.

19. *Copy of the Report of Dr Playfair and Mr Lindley on the Present State of the Irish Potato Crop, and on the Prospects of the Approaching Scarcity*, 1846, xxxviii; for breakdown of crop losses by county, see Kinealy, *Great Calamity*, Appendix 1, pp. 360–2.

20. Peel to Sir James Graham, 13 October 1845, Parker, *Peel*, p. 223.

21. *Hansard*, lxxxv, 27 April 1846.

22. Queen Victoria to Peel, 18 December 1845, Parker, *Peel*, p. 253; Ibid., 19 December 1845, p. 254.

23. Ibid., Prince Albert to Peel, 11 December 1845, p. 241.

24. *Hansard*, lxxxvii, 16 July 1847, p. 1179.

25. Ibid., xcv, 13 December 1847, p. 989.

26. Daniel O'Connell to Russell, Russell Papers, PROL 30.22.5B, 12 August 1846.

27. Ibid., Lord Enniskillen to Bessborough, Dublin Castle, 12 August 1846.

28. Ibid.

29. *Freeman's*, 3 July 1847.

30. O'Connell, quoted in Bessborough to Russell, Russell Papers, PROL, 30.22.5B, 11 September 1846.

31. Ibid.

32. Russell to Bessborough, Russell Papers, PROL 30.22.5C, 1 September 1846.

33. Wood to Labouchere, Hickleton Papers, A4/185/1/, 22 September 1846.
34. *Times*, 26 September 1846.
35. Earl of Bandon to Russell, Russell Papers, PROL 30.22.5C, 7 September 1846.
36. Ibid., Charles Wood to Bessborough, 9 September 1846.
37. Charles Trevelyan, quoted in Devine, *Highlands Famine*, p. 91.
38. Routh to Trevelyan, 29 October 1846, *Correspondence Explanatory*, p. 207.
39. Ibid., Lieutenant Col. Jones, Board of Works to Treasury, 7 April 1846, p. 346.
40. Ibid., p. 347.
41. William Henry Smith, *A Twelvemonth's Residence in Ireland during the Famine and the Public Works, with Suggestions to meet the Coming Crisis*, (London, 1848) p. 94.
42. *Globe*, 19 January 1847.
43. Trevelyan to Jones, 16 March 1846, *Correspondence Explanatory*, p. 331; Ibid., Treasury Minute, 3 April 1846, p. 343.
44. *Hansard*, xciii, 28 June 1847, p. 1005.
45. *Globe*, 11 January 1847.
46. *Freeman's*, 5 December 1846.
47. Bessborough to Russell, Russell Papers, PROL 30.22.6C, 12 April 1847.
48. *Roscommon and Leitrim Gazette*, 27 March 1847.
49. See Kinealy, *Great Calamity*, pp. 90–106.
50. Russell to Bessborough, Russell Papers, PROL 30.22.6C, 21 April 1847.
51. Ibid., Bessborough to Russell, 23 April 1847.
52. Ibid., Bessborough to Russell, 5 April 1847.
53. Circular to Inspecting officer of each Union, *Freeman's*, 3 July 1847.
54. *Northern Star*, 17 July 1847.
55. Clarendon to Wood, Clarendon Papers, Bodleian Library, 12 August 1847.
56. Ibid., Clarendon to Russell, 5 July 1847.
57. Ibid., Clarendon to Russell, 5 July 1847.
58. Ibid., Clarendon to Lord Brougham, 10 August 1847.
59. Ibid., Clarendon to Wood, 2 August 1847.
60. Ibid., Clarendon to Charles Wood, 12 July 1847.
61. Ibid., Clarendon to Wood, 12 August 1847.
62. Ibid., Clarendon to the Marquis of Sligo, 14 August 1847.
63. Ibid., Marquis of Clanricarde to Clarendon, 15 August 1847.
64. Quoted in Grey, *Famine*, p. 180.
65. James Donnelly Jr., 'Mass Eviction and the Great Famine', in Póirtéir, *Irish Famine*, pp. 155–73.
66. For example, Charles Trevelyan, *Irish Crisis* (London, 1848).
67. *Hansard*, xcii, 6 May 1847.
68. The condemnation of absentee landlords was a constant theme throughout the famine in some of the less distressed parts of the country, e.g. resolution of Waterford Guardians, *Globe*, 18 January 1847.
69. *Hansard*, xci, (House of Lords) 19 March 1847, p. 202.
70. George Nicholls, *The Irish Poor Law* (London, 1856), pp. 309, 357.
71. Clarendon to Charles Wood, Clarendon Papers, 12 July 1847.
72. Ibid.
73. Ibid., 21 July 1847.
74. Ibid., Clarendon to Russell, 10 August 1847.
75. Ibid., Marquis of Clanricarde to Clarendon, 15 August 1847.

76. Abstract of Constabulary Reports, PROL, HO45 2416, March 1848.
77. Ibid., January–April 1848.
78. Ibid., for Waterford, PROL HO45 2416, 7 March 1848.
79. Clarendon to Russell, Clarendon Papers, 23 October 1847.
80. Ibid., Clarendon to Wood, 26 October 1847.
81. Ibid., Clarendon to Lord Brougham, 10 August 1847.
82. John Prest, *Lord John Russell* (London, 1972), p. 263.
83. On agreeing to take office, Peel had assured Russell that he would guide and support him, Peel to Russell, Russell Papers, marked Confidential, PROL 30 22 5A, 27 June 1846. By 1849, however, Peel was exasperated with the failure of the Whigs on a variety of fronts and opposed the introduction of the Rate-in-Aid, *Times*, 14 April 1849.
84. Scrope had rejected the Malthusian approach to poverty and defended the old Poor Law in England whilst calling for a more liberal version to be introduced into Ireland. Redvers Opie, 'A neglected English economist: George Poulett Scrope', in *Quarterly Journal of Economics*, xliv (1929), pp. 101–37.
85. Scrope to Russell, Russell Papers, PROL 30 22 5A, 23 June 1846.
86. *Times*, 14 April 1849.
87. *Hansard*, xci, 22 March 1847, p. 306.
88. *Roscommon and Leitrim*, 3 April 1847. Soyer was a French chef who was sent by the government to devise a recipe for making soup in the government soup kitchens at the beginning of 1847, see Kinealy, *Death Dealing Famine*, pp. 99–101.
89. *Northern Star*, 3 July 1847.
90. *Hansard*, xciii, p. 1014.
91. Ibid., xci, pp. 302–6.
92. Ibid., pp. 307–310.
93. *Hansard*, xci, 29 March 1847, pp. 572–4.
94. Ibid., pp. 571–4.
95. Ibid., p. 575.
96. Labouchere, Dublin Castle, Russell Papers, PROL 30.22.16.A, 1 January 1847.
97. Ibid., Labouchere to Russell, PROL 30.22.5.A, 2 January 1847.
98. Ibid.
99. *Hansard*, xci, 23 March 1847, p. 338.
100. Labouchere, Dublin Castle, Russell Papers, PROL 30.22.16.A, 1 January 1847: ibid., 30.22.5.A., 2 January 1847.
101. Bentinck felt that a line from Dublin to Galway should be the priority in order to open up the west of the country.
102. Hansard, xciii, 28 June 1847, pp. 984–90; pp. 1002–6.
103. Ibid., p. 1006.
104. *Globe*, 5 February 1847.
105. *Hansard*, xciii, pp. 994–8.
106. *Mercury*, 13 April 1847.
107. *Times*, 22 February 1847, 12 March 1847.
108. *Freeman's Journal*, 12 July 1849.
109. *Illustrated London News*, 29 July 1848.
110. *Times*, 4 October 1848.
111. Trevelyan to Russell, Russell Papers, 21 August 1848; Clarendon to Trevelyan, Letter Books, 21 September 1848.

112. *Liverpool Mercury*, 4 May 1849.
113. *Times*, 1 February 1849.
114. Clarendon to Russell, Clarendon Papers, 23 October 1847.
115. Ibid., Clarendon to George Grey, 7 December 1848.
116. Ibid., Clarendon to Russell, 12 February 1848.
117. Ibid., Clarendon to the Duke of Bedford, 16 February 1849.
118. *Hansard*, ciii, 1 March 1849.
119. *Armagh Guardian*, 19 March 1849.
120. *Newry Telegraph*, 6 March 1849.
121. Kinealy and MacAtasney, *Hidden Famine*, Chapter 2.
122. Clarendon to the Duke of Bedford, Clarendon Papers, 29 March 1849.
123. *Hansard*, ciii, 1 March 1849.
124. Twistleton to Trevelyan, marked Confidential, PROL, T64.370.C/3, 1 March 1848; ibid, Twistleton to Trevelyan, T64.370.B/1, 13 September 1848.
125. Evidence of Edward Twistleton, *Select Committee on the Irish Poor Law*, PP, 1849, xvi, pp. 711–14.
126. Ibid., p. 717.
127. *Freeman's*, 10 July 1849.
128. Ibid., 10 July 1849.
129. *Nation*, 18 July 1849.
130. *Liverpool Mercury*, 17 August 1849.
131. *Liverpool Mercury*, 7 August 1849.
132. *Freeman's*, 14 July 1849.
133. For example, Mary Duffy was found dead near Lurgan. The verdict of the jury was 'Death from want of common necessaries of life and exposure to the night air', *Freeman's*, 18 July 1849; for other cases, see also *Freeman's*, 16 July 1849.
134. *Freeman's*, 11 July 1849.
135. The deputation consisted of Mr Bright MP; Mr Scrope MP; Mr John O'Connell MP; Mr W. T. McCullagh MP; Mr W. Fagan MP; Mr A. O. Flaherty MP; Rev. Dr Miley; Rev. Mr King; Dr Gray; Mr R. R. Moore, *Freeman's*, 16 July 1849.
136. *Freeman's*, 18 July 1849.
137. Kinealy, *Great Calamity*, Chapter 5.
138. Ibid., for more on emigration, see Chapter 6.
139. One of the most famous quarantine stations was Grosse Ile in Canada (see Marianna O'Gallagher, 'The Orphans of Grosse Ile', in Patrick O'Sullivan (ed.), *The Meaning of the Famine* (Leicester, 1997), pp. 81–111. Emigrants to Liverpool suspected of carrying disease were placed on quarantine ships in the River Mersey (see Kinealy *Great Calamity*, Chapter 6).
140. *Freeman's Journal*, 12 July 1849.
141. M. Blole to Inspector General of Constabulary, Abstract of Constabulary Reports, PROL HO45 2416, 6 December 1848.
142. *Globe*, 7 January 1847.
143. Ibid., 9 February 1847.
144. The best exponent of this view of emigration is Kerby Miller, *Emigrants and Exiles* (New York, 1985), although it has been challenged, most notably by Donald Akenson. For more on the debate, see Andy Bielenberg (ed.), *The Irish Diaspora* (Essex, 2000).

3 Philanthropy and Private Donations

1. Frank Prochaska, *The Voluntary Impulse. Philanthropy in Modern Britain* (London, 1988), pp. xiii, 39–40.
2. Ibid., p. 6.
3. Frank Prochaska, *Women and Philanthropy in Nineteenth-Century England* (Oxford, 1980), p. 16.
4. *Globe and Traveller* (hereafter, *Globe*), 6 January 1847.
5. Prochaska, *Women and Philanthropy*, pp. 8–9.
6. Ibid., p. 92.
7. Ibid., pp. 102–3.
8. Ibid., pp. 5, 39.
9. Sir James Graham to Peel, 22 October 1845, C. S Parker, *Sir Robert Peel from his Private Letters* (London, 1899, vol. iii), p. 226.
10. Cabinet Memorandum, 1 November 1845, Lord Mahon and Right Hon. Edward Cardwell (eds), *Memoirs by the Right Hon. Sir Robert Peel* (London, 1857), p. 145.
11. *Freeman's*, 25 November 1847.
12. *Times*, 28 January 1847.
13. Ibid., 5 January 1847.
14. Ibid., 9 October 1847, 12 October 1847.
15. *Freeman's*, 13 January 1847.
16. *Globe*, 14 January 1847, 4 February 1847.
17. Peter Hart, PP to Archbishop Murray, Dublin Diocesan Archives, Murray Papers, 32/4, 19 June 1848.
18. Summary of Financial Returns showing the amount of poor rates collected in 1846 and 1847, *Relief of Distress, Fifth Series*,1848, lli, p. 674.
19. Annual Reports of Irish Poor Law Commissioners, 1845–50.
20. *Globe*, 1 January 1847.
21. Ibid., 1 January 1847.
22. Ibid., 2 January 1847.
23. *Roscommon and Leitrim Gazette*, 9 January 1847.
24. Kinealy and Mac Atasney, *Hidden Famine*, Chapter 2.
25. For example, the Fishmongers Company, landowners in Co. Derry, gave a 10 per cent reduction, *Globe*, 1 January 1847.
26. Ibid., 12 January 1847.
27. Ibid., 9 January 1847, 8 May 1847.
28. *Aris's Birmingham Gazette*, 24 November 1845, 23 February 1846.
29. *Roscommon and Leitrim Gazette*, 1 May 1847.
30. Gerard Mac Atasney, 'The Famine in Lurgan, 1845–47' (unpublished MA thesis, Queens University, 1995); *Globe*, 8 May 1847.
31. *Globe*, 18 January 1847.
32. Ibid., 9 January 1847.
33. *Northern Whig*, 6 April 1847.
34. *Londonderry Sentinel*, 6 February 1847.
35. *Royal Irish Art Union Journal*, 1 May 1847.
36. Trevelyan, *Irish Crisis*, p. 90; *Globe*, 15 January 1847.
37. List of Subscribers, *Report of British Relief Association for the Relief of the Extreme Distress in Ireland and Scotland* (London, 1849).

38. Kinealy and Mac Atasney, *Hidden Famine*, Chapter 5.

39. *Freeman's*, 1 January 1847.

40. *Globe*, 2 January 47.

41. *Report of the Proceedings of the General Central Relief Committee for all Ireland* (Dublin, 1848), pp. 7–11.

42. *Times*, 19 July 1849.

43. *Transactions of the Society of Friends* (Dublin, 1852).

44. Prochaska, *Women and Philanthropy*, p. 39.

45. Rob Goodbody, *A Suitable Channel: Quaker Relief in the Great Famine* (Dublin, 1995), pp. 10–16.

46. *Globe*, 5 January 1847.

47. Ibid., 6 January 1847.

48. Goodbody, *Suitable Channel*, p. 21.

49. Ibid., p. 24.

50. Ibid. pp. 10–16.

51. James H. Tuke, *A Visit to Connaught in the Summer of 1847* (London, 1847).

52. Cited in Jeanne A. Flood 'The Forster Family and the Irish Famine', in *Quaker History* (vol. 84, no. 2, Fall 1995), p. 120.

53. James H. Tuke, *Report of the Society of Friends on Distress in Ireland* (Dublin, 1847).

54. Ibid., p. 78.

55. Application by Ballymacarrett Relief Committee to Central Relief Committee of the Society of Friends, Papers of Society of Friends, NAD, U.B. 299, 10 May 1847; see also Kinealy and Mac Atasney, *Hidden Famine*, Chapter 3.

56. Letter from Relief Commissioners in Dublin to local relief committees, 27 March 1847, cited in *Dublin Evening Mail*, 5 April 1847.

57. Trevelyan to Pim, PROL T.64 367.B2, 24 August 1848; ibid., Pim to Trevelyan, 2 June 1849.

58. *Roscommon and Leitrim Gazette*, 10 July 1847.

59. Nicholson, *Annals*, p. 57.

60. See Kinealy and Mac Atasney, *Hidden Famine*, Chapter 5.

61. *Times*, 5 January 1847.

62. *Globe*, 7 January 1847.

63. *Freeman's*, 18 November 1847.

64. Trevelyan, *Irish Crisis*, pp. 87–8.

65. *Times*, 22 January 1847.

66. Minutes of British Relief Association, National Library of Ireland (NLI), 1 January 1847.

67. Strzelecki to Trevelyan, 10 February 1847, PROL T.64 369 B3; Strzelecki to Clarendon, 26 August 1848, Clarendon Letter Books, Bodleian Library.

68. I am grateful to the late T. P. O'Neill for giving me a copy of this correspondence, the originals are in the Monteagle Papers, NLI.

69. *Times*, 22 January 1847.

70. For more on this episode, see Christine Kinealy, 'Potatoes, Providence and Philanthropy', in O'Sullivan, *Meaning of Famine*, pp. 150–1.

71. *Freeman's*, 14 July 1849.

72. *Globe*, 6 January 1847.

73. Ibid., 12 January 1847.

74. Ibid., 11 February 1847.

75. *Times*, 22 January 1847.
76. Trevelyan, *Irish Crisis*, p. 86.
77. *Times*, 15 October 1847, 19 October 1847, 20 October 1847.
78. *Times*, 15 October 1847.
79. Trevelyan, *Irish Crisis*, p. 86.
80. *Times*, 6 March 1849.
81. Trevelyan to the Chairman of the British Relief Association, 20 August 1847, *Papers relating to proceedings for the relief of distress and state of the unions and workhouses in Ireland (4th ser. 1847–8)*, liv, p. 1.
82. Memorandum by Lord John Russell, PROL, 64 367 B, 30 April 1848.
83. *Globe*, 9 February 1847.
84. *Freeman's*, 2 July 1847.
85. *Northern Whig*, 24 April 1847.
86. *Roscommon and Leitrim Gazette*, 10 July 1847.
87. For more on this, see Kinealy, *Potatoes and Private Philanthropy*, in O'Sullivan, *Meaning of Famine*, pp. 161–2.
88. *Globe*, 9 February 1847.
89. *Freeman's*, 2 July 1847.
90. See Kinealy, *Great Calamity*, pp. 327–41; Frank Neal 'The Famine Irish in England and Ireland', in O'Sullivan, *Meaning of Famine*, pp. 65–77.
91. *Times*, 29 May 1848; *The Liberal* (Barbados) 20 January 1847, published an article on the sale of guns in Ireland.
92. Trevelyan, *Irish Crisis*, pp. 84–5.
93. *Cork Examiner*, 11 June 1847.
94. *Globe*, 11 January 1847.
95. *Roscommon and Leitrim Gazette*, 1 May 1847.
96. *Boston Pilot*, 12 December 1845. The conversion of dollars to pounds is based on calculation provided in Kerr, *Nation of Beggars*, p. 57.
97. H. A. Crosby Forbes and Henry Lee, *Massachusetts Help to Ireland during the Great Famine* (Massachusetts, 1967), pp. 3–6.
98. *Hartford Courant*, 17 March 1846, cited in Phil Gallagher, *An Account of American Relief to Ireland at the Time of the Great Hunger* (St Paul, 1996), p. 4.
99. *Boston Pilot*, 30 January 1847.
100. *Charleston Courier*, 8 February 1847.
101. *Boston Pilot*, 28 November 1846.
102. Ibid., 12 December 1846.
103. Ibid., 13 March 1847.
104. Gallagher, *American Relief*, p. 6.
105. *Boston Pilot*, 6 March 1847.
106. Nicholson, *Annals*, p. 55.
107. *Boston Pilot*, 10 April 1847.
108. John Hughes, Bishop of New York, *Antecedent Causes of the Irish Famine* (New York, 1847).
109. *National Intelligencer*, 11 February 1847.
110. *Charleston Courier*, 17 February 1847, 2 April 1847.
111. *Boston Pilot*, 13 March 1847.
112. *Charleston Courier*, 2 April 1847.
113. *Cork Examiner*, 16 April 1847.

114. *Boston Pilot*, 3 April 1847.

115. Ibid., 20 March 1847.

116. *Hansard*, xcii, 29 April 1847, pp. 127–8.

117. *Liverpool Mercury*, 10 April 1847.

118. Forbes and Lee, *Massachusetts Help*, p. 49.

119. Francis Costello, 'The Deer Island Graves, Boston', in O'Sullivan, *Meaning of Famine*, p. 117.

120. *Cork Examiner*, 16 April 1847.

121. *Cork Advertiser*, 15 April 1847.

122. *Connecticut Courant*, 8 May 1847, cited in Gallagher, *American Relief*, p. 15.

123. Forbes and Lee, *Massachusetts Help*, pp. 51–3.

124. Costello, 'Deer Island', p. 116.

125. Rourke, *Famine*, p. 508.

126. *Roscommon and Leitrim*, 27 March 1847.

127. *Boston Pilot*, 10 April 1847.

128. New York Roundtable, *New York and the Irish Famine* (New York, 1994).

129. *Boston Pilot*, 27 March 1847.

130. Ibid., 13 March 1847, 20 March 1847.

131. Ibid., 13 March 1847.

132. *Arkansas Intelligencer*, 8 May 1847.

133. Ibid.

134. *Cherokee Nation*, 6 May 1847.

135. Ibid., 10 June 1847.

136. Ibid., 13 May 1847.

137. Ibid., 15 July 1847.

138. Ibid.

139. Goodbody, *Suitable Channel*, p. 21.

140. *Charleston Courier*, 8 February 1847, 11 February 1847.

141. Earl of Elgin, Montreal, to Earl Grey, *Copies of Despatches to the Secretary of State for the Governors of Her Majesty's Colonial Possessions* (hereafter, *Copies of Despatches*), PP 1847 (853), liii, 28 May 1847.

142. *Hansard*, xci, pp. 821–4.

143. *Roscommon and Leitrim Gazette*, 17 April 1847.

144. *Report of General Relief Committee*, pp. 7–11.

145. Earl of Elgin, Montreal to Lord Grey, Colonial Office, 28 May 1847, *Copies of Despatches*, p. 7.

146. *Northern Star*, 24 July 1847.

147. *Northern Whig*, 8 May 1847.

148. Lieutenant Governor Graeme to Earl Grey, *Copies of Despatches*, 19 March 1847, p. 17.

149. O'Farrell 'Famine Irish in Australia', in O'Sullivan, *Meaning of Famine*, p. 128.

150. Ibid., pp. 129–30.

151. Ibid., p. 134.

152. Donal P. McCracken, 'The Land the Famine Irish Forgot', in E. Margaret Crawford (ed.), *The Hungry Stream Essays on Emigration and Famine* (Belfast, 1997), pp. 42–4.

153. *Freeman's*, 2 July 1847.

154. McCracken, *Land Famine Forgot*, p. 44.

155. *Roscommon and Leitrim Gazette*, 17 April 1847.

156. Trevelyan, *Irish Crisis*, p. 87.
157. *Report of British Relief Association*.
158. Trevelyan, *Irish Crisis*, pp. 87–8.
159. Kerr, *Nation of Beggars*, p. 59.
160. The main source for the role of Murray is the Murray Papers, in the Dublin Diocesan Archives.
161. David C. Sheehy, 'Archbishop Daniel Murray of Dublin and the Response of the Catholic Church to the Great Famine in Ireland', in *Link Up*, (December 1995), p. 41.
162. Ibid., p. 42.
163. *Globe*, 4 January 1847.
164. *Tablet*, 2 January 1847, 9 January 1847.
165. *Boston Pilot*, 6 March 1847.
166. Kerr, *Nation of Beggars*, p. 49.
167. *Tablet*, 12 May 1849.
168. *Times*, 30 January 1847.
169. Kerr, *Nation of Beggars*, p. 53.
170. *Times*, 20 May 1847.
171. Pius XI, *Pontificus Maximi Acta* (January 1847), Vatican Archives, Rome.
172. Kerr, *Nation of Beggars*, p. 53.
173. Report of the British Relief Association.
174. Sheehy, *Catholic Church*, p. 41.
175. *Freeman's*, 17 July 1847.
176. Ibid., 12 July 1849.
177. *Freeman's* 18 July 1849.
178. Ibid., 12 July 1849.
179. For example, Archbishop Crolly in Armagh donated £5, *Armagh Guardian*, 19 March 1849.
180. *Liverpool Mercury*, 7 August 1849.
181. *Times*, 6 March 1849.
182. *Banner of Ulster*, 12 January 1849.
183. *Times*, 12 May 1849.
184. *Freeman's*, 16 July 1849.
185. Ibid., 14 July 1849.
186. Ibid.
187. *Times*, 6 July 1849.
188. Russell to Clarendon, cited in Peter Mandler, *Aristocratic Government in the age of Reform; Whigs and Liberals 1830–52* (Oxford, 1990), p. 252.
189. *Boston Pilot*, 14 August 1847.
190. Ibid., 11 December 1847.
191. Ó Gráda, *Ireland Before and After the Famine*, p. 117.

4   Food Supply and Trade

1. J. Mitchel, *Jail Journal of Five Years in British Prisons* (New York, 1854), Introduction.
2. J. Mitchel, *The Last Conquest of Ireland (Perhaps)* (Glasgow, 1876), p. 219.

3. Patrick O'Farrell, 'Whose reality? The Irish Famine in History and Literature', in *Historical Studies* (vol. 20, 1982), pp. 1–13.
4. Graham Davis, 'The historiography of the Irish Famine', in O'Sullivan, *Meaning of Famine*, pp. 16–17.
5. Proponents of this viewpoint include diverse writers such as Mary Daly and Peter Gray. For an alternative interpretation, see Christine Kinealy, 'Food Exports from Ireland, 1846–47', in *History Ireland* (vol. 5, no. 1, 1997), pp. 32–6.
6. From the 1830s there was a cluster of extensive government enquiries into the condition of Ireland, the Poor Enquiry led by Archbishop Whately, 1833–6, is particularly valuable; overseas visitors such as de Tocqueville, Alexis de Tocqueville, *Journey in Ireland July to August 1835* (translated by Emmet Larkin, Washington, 1995).
7. Trevelyan, for example, estimated that planting took two weeks and digging between seven to ten days, Trevelyan, *Irish Crisis*, p. 4; for a contemporary description of the potato economy, see Mr and Mrs Hall, *Ireland, Its Scenery, Character etc.* (vol. 1, first pub. London, 1841).
8. Ibid.
9. Peter Solar, 'Agricultural Productivity and Economic Development in Ireland and Scotland in the early nineteenth century', in T. M. Devine and D. Dickson (eds), *Ireland and Scotland, 1600–1850* (1983), pp. 76–81.
10. Ó Gráda, *New Economic History*, pp. 24–9.
11. Roy Foster, *Modern Ireland*, pp. 200–1.
12. Ó Gráda, *Economic History*, p. 120.
13. Roger Scola, *Feeding the Victorian City: The Food Supply of Manchester 1770–1870* (Manchester, 1992), p. 45.
14. Ibid., p. 65.
15. Ibid., p. 82.
16. Cormac Ó Gráda, 'Poverty, population and agriculture, 1801–45', in W. J. Vaughan (ed.), *A New History of Ireland: Ireland Under the Union* (vol. v, Oxford, 1989).
17. Ó Gráda, *Economic History*, pp. 112–21.
18. The idea of a dual economy was most clearly stated by P. Lynch and J. Vaizey, *Guinness's Brewery in the Irish Economy, 1759–1876* (Cambridge, 1960).
19. *Hansard*, xciii, 28 June 1847, p. 1014.
20. John Killen, *The Famine Decade: Contemporary Accounts 1841–51* (Belfast, 1995), p. 2.
21. Christine Kinealy, 'Peel, rotten potatoes and providence: The repeal of the Corn Laws and the Irish Famine', in Andrew Marrison, *Free Trade and its Reception* (Routledge, 1998), pp. 50–62.
22. Poulett Scrope to Russell, Russell Papers, PROL, 30.22.5A, 23 June 1846.
23. *Belfast News-Letter*, 27 January 1847.
24. Ibid., 23 January 1846.
25. Richard Cobden to Russell, Russell Papers, PROL 30.22.5B, 4 July 1846.
26. *Belfast News-Letter*, 27 January 1846.
27. Ibid., 6 January 1846, 16 January 1846.
28. *Hansard*, lxxxv, 17 April 1847, p. 707.
29. Also see Chapter 5 for more details.
30. For more on riots in Dungarvon, see William Fraher, 'The Dungarvan Disturbances of 1846 and Sequels', in Des Cowman and Donald Brady (eds), *The Famine in Waterford* (Dublin, 1995), pp. 137–9.
31. Ibid., pp. 144–5.

32. Sir James Graham to Peel, 22 October 1845, *Peel*, p. 226.
33. Lord Heytesbury to Peel, Lord Mahon and Right Hon. Edward Cardwell (eds), *Memoirs by the Right Honourable Sir Robert Peel* (London, 1857) 17 October 1845, p. 125; ibid., Sir James Graham to Peel 19 October 1845, pp. 126–7.
34. *Belfast Vindicator*, 1 November 1845.
35. Ibid., 15 October 1845.
36. Cited in Canon John O'Rourke, *The Great Irish Famine* (first pub. 1874, reprinted Dublin, 1989), pp. 41–42.
37. *Northern Whig*, 25 November 1845.
38. Lord Heytesbury to Peel, Mahon, *Memoirs by Peel*, 27 October 1845, p. 138.
39. *Belfast Vindicator*, 15 October 1845.
40. *Belfast News-Letter*, 4 November 1845.
41. *Banner of Ulster*, 21 April 1846.
42. *Roscommon and Leitrim Gazette*, 2 January 1847.
43. *Northern Whig*, 26 December 1846.
44. *Vindicator*, 2 January 1847.
45. *Northern Whig*, 26 December 1846.
46. *Report of the House of Lords, to consider extending the functions of the Constabulary to suppressing Illicit Distilling*, PP 1854, x, pp. 458–9.
47. Ibid., *An Account Showing the Number of gallons of Proof Spirits . . . and materials from which made*, pp. 448–9.
48. *Vindicator*, 13 January 1847.
49. Ibid., p. 34.
50. Ibid., p. 50.
51. *Mark Lane Express*, 4 January 1847.
52. *Nation*, 12 June 1847.
53. *Hansard*, xci, 22 March 1847, pp. 312–3.
54. Bessborough to Russell, Russell Papers, PROL 30.22.6C, 12 April 1847.
55. *Roscommon and Leitrim*, 27 March 1847.
56. *Banner*, 17 November 1846.
57. *News-Letter*, 18 December 1846.
58. Ibid.
59. Petition of Richardson Bros., Belfast Merchants, and response, 26 August 1846, *Famine Papers* (Irish University Press, 1846–7), vol. v, pp. 455–6.
60. *Roscommon and Leitrim Gazette*, 2 January 1847
61. *Freeman's*, 13 March 1847.
62. *Roscommon and Leitrim Gazette*, 27 March 1847.
63. *Times*, 22 January 1847.
64. *Roscommon and Leitrim Gazette*, 27 March 1847.
65. *New York Herald* (hereafter *NY Herald*), 21 November 1846.
66. *Roscommon and Leitrim Gazette*, 2 January 1847.
67. Ibid., 9 January 1847.
68. *Galway Vindicator*, published in *Freeman's Journal*, 2 July 1847.
69. *Times*, 4 January 1847.
70. *Northern Star*, 3 July 1847.
71. Russell to Bessborough, Russell Papers, PROL 30.22.16.A, 30 January 1847; Roger Price, 'Poor Relief and Social Crisis in mid-Nineteenth Century France', in *European Studies Review* (October 1983), pp. 440–5.

72. Clarendon to Charles Wood, Clarendon Papers, 12 July 1847.
73. Bessborough to Russell, Russell Papers, PROL 30.22.16.A, 23 January 1847.
74. *Hansard*, xcii, 11 May 1847.
75. Ibid., xcii, 17 May 1847.
76. Ibid.
77. Trevelyan, *Irish Crisis*.
78. Sir James Graham cited in *Coleraine Chronicle*, 2 May 1846.
79. *Belfast News-Letter*, 13 January 1846.
80. *NY Herald*, 21 November 1846.
81. David Sheehy, 'Archbishop Daniel Murray of Dublin and the Response of the Catholic Church to the Great Famine in Ireland', in *Link-Up* (December 1995), p. 40.
82. Charles Trevelyan, *The Irish Crisis* (Edinburgh Review, 1848).
83. Isaac Butt, *A Voice for Ireland: The Famine in the Land* (Dublin, 1847); Butt, from being a defender of the Union, went on to become a founder of the Home Rule movement.
84. *Nation*, 12 June 1847.
85. Ibid.
86. Charles Trevelyan, *The Irish Crisis*.
87. Ibid., p. 52.
88. *The Globe and Traveller*, 2 January 1847.
89. This view that reduction in exports was due to higher consumption in the home market, propagated by the Whig government at the time, has widely been accepted by contemporary historians, for example Graham Davis, 'The Historiography of the Irish Famine', in O'Sullivan, *The Meaning of the Famine*, p. 31.
90. See Chapter 2.
91. *Hansard*, xciii, 30 June 1847, pp. 1057–9.
92. *Times*, 22 January 1847.
93. Ibid., 18 March 1847.
94. Cited in *Times*, 18 March 1847.
95. *Times*, 27 February 1847.
96. *Northern Star*, 3 July 1847.
97. *Mercury*, 13 April 1847.
98. *Times*, 6 February 1847.
99. Ibid., 8 March 1847.
100. Ibid., 18 March 1847.
101. *Hansard*, xci, 22 March 1847, p. 306.
102. Ibid., p. 310.
103. Ibid., p. 313.
104. Bessborough to Clarendon, Russell Papers, PROL 30.22.16.A, 23 January 1847.
105. Clarendon to Russell, Clarendon Papers, Bodleian Library, 12 July 1847.
106. Ibid., Clarendon to Russell, 15 July 1847.
107. Ibid., Clarendon to Charles Wood, 12 July 1847.
108. *Globe*, 7 January 1847.
109. Ibid., 9 January 1847.
110. Ibid., 11 February 1847.
111. *NY Herald*, 21 November 1846.
112. Gray, *The Irish Famine*, p. 46.

113. Ó Gráda, *Black '47*, p. 124.
114. Bourke, *Visitation*, p. 168.
115. Sen, *Entitlements*.
116. *Nation*, 12 June 1847.
117. *Mark Lane Express*, 18 January 1847.
118. All the data provided is extracted from the Bills of Entry.
119. *Supplementary Appendix to Seventh Report of Relief Commissioners*, PP 1847–8, xxix, p. 58.
120. Captain Kennedy to P. L. Commissioners, 13 April 1847, *Copies of the correspondence between the Poor Law Commissioners of Ireland and their Inspector, relative to the statements contained in an extract from a book entitled, 'Gleanings in the west of Ireland'*, 1851, xlix, p. 6.
121. *Report of the Select Committee appointed to enquire into the Administration of the Poor Law in the Kilrush Union since 19 September 1848*, PP 1850, xi.
122. *Fourth Annual Report of P. L. Commissioners*, 1851, pp. 4–8; *Fifth Annual Report of P. L. Commissioners*, 1852.
123. *Seventh Report of Relief Commissioners*, p. 19.
124. Bills of Entry.
125. *Seventh Report of Relief Commissioners*, p. 21.
126. Kinealy, *Great Calamity*, pp. 175–80.
127. Minutes of Westport Union, (NLI) 25 August 1847, 8 September 1847.
128. Kinealy, *Great Calamity*, pp. 207–8.
129. Bills of Entry.
130. B. Poole, *Statistics of British Commerce* (London, 1852), p. 148.
131. *Mark Lane Express*, 18 January 1847.
132. *Freeman's*, 16 July 1849.
133. Ibid.
134. *Banner of Ulster*, cited in *Freeman's*, 18 July 1849.
135. Ibid.
136. Thomas Carlyle, *Reminiscences of My Irish Journey in 1849* (London, 1882), p. 182.

5 Riot, Protest and Popular Agitation

1. See, for example, Nicholson, *Annals of the Famine*, pp. 77–8; *Cork Examiner*, 1 January 1847.
2. Michael Davitt, *The Fall of Feudalism in Ireland* (London, 1904), p. 48.
3. Tom Garvin, 'Defenders, Ribbonmen and Others; underground political networks in pre-Famine Ireland', in *Past and Present*, 96 (1982), pp. 133–55.
4. Earl Grey in House of Lords, *Hansard*, 23 March 1846.
5. Nicholson, *Annals*, p. 28.
6. Curtis, *Cause of Ireland*, pp. 32–3.
7. John Saville, *1848: The British State and the Chartist Movement* (Cambridge, 1990), pp. 35–6.
8. James McKnight, *The Ulster Tenants' Claim of Right, or, Land Ownership a State Trust* (Dublin, 1848).
9. *Hansard*, xxx, 26 August 1835.

10. Peel to Wellington, Parker, *Peel*, ii, p. 120.

11. *Report from Her Majesty's Commissioners of Inquiry into the State of the Law and Practice in Relation to the Occupation of Land in Ireland* (Devon Commission), PP 1845 xix, pp. 37–8.

12. Memorandum of Sir Robert Peel, 12 January 1829.

13. Sir James Graham, quoted by Earl Grey, *Hansard*, House of Commons, 23 March 1846.

14. Sean Connolly (ed.), *Oxford Companion to Irish History* (Oxford, 1998), p. 101.

15. *Hansard*, xxiv, 802–4, 23 June 1834.

16. Ibid., xlvii, 18 April 1839.

17. Cited in Grey, *Famine and Land*, p. 32.

18. Duke of Wellington to Peel, 25 January 1845, Charles Stuart Parker, *Sir Robert Peel from his Private Papers* (2nd edn., London, 1899, vol. iii), p. 178.

19. Devon Commission, pp. 37–8.

20. Sir James Graham to Peel, 3 October 1845, Parker, *Robert Peel*, p. 190.

21. *Fraser's Magazine*, vol. xxviii, December 1843.

22. *Blackwood's Edinburgh Magazine*, lix, May 1846.

23. *Hansard*, lxxxv, 30 March 1846, pp. 338–9.

24. Ibid., lxxxiii, 23 February 1846.

25. Ibid., 23 February 1847, pp. 137–8.

26. Mr Arbuthnot to Peel, 8 June 1848, Parker, *Robert Peel*, p. 351.

27. Ibid., 7 June, p. 351.

28. *Morning Chronicle*, 21 January 1846.

29. Russell to Clarendon, marked Confidential, Russell Papers, PROL 30 22 5A, 29 June 1846.

30. *Freeman's*, 4 August 1846.

31. *Hansard*, xcii, 11 May 1847, 15 May 1847.

32. The best insight into the workings of the moral economy continues to be E. P. Thompson, 'The Moral Economy of the English Crowd in the Eighteenth Century', in *Past and Present*, 50 (1971).

33. *Roscommon and Leitrim Gazette*, 2 January 1847.

34. Ibid., 2 January 1847.

35. *NY Herald*, 21 November 1846.

36. *Illustrated London News*, 25 June 1842.

37. Ibid.

38. Andrés Eiríksson, 'Food Supply and Food Riots', in Cormac Ó Gráda, *Famine 150* (Dublin, 1997), p. 75.

39. John Coghlan PP to Bernard Owen JP, Relief Commission Papers, NAD, Z.5748, 18 March 1846.

40. *Illustrated London News*, 18 April 1846.

41. Abstract of Constabulary Reports, PROL, HO45 1080, March and April 1846.

42. Grey, *Famine and Land*, p. 121.

43. Dobree to Trevelyan, 24 April 1846, *Correspondence Explanatory of Relief Measures . . .* , Commissariat Series, PP 1846, [735] xxxvii, pp. 174–5.

44. Dobree to Trevelyan, 24 April 1846, Correspondence Explanatory, Commissariat Series, PP 1846, [735] xxxvii, pp. 174–5.

45. Daniel O'Connell to Russell, Russell Papers, PROL 30.22.5B, 12 August 1846.

46. *Times*, 4 January 1847, 7 January 1847.

47. *Roscommon and Leitrim Gazette*, 2 January 1847.
48. Routh to Trevelyan, 29 September 1846, *Correspondence Relating to the Relief of Distress in Ireland*, Commissariat Series, 1847, li, p. 119.
49. Ibid., Trevelyan to the Earl of Auckland, 1 October 1846, pp. 127–8.
50. Ibid., Mr Lowe to Sir H. Pigot, 20 October 1846, p. 219.
51. *NY Herald*, 21 November 1846.
52. *Roscommon and Leitrim Gazette*, 9 January 1847.
53. Edward Waldren PP to Lord Lieutenant, CSORP, NAD, I. 6336, 21 May 1847.
54. Memorial of the Parish Priest and Inhabitants of Erris to the Lord Lieutenant, NAD, Distress Papers 4467, 24 August 1846.
55. Quoted in Kerr, *Catholic Church*, p. 11.
56. Ibid., pp. 11–13.
57. Abstract of Constabulary Reports (ACR) for Clare, PROL HO45, 2416, 15 March 1848.
58. ACR, PROL, HO45 1080, March and April 1846.
59. From *Kerry Examiner*, quoted in *Freeman's Journal*, 30 November 1846.
60. *Roscommon and Leitrim Gazette*, 24 April 1847.
61. Kinealy and Mac Atasney, *Hidden Famine*, Chapter 2.
62. *Freeman's*, 30 November 1846.
63. Ibid.
64. *Illustrated London News*, 16 January 1847.
65. Ibid., 9 January 1847.
66. *Freeman's*, 13 January 1847.
67. *The Globe and Traveller*, 11 January 1847.
68. Ibid., 12 January 1847.
69. Ibid., 11 January 1847.
70. *Cork Examiner*, 8 February 1847.
71. Devine, *Highland Famine*.
72. *Roscommon and Leitrim Gazette*, 15 May 1847.
73. From *John O Groats Journal*, quoted in *Freeman's*, 13 March 1847.
74. *NY Herald*, 24 July 1846.
75. Ibid.
76. *Roscommon and Leitrim Gazette*, 13 March 1847, 15 May 1847.
77. *Freeman's*, 2 July 1847.
78. Kerr, *Catholic Church*, p. 7.
79. ACR, PROL, HO45 1080, 18 October 1846.
80. *Roscommon and Leitrim Gazette*, 2 January 1847.
81. 'A Return of Outrages showing the names of the persons injured etc.', *Correspondence from January to March 1847 relating to the Measures adopted for the relief of distress in Ireland*, 797, ii, pp. 60–4.
82. Ibid., pp. 60–9.
83. Analysis of the variation of Employment on the Public Works in 1846 in Kinealy, *Great Calamity*, pp. 363–5.
84. *Limerick Reporter*, 21 August 1846.
85. Ibid., 16 October 1846.
86. Ibid.
87. Ibid.
88. ACR, PROL, HO45 1080, October 1846.

89. Fraher, 'Dungarvan Disturbances', in *Famine in Waterford*, pp. 138–9.
90. *Cork Examiner*, 30 September 1846.
91. *Illustrated London News*, 7 November 1846.
92. Fraher, 'Dungarvan Disturbances', in *Famine in Waterford*, pp. 143–4.
93. Memorial of the Dungarvan Union, Relief Commission Papers, 0.4194, NAD, 22 March 1847.
94. *Roscommon and Leitrim Gazette*, 27 March 1847.
95. Póirtéir, *Famine Echoes*, pp. 68–84.
96. *Times*, 18 March 1847.
97. *Mercury*, 13 April 1847.
98. *Cork Examiner*, 2 April 1847.
99. *Roscommon and Leitrim Gazette*, 24 April 1847.
100. *Cork Examiner*, 19 April 1847.
101. *Roscommon and Leitrim Gazette*, 22 May 1847.
102. *Northern Whig*, 8 May 1847, 13 May 1847.
103. From *Ballinasloe Star*, quoted in *Northern Whig*, 13 May 1847.
104. Galway Guardians to Relief Commissioners, PROL, HO45 1942, 1 June 1847.
105. *Roscommon and Leitrim Gazette*, 10 July 1847.
106. *Meath Herald*, in *Roscommon and Leitrim Gazette*, 29 May 1847.
107. From *Clare Journal*, in *Roscommon and Leitrim Gazette*, 22 May 1847.
108. *Limerick Reporter*, 11 May 1847, 18 May 1847.
109. *Roscommon and Leitrim Gazette*, 3 July 1847.
110. Ibid.,12 June 1847.
111. Joseph Burke, PLI to PLC, Letter Books of Joseph Burke, NAD, 29 December 1847, 12 October 1847, 12 January 1848, 17 April 1848.
112. Fraher, 'Disturbances in Dungarvan', in *Famine in Waterford*, pp. 148–50.
113. Eiríksson, 'Food Supply', in *Famine 150*, p. 68.
114. Irish Crime Records, National Archives, Dublin.
115. Stephen J. Campbell, *The Great Irish Famine: Words and Images from the Famine Museum, Strokestown Park, County Roscommon* (Roscommon, 1994).
116. *Criminal Tables for the Year 1848*, PP 1849, xliv, p. 132.
117. Clarendon to Russell, Clarendon Papers, Bodleian Library, 5 July 1847.
118. Confidential Report from Dublin Castle to Magistrates, PROL HO45 1793, 4 November 1847.
119. *Criminal Tables*, p. 131.
120. Ibid.
121. *Return from the County Gaols and Workhouses in Ireland of the Daily Diet allowed to an Able-Bodied Man*, PP 1847–48 (486), liii.
122. *Times*, 30 July 1849.
123. *Twenty-Sixth Report of the Inspectors-General of Prisons in Ireland*, PP 1847, xxxiv.
124. Ibid.
125. Nicholson, *Annals*, pp. 152–3.
126. *Twenty-Seventh Report of the Inspectors-General of Prisons in Ireland* (373) xxvi.
127. *Criminal Tables*, p. 131.
128. 10 & 11 Vict. Cap. 84. *An Act to Make Provision for the Punishment of Vagrants and Persons offending against the Laws in Force for the Relief of the Destitute Poor In Ireland*, 22 July 1847.

129. Captain Hellard, PLI to P. L. Commissioners, 19 December 1847, *Papers Relating to the Proceedings for Relief of Distress, and the state of Unions and Workhouses in Ireland*, 5th series, 1848, lli, p. 455.
130. *Cork Examiner*, 22 October 1847.
131. *Vindicator*, 13 January 1847.
132. For more on folk memories of theft, see 'No Sin and You Starving', in Póirtéir, *Famine Echoes*, pp. 68–84.
133. *Criminal Tables*, p. 131
134. *Cork Examiner*, 10 May 1847.
135. Tables of Deaths, Census for 1851, quoted in Killen, *Famine Decade*, p. 247.
136. See Gerard Mac Atasney, *This Dreadful Visitation: The Famine in Lurgan//Portadown* (Belfast, 1997), p. 44.
137. *Roscommon and Leitrim Gazette*, 22 May 1847.
138. Outrage Papers for County Mayo, NAD, 12 May 1847.
139. Ibid. Petition of 34 Petitioners to Lord Lieutenant, 29 May 1847.
140. *Cork Examiner*, 31 March 1847.
141. Clarendon to Russell, Clarendon Papers Bodleian, 8 August 1847.
142. *Times*, 4 January1847.
143. Ibid., 22 January 1847.
144. Ibid., 24 March 1847.
145. *Roscommon and Leitrim Gazette*, 15 May 1847.
146. *Times*, 15 October 1847.
147. *Vindicator*, 13 January 1847.
148. *NY Herald*, 21 November 1846.
149. *Mercury*, 13 April 1847.
150. Memorial from Magistrates in Nenagh to Lord Lieutenant, PROL, HO45 1793, 15 November 1847.
151. *Hansard*, xcii, 6 May 1847.
152. *Morning Chronicle*, quoted in *Cork Examiner*, 15 November 1847.
153. *Times*, 6 October 1847, 22 April 1850.
154. The clause regarding rating had been introduced in 1843; Lucius O'Brien, *Hansard*, xciii, 4 July 1848.
155. James Connolly Jr., 'Mass Evictions and the Great Famine', in Póirtéir, *Irish Famine*, pp. 155–73.
156. *Hansard*, lxxxv, 485, 2 April 1846.
157. *Illustrated London News*, 4 April 1846.
158. *NY Herald*, 21 November 1846.
159. Russell to Clarendon, Clarendon Papers, 8 November 1847.
160. *Times*, 22 April 1850.
161. *Illustrated London News*, 30 October 1847.
162. *Times*, 12 July 1849.
163. *Freeman's*, quoted in *Cork Examiner*, 5 November 1847.
164. *Times*, 17 November 1847.
165. Palmerston to Clarendon, Clarendon Papers, 13 November 1847.
166. Grey, *Famine and Land*, p. 183.
167. Russell to Clarendon, Clarendon Papers, 10 November 1847.
168. *Hansard*, xcv, 3225–8, 29 November 1847.
169. Proclamation under the Act for the Prevention of Crime and Outrage in Ireland.

170. Clarendon to Peel, 24 Oct. 1849, Parker, *Peel*, iii, p. 517.

171. Russell to Clarendon, Clarendon Papers, 5 February 1849.

172. Theodore K. Hoppen, *Elections, Politics and Society in Ireland*, p. 414

173. Ibid., p. 371.

174. Russell to Clarendon, Russell Papers, PROL, 30 22 5A, 23 June 1847; Russell to Clarendon, 15 November 1847, H. E. Maxwell, *The Life and Letters of the Fourth Earl of Clarendon* (2 vols, London, 1913), p. 282.

175. Kerr, *Nation of Beggars*, p. 201.

176. *Banner of Ulster*, 27 February 1849.

177. J. S. Kennedy, *Standing Rules and Regulations for the Government and Guidance of the Constabulary Force in Ireland* (Dublin, 1837).

178. Appendix P. , *The Consequences of Extending the Functions of the Constabulary in Ireland to the Suppression or Distillation of Illegal Distillation*, PP, 1854, x.

179. Trevelyan to the Earl of Auckland, 1 October 1846, *Commissariat Correspondence*, p. 127.

180. Clarendon to Russell, Clarendon Papers, Bodleian Library, 5 July 1847.

181. Lady Wilde (Speranza), *The Famine Year*, reprinted in Christopher Morash (ed.), *The Hungry Voice: The Poetry of the Irish Famine* (Irish Academic Press, 1989), p. 221. Jane Elgee married William Wilde in 1851 and was the mother of Oscar Wilde.

182. Quoted in Woodham-Smith, *Great Hunger*, p. 132.

183. *Times*, 6 October 1847.

184. Palmer Kirkwood, rate collector, Killala to Poor Law Commission, 26 May 1847, quoted in Swords, *In Their Own Words*, p. 186.

185. *NY Herald*, 21 November 1846.

186. For more on conflict between Routh and Trevelyan, see Kinealy, *Great Calamity*, pp. 43–51.

187. *Globe and Traveller*, 12 January 1847.

188. W. J. Lowe, 'Policing Famine Ireland', in *Eire-Ireland* (1994), pp. 47–67.

189. *Cork Examiner*, 4 November 1846.

190. Charles Trevelyan, *The Irish Crisis* (London, 1848), p. 84.

191. *Royal Irish Art Union Monthly Journal*, 1 May 1847.

192. *Freeman's*, 2 July 1847.

193. Recollection of Philib Ó Connaill, national teacher, Navan, County Meath, in Cathal Póirtéir, *Famine Echoes*, p. 71.

6 Religion and the Churches

1. A small publication which provides a valuable insight into the work of the Catholic Church is Donal Kerr, *The Catholic Church and the Famine* (Dublin, 1996).

2. *Transactions of the Central Relief Committee of the Society of Friends during the Famine in Ireland in 1846 and 1847* (Dublin, 1852).

3. Póirtéir, *Famine Echoes*, particularly Chapter 11, 'Soupers, Jumpers and Cat Breacs' – all of which were pejorative terms for those who 'took the soup'.

4. Irene Whelan, 'The Stigma of Souperism', in Cathal Póirtéir (ed.), *The Great Irish Famine* (Cork, 1995), p. 135.

5. E. Larkin, *The Consolidation of the Roman Catholic Church in Ireland, 1860–70* (Chapel Hill, 1987).

6. Kerr, *Nation of Beggars*, pp. 14–15.

7. *Freeman's*, 11 January 1847.

8. *Freeman's*, 11 November 1846.

9. *Northern Star*, 3 July 1847.

10. For example, on 3 July 1847 the *Freeman's Journal* when reporting the death of Dr Cummins, the parish priest of Killenaule, who although 'in the prime of his life' died from 'malignant fever in administering to the spiritual and temporal wants and necessities of the poor of his parish'. It also recorded the death of the eighth Roman Catholic clergyman in Liverpool from 'famine fever'.

11. *Globe*, 12 January 1847.

12. *Banner of Ulster*, 30 March 1849.

13. Routh to Trevelyan, *Correspondence relating to the Relief of Distress in Ireland (Commissariat Series)* PP 1847, li, 15 December 1846; ibid., Trevelyan to Routh, 18 December 1846.

14. *Times*, 24 December 1846, 7 January 1847.

15. For example, Lord Dufferin and the Hon. Boyle, two Oxford students, travelled to Skibbereen to judge if descriptions of the suffering had been exaggerated. They found the opposite to be true and published *Narrative of the Journey from Oxford to Skibbereen during the Year of the Irish Famine by Lord Dufferin and the Honourable G. F. Boyle* (Oxford, 1847).

16. Patrick Hickey, 'The Famine in the Skibbereen Union', in Póirtéir, *Great Irish Famine*, pp. 197–8.

17. *Freeman's*, 16 July 1849.

18. *Times*, 22 January 1847.

19. *Hansard*, xci, 23 March 1847, pp. 335–7.

20. Minutes of Fisherwick Presbyterian Church, Belfast, Presbyterian Church House, Mic/1P/92, 24 March 1847.

21. Charles Trevelyan, *Irish Crisis*, p. 86.

22. *Times*, 19 October 1847.

23. *Wexford Independent*, 1 January 1848.

24. *Freeman's*, 12 July 1849.

25. Kerr, *Nation of Beggars*, pp. 49–50.

26. *Freeman's*, 11 July 1849.

27. Ibid., 5 August 1846.

28. Ibid., 22 August 1846.

29. *Times*, 6 March 1847, 27 March 1847.

30. *Northern Whig*, 11 March 1847.

31. *Roscommon and Leitrim Gazette*, 2 January 1847, 24 April 1847.

32. *Banner of Ulster*, 15 January 1847.

33. Evidence of Joseph Bewley, *Report of the Select Committee of the House of Commons on the Poor Law (Ireland) 1849*, xv, 2nd part, pp. 952, 964.

34. James H. Tuke, 'Report of the Society of Friends on Distress in Ireland', NLI, Ms. Ir.9410859.

35. Trevelyan to Lord Lieutenant, PROL, T.64.369 B 1, 14 December 1847; ibid., Trevelyan to Jonathan Pim, Society of Friends, T.64.367.B 2, 24 August 1848; Pim to Trevelyan, 5 June 1849, *Transactions of the Society of Friends* (Dublin, 1852), pp. 452–4.

36. Minutes of Fisherwick Place, 24 March 1847.
37. *Freeman's*, 5 November 1846. In 1850 Wiseman was at the centre of a controversy when the Pope decided to restore ecclesiastical titles to the Catholic hierarchy in England, thus making Wiseman the Archbishop of Westminster.
38. Desmond Bowen, *The Protestant Crusade in Ireland, 1800–1870* (Dublin, 1978).
39. Kerr, *Nation of Beggars*, p. 206.
40. *Ulster Times*, 21 July 1838.
41. Ibid., 20 November 1838.
42. For example, *Ulster Times*, 20 November 1838; *Belfast Protestant Journal*, 4 July 1846; and in Dublin, *Protestant Watchman*.
43. Ibid., 27 November 1838.
44. Presbyterian Registers of Fitzroy Congregation, (Alfred Street) PRONI, 1P/14/1, 11 October 1846, 11 July 1847, 10 November 1847.
45. *Protestant Watchman* (Dublin), 13 December 1838.
46. Ibid., 20 December 1838.
47. Jonathan Bardon, *A History of Ulster* (Belfast, 1997), pp. 252–3.
48. Alexander Somerville, *Letters from Ireland during the Famine of 1847* ed. D. K. M. Snell (Dublin, 1994), pp. 76–7.
49. *History Ireland*, pp. 35–6.
50. *Freeman's Journal*, 25 September 1847.
51. William Marrable, *The Rise and Progress of the Irish Church Missions* (Dublin, 1850).
52. Cited in Flan Campbell, *Protestant Dissenting Tradition*, p. 206.
53. *Protestant Watchman* (Dublin), 12 May 1848.
54. Ibid., p. 37.
55. Niall R. Branch, 'Edward Nangle and the Achill Island Mission', in *History Ireland*, 8:3, (Autumn 2000), p. 38.
56. Ibid.
57. William Flannelly, PP to Archbishop Murray, 6 April 1848, quoted in Kerr, *Nation of Beggars*, p. 208.
58. Póirtéir, *Famine Echoes*, pp. 166–81. This publication is based on a survey undertaken by the Irish Folklore Commission in the 1830s, which is now housed in University College, Dublin.
59. *Freeman's*, 25 September 1847.
60. *Cork Examiner*, 25 October 1847.
61. *Belfast News-Letter*, 9 July 1847.
62. *Belfast Protestant Journal*, 18 July 1846.
63. Ibid., 7 November 1846.
64. Ibid., 17 July 1847.
65. *Times*, 6 October 1847.
66. *Hansard*, xcii, 11 March 1847.
67. Ibid., 20 November 1847.
68. *Banner of Ulster*, 9 January 1849.
69. Ibid., 20 February 1849.
70. Michael Brannigan, Missionary of the General Assembly of the Presbyterian Church in Ireland, *Banner of Ulster*, 12 January 1849.
71. Ó Gráda, *Black '47*, p. 185.
72. *Western Times*, cited in *Freeman's*, 13 January 1847.
73. *Banner of Ulster*, 8 January 1847.

74. R. Whately, *The Right use of National Afflictions being a charge delivered on 19 and 22 September 1848* (Dublin, 1848).

75. *Liverpool Mercury*, 3 August 1849.

76. Nicholson, *Annals*, pp. 181–2.

77. Ibid., p. 106.

78. Ibid., p. 125.

79. *Freeman's*, 2 July 1847.

80. Ibid., 25 September 1847.

81. *Mercury*, 20 April 1847.

82. Nicholson, *Annals*, p. 182.

83. Abstract of Constabulary Reports, PROL HO45 2416, 31 March 1848.

84. *Banner of Ulster*, 23 January 1849.

85. *Times*, 17 August 1849.

86. *Freeman's*, 26 August 1847.

87. Kerr, *Nation of Beggars*, pp. 209–10.

88. Kerr, *Catholic Church*, p. 88.

89. Kerr, *Nation of Beggars*, p. 212.

90. P. C. Barry, 'The Legislation of the Synod of Thurles, 1850', in *Irish Theological Quarterly*, 26 (1959), pp. 131–66.

91. *Banner of Ulster*, 16 February 1849.

92. A. Dallas, *The Story of the Irish Church Missions, continued to 1869* (London, 1875).

93. John Edgar DD, *Ireland's Field Mission*, A Paper read at the Sixth Annual Conference of the British Organization, 1852.

94. T. P. O'Neill, 'Sidelights on Souperism', in *Irish Ecclesiastical Record*, 71 (5th ser., 1949), pp. 50–64.

95. *Ulster Times*, 21 July 1838.

96. *Ulster Times*, 20 November 1838.

97. *Belfast Protestant Journal*, 18 March 1848.

98. Ibid.,11 July 1846.

99. Ibid., 17 July 1847, 18 July 1846

100. *Wexford Independent*, 19 July 1848.

101. *Belfast Protestant Journal*, 7 November 1846.

102. Russell to Monteagle, Monteagle Papers, NLI, 12 November 1848.

103. Clarendon to Russell, Clarendon Papers, 12 July 1847.

104. Ibid., Clarendon to Hon. Blake, 26 July 1847

105. Ibid., Clarendon to Russell, 16 July 1847.

106. Ibid., Clarendon to Hon. Blake, 26 July 1847.

107. Ibid., Clarendon to Russell, 31 July 1847.

108. Ibid., Clarendon to Russell, 26 October 1847.

109. *St James Chronicle*, 26 October 1847.

110. Clarendon to Marquis of Lansdowne, Clarendon Papers, 26 October 1847.

111. *St James's Chronicle*, 26 October 1847.

112. *St James's Chronicle*, 26 October 1847.

113. E. E. Y. Hayes, *Pio Nono: A Study in European Politics and Religion in the Nineteenth Century* (London, 1954), pp. 17–81.

114. Clarendon to Russell, Clarendon Papers, 23 October 1847.

115. *Nation*, 13 May 1848.

116. *Wexford Independent*, 12 July 1848.

117. *Hansard*, c, 21 July 1848, p. 639.
118. Abstract of Constabulary Reports, PROL, HO45 2416, 16 March 1848.
119. *Hansard*, c, 21 July 1848, p. 632.
120. Ibid.,c, 24 July 1848, pp. 755–6.
121. *Illustrated London News*, 5 August 1848.
122. Clarendon to Monteagle, Monteagle Papers, NLI, 20 February 1849.
123. *Freeman's*, 14 July 1849.
124. There were only three archbishops at the time because the vacancy in Armagh had not been filled.
125. Kerr, *Nation of Beggars*, pp. 203–4.
126. *Banner of Ulster*, 14 August 1849.
127. *Times*, 30 July 1849.
128. *Banner of Ulster*, 3 August 1849.
129. *Belfast News-Letter*, 11 August 1849.
130. Mr Anson, Secretary to Queen to Providence Home, cited in *Liverpool Mercury*, 3 August 1849.
131. *Times*, 30 August 1849.
132. *Banner of Ulster*, 10 August 1849.
133. Ibid., 14 August 1849.
134. Ibid., 17 August 1849.
135. *Liverpool Mercury*, 7 August 1849.
136. Lee, *The Modernization of Irish Society* (Dublin, 1973), p. 47.
137. *Banner of Ulster*, 3 March 1849.
138. Ibid., 9 March 1849.
139. Kinealy and Mac Atasney, *Hidden Famine*, Chapter 1.
140. Ó Gráda, *Black '47*, p. 86,based on his study of Anglican parish registers in Cork and Dublin; Kinealy and Parkhill, *Famine in Ulster*.
141. *Times*, 27 October 1850.
142. Ibid., 6 November 1850.
143. *Times*, cited in *Wexford Independent*, 4 January 1851.
144. *Nation*, 22 February 1851.
145. Ibid., 1 March 1851.
146. *Wexford Independent*, 1 January 1851.
147. *Nation*, 1 March 1851.
148. Clarendon to Russell, Clarendon Papers, 28 March 12851; ibid., Clarendon to George Grey, 1 April 1851.
149. *Hansard*, cxiv, 7 February 1851.
150. Clarendon to Russell, Clarendon Papers, 13 October 1847; *St James's Chronicle*, 26 October 1847.
151. 'Lord Clarendon's Policy in Ireland', in *Dublin University Magazine*, 37 (1851), pp. 136–58.
152. *Nation*, 22 February 1851.
153. *Hansard*, cxv, 20 March 1851.
154. *Wexford Independent*, 15 January 1851, 25 January 1851.
155. *Times*, 9 December 1850.
156. Clarendon to Russell, Clarendon Papers, 23 February 1851.
157. R. K. Webb, *Modern England: From the Eighteenth Century to the Present* (2nd edn, Routledge, 1994), p. 306.

158. Ibid.
159. *Freeman's*, 27 December 1851.
160. *Tablet*, 23 August 1851.
161. Kerr, *Nation of Beggars*, pp. 310–24.

7   Repeal, Relief and Rebellion

1. There are many publications on Daniel O'Connell: Oliver MacDonagh, *The Hereditary Bondsman: Daniel O'Connell 1775–1829* (London, 1988); Oliver MacDonagh, *The Emancipist: Daniel O'Connell 1830–47* (London, 1989).
2. K. Theodore Hoppen, 'Politics, the law, and the nature of the Irish electorate 1832–1850', in *English Historical Review*, xcii (1977), p. 751.
3. K. Theodore Hoppen, *Elections, Politics and Society in Ireland 1832–1885* (Oxford, 1984), pp. 16–7.
4. 13 and 14 Vict., *c.* 69.
5. *Times*, 22 January 1847.
6. Since 1835, O'Connell and the Whig government had an informal understanding known as The Lichfield House Pact.
7. Brigitte Anton, 'Women of the Nation', in *History Ireland* (1993, Autumn), pp. 34–7.
8. *Freeman's*, 18 November, 2 December 1845.
9. *Hansard*, lxxxiv , 13 March 1846, 16 March 1846.
10. *Nation*, 12, 19, 26 December 1846.
11. *Hansard*, lxxxix, 19 January 1847, pp. 77–80.
12. *Mercury*, 13 April 1847.
13. *Hansard*, lxxxix, 8, 11, 12 February 1847.
14. *Nation*, 7 May 1847.
15. This point is made by Sloan, *William Smith O'Brien*, p. 142.
16. Petition from Loyal Orange Lodge, No. 356, Castlewellan, Outrage Papers for County Down, National Archives Dublin (NAD), 29 July 1848.
17. *Nation*, 18 March 1848, 25 March 1848.
18. Sloan, *Smith O'Brien*, p. 219.
19. Charles Gavan Duffy, *Four Years of Irish History, 1845–9* (Dublin, 1887).
20. *Times*, 16 May 1843.
21. *Report of Her Majesty's Commissioners of Inquiry into the state of the law and practice in respect to the occupation of land in Ireland, together with minutes of evidence, parts i–v, (Devon Commission)*, PP 1845, xix, Part 1, pp. 15–21.
22. *Times*, 3 April 1845.
23. *Nation*, 24 June 1843.
24. Ibid., 8 November 1845.
25. Heytesbury to Graham, Graham Papers, 17 April 1846.
26. *NY Herald*, 21 November 1846.
27. B. Holmes RM, Cavan to Lord Lieutenant, PROL HO45 2416, 5 December 1847.
28. Poster issued by Somerville, Dublin Castle, PROL HO45 OS2035, 9 November 1847.
29. Ibid.

30. *Nation*, 7, 15 July 1848.
31. *Times*, 11 December 1848.
32. Confidential Reports on the State of the Lately Disturbed Districts by Resident Magistrates, PROL, Colonial Office Papers, CO 904/9.
33. *Wexford Independent*, 1 January 1848.
34. *Devon Commission*, pp. 14–15.
35. *St James's Chronicle*, 26 October 1847.
36. J. M'Caunce RM to Dublin Castle, Constabulary Reports, PROL HO45 2416, 15 March 1848.
37. David N. Buckley, *James Fintan Lalor: Radical* (Cork, 1990).
38. Times, 22 September 1847.
39. *Nation*, 24 April 1847.
40. *Freeman's*, 4 August 1846.
41. MacDonagh, *The Emancipist*, pp. 295–7.
42. Kevin B. Nowlan, *The Politics of Repeal: A Study of Relations between Great Britain and Ireland, 1841–50* (London, 1965).
43. *Roscommon and Leitrim Gazette*, 9 January 1847, 13 March 1847.
44. *Wexford Independent*, 1 January 1848.
45. *Roscommon and Leitrim Gazette*, 13 March 1847.
46. Ibid., 3 April 1847.
47. *Nation*, cited in *Northern Star*, 3 July 1847.
48. *Northern Star*, 10 July 1847.
49. John Prest, *Lord John Russell* (London, 1972), p. 263.
50. *Wexford Independent*, 1 January 1848.
51. *Nation*, 14 August 1847.
52. Ibid., 18 August 1847.
53. Lord Palmerston to Russell, PROL, Russell Papers, 30 20 6E, 19 August 1847.
54. Prest, *Russell*, pp. 262–3.
55. Russell to Clarendon, Clarendon Papers, Bodleian Library, 2 August 1847.
56. Report of RM, Clonmel, Tipperary, PROL, HO 45 2416, 17 March 1848.
57. R. Ryan, RM, Magistrates Reports, PROL HO 45 2416, 18 March 1848.
58. Magistrates Report, Leitrim, PROL HO 45 2416, 18 March 1848.
59. Ibid., RM, Limerick to Redington, 13 March 1848.
60. Abstract of Constabulary Reports (hereafter ACR) PROL HO45 2416, 16 March 1848.
61. Ibid., ACR for Clogher, Kings County, 20 March 1848.
62. Ibid., ACR for Wicklow, 18 March 1848.
63. Ibid., ACR for Queen's County, 20 March 1848.
64. Ibid., ACR for Cork, 8 April 1848.
65. Ibid., ACR for Tipperary, 5 April 1848.
66. ACR, Meath, PROL HO45 2416, 18 March 1848.
67. Kevin Whelan, 'Origins of the Orange Order', *Bullan*, pp. 19–24.
68. *Nation*, 1 April 1843.
69. Ibid., 27 June 1846.
70. *Freeman's*, 29 April 1845.
71. *Nation*, 14 December 1844.
72. Wayne Hall, 'A Tory Periodical in a Time of Famine', in Arthur Gribben (ed.), *The Great Famine and the Irish Diaspora in America* (Massachusetts, 1999), pp. 48–65.

73. *Nation*, 15, 22 May 1847.
74. *Protestant Journal*, 13 November 1847.
75. Ibid., 20 November 1847.
76. *Northern Whig*, 16 November 1847.
77. Thomas Verner SM to Dublin Castle, NAD, Outrage Papers for Co. Antrim, 1847. 19 November 1847.
78. *Belfast News-Letter*, 14 March 1847.
79. Ibid., 17 March 1847.
80. Ibid., 28 March 1847.
81. ACR for Tyrone, PROL HO45 2416, 21 March 1848.
82. George Suffren, Mayor of Belfast, to Chief Secretary, Dublin Castle, NAD, Outrage Papers for Co. Antrim, 1848, 8 April 1848.
83. *Nation*, 8 April 1848.
84. Ibid., 29 April 1848.
85. Richard Davis, *Revolutionary Imperialist: William Smith O'Brien* (Dublin, 1998), p. 251.
86. Ibid., 13 May 1848, 20 May 1848.
87. Belfast Petty Sessions to Chief Secretary, Dublin Castle, NAD, Outrage Papers for Co. Antrim, 1848, 26 July 1848.
88. Davis, *Young Ireland*, p. 228.
89. Memorial of Inhabitants of Belfast to Lord Lieutenant, PROL, HO 45 OS 2488, 15 April 1848.
90. *Belfast News-Letter*, 14 March 1847.
91. Petition from Loyal Orange Lodge No. 356, NAD, Outrage Papers, Co. Down, 29 July 1848.
92. Russell to Clarendon, Clarendon Letter Books, 17 July 1848.
93. *Warder*, 10 July 1848.
94. Ibid., 10 July 1848.
95. Kinealy and Mac Atasney, *The Hidden Famine*, Chapter 6.
96. *Northern Whig*, cited in *Wexford Independent*, 19 July 1848.
97. *Belfast News-Letter*, 12 July 1848.
98. Town Clerk, Belfast to Chief Secretary, Dublin Castle, NAD, Outrage Papers for Co. Antrim, 1848, 26 July 1848.
99. Ibid., George Bentinck, RM, Belfast to Chief Secretary, Dublin Castle, 29 July 1848.
100. *Nation*, 29 July 1848.
101. *Warder*, 14 July 1849.
102. Russell to Clarendon, Russell Papers, PROL, 30 22 5A, 29 June 1847.
103. Clarendon to Russell, Clarendon Papers, Bodleian Library, 17 July 1847.
104. Clarendon to Russell, 30 March 1848, cited in G. P. Gooch (ed.), *The Later Correspondence of Lord John Russell 1840–78* (London, 1925), p. 221.
105. *Nation*, 8 January 1848.
106. Redington, Dublin Castle to Home Office, PROL HO 45 2416, 4 March 1848.
107. *United Irishman*, 12 February 1848.
108. T. F. O'Sullivan, *The Young Irelanders* (Tralee, 1944), pp. 78–9.
109. *Nation*, 11 March 1848.
110. Ibid., 6 April 1848, 20 April 1848.
111. Redington to Home Office, PROL HO 45 2416, 4 March 1848.
112. *United Irishman*, 26 February 1848.

113. The leader of the Chartist movement, Fergus O'Connor, was Irish and a supporter of repeal; not all Chartists, however, supported repeal, for example, Thomas Carlyle in *Chartism* (1839) warned the English radicals not to trust Irish immigrants.

114. Dorothy Thompson, 'Ireland and the Irish in English Radicalism before 1850', in James Epstein and Dorothy Thompson (eds), *The Chartist Experience* (Macmillan – now Palgrave, 1985), pp. 139–46.

115. Dermot Power, 'The Politicization of the People? Strange Episodes in 1848–9, in *Famine in Waterford*, pp. 293–6.

116. *Wexford Independent*, 15 July 1848.

117. *Waterford Chronicle*, 12 July 1848.

118. *Wexford Independent*, 12 July 1848.

119. *Tribune*, cited in *Wexford Independent*, 12 July 1848.

120. *Nation*, 10 April 1847.

121. Ibid., 25 March 1848.

122. *United Irishman*, 22 April 1848.

123. Nation, 6 May 1848.

124. *Freeman's*, 4 May 1848.

125. Clarendon to Russell, Clarendon Papers, 2 May 1848.

126. *Nation*, 6 May 1848.

127. Quoted in Sloan, *Smith O'Brien*, p. 169.

128. ACR, Louth, PROL HO45 2416, 21 March 1847.

129. Ibid., Edward Fraser, Sub-Inspector, Blacklion, Cavan to Lord Lieutenant, 20 December 1847.

130. Ibid., ACR for Cavan, 21 March 1848.

131. Letter from Catholic clergy of the Deanery of Tuam; Resolution adopted by Catholic priests in the Deanery of Ardagh, *Wexford Independent*, 12 July 1848.

132. *Erne Packet*, cited in *Wexford Independent*, 12 July 1848.

133. Address of the Peers and Members of the House of Commons connected with Ireland, *Wexford Independent*, 12 July 1848.

134. Ibid., 19 July 1848.

135. *Freeman's*, 13 April 1848.

136. Nowlan, *The Politics of Repeal*, p. 195.

137. Clarendon to Russell, Clarendon Papers, Bodleian Library, 16 April 1848.

138. Ibid., Clarendon to Bedford, 8 July 1848.

139. Ibid., Clarendon to George Grey, 5 July 1848.

140. Ibid., Clarendon to the Marquess of Lansdowne, 16 July 1848.

141. Report of Wellington, PROL W0 30 111, April 1848.

142. *Hansard*, lxxxxviii, 10 April 1848.

143. *Freeman's Journal*, 17 May 1848.

144. Clarendon to Russell, Clarendon Papers, Bodleian Library, 16 May 1848.

145. Ibid., 21 May 1848.

146. Saville, *1848*, pp. 133–4.

147. *Wexford Independent*, 12 July 1848.

148. Ibid., 19 July 1848.

149. Ibid., 12 July 1848.

150. Charles Gavan Duffy, *Four Years of Irish History* (London, 1883), p. 641.

151. Ibid.

152. Davis, *Revolutionary Imperialist*, pp. 270–5.
153. Clarendon to Russell, Clarendon Papers, 10 August 1848.
154. *Times*, 3 August 1848.
155. Antony M. Breen, 'Cappoquin and the 1849 Movement', in *History Ireland*, 7:2 (1999 Summer), pp. 31–3.
156. Allan Todd, *Revolutions 1789–1917* (Cambridge,1998), pp. 61–3.
157. *Illustrated London News*, 29 July 1848.
158. *Times*, 3 August 1848.
159. See Kinealy, *Disunited Kingdom*.
160. Saville, *1848*; in Saville's words, 'It was the working compact between the Irish nationalists and the English radicals that made 1848 such a promising year', p. 223.
161. *Freeman's*, 27 April 1848.
162. Kerr, *Nation of Beggars*, pp. 153–7.
163. Memorandum of Orange Lodge to Clarendon, Clarendon Papers, Bodleian Library, 19 October 1848.

Epilogue

1. *Times*, 18 July 1849.
2. *General Report of Census Commissioners for 1851*, p. lviii.
3. Third Annual Report of PLC, 1850, pp. 5–7; Fourth Annual Report of PLC, 1851, pp. 9–10.
4. *Times*, 29 April 1850.
5. *Illustrated London News*, 15 December 1849.
6. *A Return of the Outrages specially reported by the constabulary as committed within the barony of Kilmacrenan, County Donegal, during the last ten years*, PP, 1861, lii, describes the killing of hundreds of sheep on the estate of Lord George Hill in Gweedore, County Donegal.
7. *Freeman's*, 10 March 1855.
8. Ó Gráda, *New Economic History*, p. 250.
9. Tim P. O'Neill, 'The Persistence of Famine in Ireland', in Póirtéir, *Irish Famine*, p. 205.
10. Ibid., p. 204.
11. H. M. Boot, *The Commercial Crisis of 1847* (Hull, 1984).
12. Saville, *1848*, p. 202.
13. *Irish Quarterly Review*, 1853.
14. W. E. Vaughan, *Landlords and Tenants in Ireland 1848–1904* (Dublin, 1984), p. 6.
15. *Freeman's*, 10 March 1855.
16. W. E. Vaughan, *Sin, Sheep and Scotsmen: John George Adair and the Derryveagh Evictions, 1861* (Belfast, 1983).
17. *Nation*, 13 April 1861.
18. *Freeman's*, 13 January 1855.
19. Carla King, *Michael Davitt* (Dublin, 1999), pp. 19–21.
20. Moody and Martin, *The Course of Irish History*, pp. 285–7.
21. Liz Curtis, *The Cause of Ireland: From the United Irishmen to Partition* (Belfast, 1994).

22. *Freeman's*, 30 December 1854, 11 January 1855.
23. Ibid., 7 March 1855.
24. Kerr, *Nation of Beggars*, p. 337.
25. Linda Colley, *Britons: Forging the Nation 1707–1837* (London, 1994), pp. 328–34.
26. *Times*, 6 March 1849.
27. *Freeman's*, 1854–5, *passim*.
28. D. P. McCracken, *The Irish Pro-Boers, 1877–1902* (Johannesburg, 1989).
29. *United Irishman*, 21 April 1900.
30. *Times*, 9 March 1847.
31. Thirteenth Annual Report of PLC, 1860, pp. 4–6.
32. See Kinealy, *Administration of Poor Law*.
33. *Times*, 10 February 1847.
34. *Hansard*, cvii, 23 July 1849, pp. 839–42.
35. Ibid., pp. 843–4.
36. Ibid., pp. 834–8.
37. *Report on Kilrush Union*, p. xiii.
38. Twistleton to Trevelyan, PROL T64 366A, 21 January 1849.
39. Clarendon to Russell, Clarendon Papers, 12 March 1849.
40. Evidence of Edward Twistleton, *Select Committee on the Poor Law*, p. 717.
41. Sligo to Clarendon, Clarendon Papers, 18 November 1848.
42. Ibid., Clarendon to Russell, 28 April 1849.

SELECT BIBLIOGRAPHY

Bielenberg, Andy (ed.), *The Irish Diaspora* (Essex, 2000).

Bourke, Austin, *The Visitation of God? The Potato and the Irish Famine* (Dublin, 1993).

Boylan, T. A., and Foley T. P., *Political Economy and Colonial Ireland* (London, 1992).

Bradshaw, Brendan, 'Nationalism and Historical Scholarship in Modern Ireland', in *Irish Historical Studies* xxvi (November 1989).

Butt, Isaac, *A Voice for Ireland: Famine in the Land* (Dublin, 1847).

Campbell, Stephen J., *The Great Irish Famine: Words and Images from the Famine Museum, Strokestown Park, County Roscommon* (Strokestown, 1994).

Central Relief Committee, *Transactions of the Central Relief Committee of the Society of Friends during the Famine in Ireland in 1846 and 1847* (Dublin, 1852, 1996).

Colley, Linda, *Britons: Forging the Nation 1707–1837* (London, 1992).

Cowman, Des, and Donald Brady, *The Famine in Waterford* (Dublin, 1995).

Crawford, E. Margaret, *Famine: The Irish Experience, 900–1900* (Edinburgh, 1989).

Crawford, E. M., *The Hungry Stream: Essays on Emigration and Famine* (Belfast, 1997).

Crosby Forbes, H. A., and Henry Lee, *Massachusetts Help to Ireland During the Great Famine* (Massachusetts, 1967).

Curtis, Liz, *The Cause of Ireland: From the United Irishmen to Partition* (Belfast, 1995).

Daly, Mary, *The Famine in Ireland* (Dundalk, 1986).

Davis, Richard, *Revolutionary Imperialist: William Smith O'Brien 1803–1864* (Dublin, 1998).

Devine, T. M., *The Highland Famine: Hunger, Emigration and the Scottish Highlands in the Nineteenth Century* (Edinburgh, 1988).

Donnelly, J. S., *The Land and People of Nineteenth-Century Cork* (London, 1975).

Donnelly, J. S., 'The Famine its Interpreters, Old and New' in *History Ireland* 1:3 (1993).

Dufferin, Lord, and the Hon. G. F. Boyle, *Narrative of a journey from Oxford to Skibbereen during the year of the Irish Famine* (Oxford, 1847).

Duffy, Charles Gavan, *Four Years of Irish History 1845–49* (London, 1983).

Eagleton, Terry, *Heathcliff and the Great Hunger* (Verso, 1995).

Eagleton, Terry, *Scholars and Rebels in Nineteenth-Century Ireland* (Oxford, 1999).

Edwards R. D., and T. D. Williams, *The Great Famine: Studies in Irish History, 1845–52* (Dublin, 1956, 1995).

Egan, Desmond, *Famine* (Dublin, 1997).

Goodbody, Rob, *A Suitable Channel: Quaker Relief in the Great Famine* (Dublin, 1995).

Grace, Daniel, *The Great Famine in Nenagh Poor Law Union* (Tipperary, 2000).

Grant, James, 'The Great Famine and the Poor Law in the Province of Ulster: the rate in aid issue of 1849', in *Irish Historical Studies*, 27: 105 (1990), pp. 30–47.

Gray, Peter, *The Irish Famine* (London, 1995).

Gray, Peter, *Famine, Land and Politics: British Government and Irish Society* (Dublin, 1999).

Gribben, Arthur (ed.), *The Great Famine and the Irish Diaspora in America* (Massachusetts, 1999).

Gooch, A. P. (ed.), *The Later Correspondence of Lord John Russell 1840–78* (London, 1925).

Griffiths, A. R. 'The Irish Board of Works during the Famine Years', in *Historical Journal*, xiii (1970).

Haddick-Flynn, Kevin, *Orangeism: The Making of a Tradition* (Dublin, 1999).

Hall, S. C., and A. M. Hall, *Ireland, its Scenery, Character etc*. (3 vols, London, 1841–3).

Hart, Jennifer, 'Sir Charles Trevelyan at the Treasury', in *English Historical Review*, lxxv (1960).

Hayden, Tom, *Irish Hunger: Personal Reflections on the Legacy of the Famine* (Colorado, 1997).

Hilton, Boyd, *The Age of Atonement: The Influence of Evangelicalism on Social and Economic Thought, 1785–1865* (Oxford, 1988).

Keegan, Gerald, *Famine Diary: Journey to a New World* (Dublin, 1991).

Kelly, James 'Scarcity and Poor Relief in Eighteenth-Century Ireland: the subsistence crisis of 1782–4', in *Irish Historical Studies*, xxviii (May 1992).

Kelleher, Margaret, *The Feminization of Famine: Expressions of the Inexpressible?* (Cork, 1997).

Kerr, Donal, *'A Nation of Beggars?' Priests, People and Politics in Ireland 1846–52* (Oxford, 1994).

Kerr, Donal, *The Catholic Church and the Famine* (Columbia Press, 1996).

Kierse, Seán, *The Famine Years in the Parish of Killaloe* (Killaloe, 1994).

Kildare County Council (ed.), *Lest We Forget: Kildare and the Great Famine* (Kildare, 1995).

Killen, John (ed.), *The Famine Decade: Contemporary Accounts 1841–1851* (Belfast, 1995).

Kinealy, Christine, *This Great Calamity: The Irish Famine 1845–52* (Dublin, 1994).

Kinealy, Christine, *A Death-Dealing Famine: The Great Hunger in Ireland* (Pluto, 1997).

Kinealy, Christine, and Trevor Parkhill (eds), *The Famine in Ulster* (Belfast, 1997).

Kinealy, Christine, *A Disunited Kingdom? England, Ireland, Scotland and Wales 1800–1949* (Cambridge University Press, 1999).

Kinealy, Christine, and Gerard Mac Atasney, *The Hidden Famine: Hunger, Poverty and Sectarianism in Belfast 1840* (Pluto Press, 2000).

King, Carla, *Life and Times of Michael Davitt* (Dublin, 1999).

Kissane, Noel, *The Irish Famine: A Documentary History* (Dublin, 1995).

Kohl, J. G., *Travels in Ireland* (London, 1844).

Mac Atasney, Gerard, *'This Dreadful Visitation': The Famine in Lurgan/Portadown* (Belfast, 1997).

Mac Atasney, Gerard, *Leitrim and the Great Hunger* (Carrick-on-Shannon, 1997).

MacGregor, Pat, 'Demographic Pressure and the Irish Famine: Malthus after Mokyr' in *Land Economics*, 65 (1989), pp. 228–38.

MacGregor, Pat, *The Great Irish Famine: An Empirical Analysis* (unpub. paper presented to fourteenth World Congress on Sociology, Montreal, 1998).

MacRaild, Donald M. (ed.), *The Great Famine and Beyond: Irish Migrants in Britain in the Nineteenth and Twentieth Centuries* (Dublin, 2000).

Marrison, Andrew (ed.), *Free Trade and its Reception* (*Freedom and Trade*, Vol. 1, London, 1998).

Miller, Kerby, *Emigrants and Exiles: Ireland and the Irish Exodus to North America* (Oxford, 1985).

Mokyr, Joel, *Why Ireland Starved: An Analytical and Qualitative History of the Irish Economy, 1800–1850* (2nd edn, London, 1985).

Mooney, T. A., *Compendium of the Irish Poor Law* (Dublin, 1887).

Moran, Gerard P., *The Mayo Evictions of 1860* (Westport, 1986).

Morash, Chris, *The Hungry Voice: The Poetry of the Irish Famine* (Dublin, 1989).

Mullen, Don (ed.), *A Glimmer of Light: An Overview of Great Hunger Commemorative Events in Ireland and Throughout the World* (Dublin, 1995).

Murphy, Ignatius, *The Diocese of Killaloe, 1800–50* (Dublin, 1992).

Neal, Frank, *Sectarian Violence: The Liverpool Experience 1819–1914. An Aspect of Anglo-Irish History* (Manchester, 1988).

Nicholls, George, *A History of the Irish Poor Law* (London, 1856).

Nicholson, Asenath, *Annals of the Famine in Ireland* (first pub. 1851: repub. Dublin, 1998, Maureen Murphy, ed.).

O'Brien, William, *Dingle: Its Pauperism and Proselytism* (Dublin, 1852).

O'Ceallaigh, Daltún, (ed.), *Reconsiderations of Irish History and Culture* (Dublin, 1994).

O'Ciosáin, Niall, 'Was there a "silence" about the Famine?', in *Irish Studies Review*, 13 (1995–6), pp. 7–10.

Ó Gráda, Cormac, 'Making History in Ireland in the 1940s and 1950s: The Saga of the Great Famine', in *Irish Review*, 12 (1992).

Ó Gráda, Cormac, *Ireland: A New Economic History, 1780–1939* (Oxford, 1994).

Ó Gráda, Cormac, *Famine 150* (Dublin, 1997).

Ó Gráda, Cormac, *Black '47 and Beyond: The Great Irish Famine in History, Economy and Memory* (Princetown, 1999).

O'Rourke, John, *History of the Great Irish Famine of 1847* (Dublin, 1875).

O'Rourke, Kevin, 'Did the Great Irish Famine Matter?', in *Journal of Economic History*, 51 (1991).

Osborne, S. Godolphin, *Gleanings from the West of Ireland* (London, 1850).

O'Sullivan, Patrick, *The Meaning of the Famine* (vol. 6. London, 1996).

Parker, C. S., *Sir Robert Peel from his Private Papers* (London, 1891).

Póirtéir, Cathal, *Famine Echoes* (Dublin, 1995).

Póirtéir, Cathal, *The Great Irish Famine* (Cork, 1995).

Prochaska, F. K., *The Voluntary Impulse: Philanthropy in Modern Britain* (London, 1988).

Prochaska, F. K., *Women and Philanthropy in Nineteenth-Century England* (Oxford, 1980).

Robinson, Mary, *A Voice for Somalia* (Dublin, 1994).

Saville, John, *The British State and the Chartist Movement* (Cambridge, 1990).

Scally, R. J., *The End of Hidden Ireland: Rebellion, Famine and Emigration* (Oxford, 1995).

Scola, Roger, *Feeding the Victorian City: The Food Supply of Manchester 1770–1870* (Manchester, 1992).

Sen, Amartya K., *Poverty and Famines: An Essay on Entitlement and Deprivation* (Oxford, 1981).

Sen, A. K., 'Nobody Need Starve', in *Granta*, 52 (1995).

Sheehy, David C., 'Archbishop Daniel Murray and the Response of the Catholic Church to the Great Famine in Ireland', in *Linkup: A Journal for the Dublin Diocese* (December 1995).

Sloan, Robert, *William Smith O'Brien and the Young Ireland Rebellion of 1848* (Dublin, 2000).

Smith, William Henry, *A Twelvemonth's Residence in Ireland during the Famine and the Public Works in 1846 and 1847* (London, 1848).

Swift, Roger, and Sheridan Gilley (eds), *The Irish in Victorian Britain: The Local Dimension* (Dublin, 1999).

Swords, Liam, *In Their Own Words: The Famine in North Connacht 1845–49* (Dublin, 1999).

Trevelyan, Charles E., *The Irish Crisis* (London, 1848).

Tuke, James Hack, *A Visit to Connaught in the Autumn of 1847* (London, 1848).

Vaughan, W. E., *Sin, Sheep and Scotsmen: John George Adair and the Derryveagh Evictions, 1861* (Belfast, 1983).

Vaughan, W. E., *Landlords and Tenants in Ireland 1848–1904* (Dublin, 1984).

Turner, Michael, *After the Famine. Irish Agriculture 1850–1914* (Cambridge, 1996).

Williams, T. D. (ed.), *Secret Societies in Ireland* (Dublin, 1973).

Whyte, J. H., *The Tenant League and Irish Politics in the Eighteen-Fifties* (Dundalk, 1963).

Woodham-Smith, Cecil, *The Great Hunger 1845–49* (London, 1962).

INDEX